A Century in Captivity

Revisiting New England: The New Regionalism

SERIES EDITORS

Siobhan Senier, University of New Hampshire
Darren Ranco, Dartmouth College
Adam Sweeting, Boston University
David H. Watters, University of New Hampshire

This series presents fresh discussions of the distinctiveness of New England culture. The editors seek manuscripts examining the history of New England regionalism; the way its culture came to represent American national culture; the interaction between that "official" New England culture and the people who lived in the region; and local, subregional, or even biographical subjects as microcosms that explicitly open up and consider larger issues. The series welcomes new theoretical and historical perspectives and is designed to cross disciplinary boundaries and appeal to a wide audience.

RECENT BOOKS IN THIS SERIES:

Paul M. Searls, *Two Vermonts: Geography and Identity, 1865–1910*
Judith Bookbinder, *Boston Modern: Figurative Expressionism as Alternative Modernism*
Donna M. Cassidy, *Marsden Hartley: Race, Region, and Nation*
Joseph A. Conforti, editor, *Creating Portland: History and Place in Northern New England*
Maureen Elgersman Lee, *Black Bangor: African Americans in a Maine Community, 1880–1950*
T. A. Milford, *The Gardiners of Massachusetts: Provincial Ambition and British-American Career*
David L. Richards, *Poland Spring: A Tale of the Gilded Age, 1860–1900*
Donald W. Linebaugh, *The Man Who Found Thoreau: Roland W. Robbins and the Rise of Historical Archaeology in America*
Pauleena MacDougall, *The Penobscot Dance of Resistance: Tradition in the History of a People*
Jennifer C. Post, *Music in Rural New England Family and Community Life, 1870–1940*
Mark J. Sammons and Valerie Cunningham, *Black Portsmouth: Three Centuries of African-American Heritage*
Christopher J. Lenney, *Sightseeking: Clues to the Landscape History of New England*
Priscilla Paton, *Abandoned New England: Landscape in the Works of Homer, Frost, Hopper, Wyeth, and Bishop*
Adam Sweeting, *Beneath the Second Sun: A Cultural History of Indian Summer*
James C. O'Connell, *Becoming Cape Cod: Creating a Seaside Resort*
Richard Archer, *Fissures in the Rock: New England in the Seventeenth Century*
Sidney V. James, *The Colonial Metamorphoses in Rhode Island: A Study of Institutions in Change*
Diana Muir, *Reflections in Bullough's Pond: Economy and Ecosystem in New England*
Nancy L. Gallagher, *Breeding Better Vermonters: The Eugenics Project in Vermont*

For a complete list of books in this series, please visit www.upne.com
and www.upne.com/series/RVNE.html

A Century in Captivity

*The Life and Trials of Prince Mortimer,
a Connecticut Slave*

Denis R. Caron

University of New Hampshire Press
Durham, New Hampshire
PUBLISHED BY UNIVERSITY PRESS OF NEW ENGLAND
HANOVER AND LONDON

University of New Hampshire Press
Published by University Press of New England, One Court Street, Lebanon, NH 03766
www.upne.com

Printed in the United States of America

5   4   3   2   1

LIBRARY OF CONGRESS CATALOGING-IN-PUBLICATION DATA
Caron, Denis R.
A century in captivity : the life and trials of Prince Mortimer, a Connecticut slave / Denis R. Caron.
p.   cm.
Includes bibliographical references and index.
ISBN-13: 978-1-58465-539-8 (cloth : alk. paper)
ISBN-10: 1-58465-539-9 (cloth : alk. paper)
ISBN-13: 978-1-58465-540-4 (pbk. : alk. paper)
ISBN-10: 1-58465-540-2 (pbk. : alk. paper)
1. Mortimer, Prince, d. 1834. 2. Mortimer, Prince, d. 1834—Trials, litigation, etc. 3. Slaves—
Connecticut—Biography. 4. African Americans—Connecticut—Biography. 5. Trials
(Murder)—Connecticut. 6. Prisoners—Connecticut—Biography. 7. Newgate Prison (East Granby,
Conn.) 8. African Americans—Legal status, laws, etc.—Connecticut—History. 9. Prisoners—
Connecticut—Social conditions. 10. Prisons—Connecticut—History. I. Title.
E444.M67C37   2006
306.3'62092—dc22   2005025766

For Judy,
who makes me proud

Contents

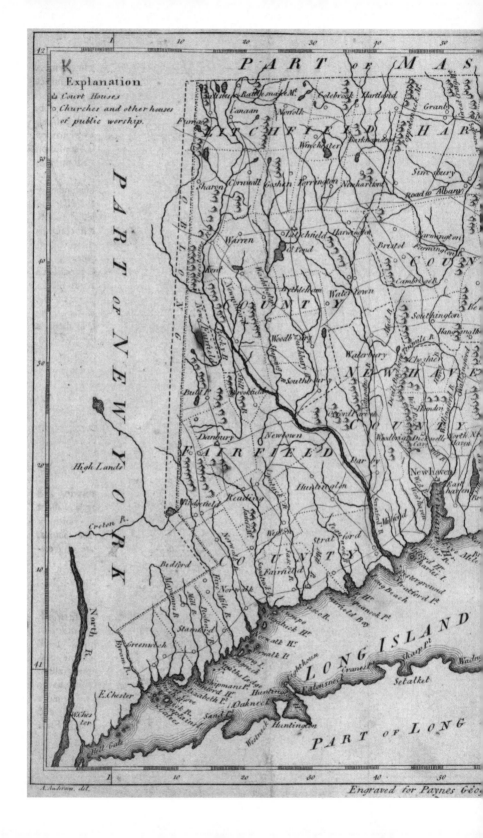

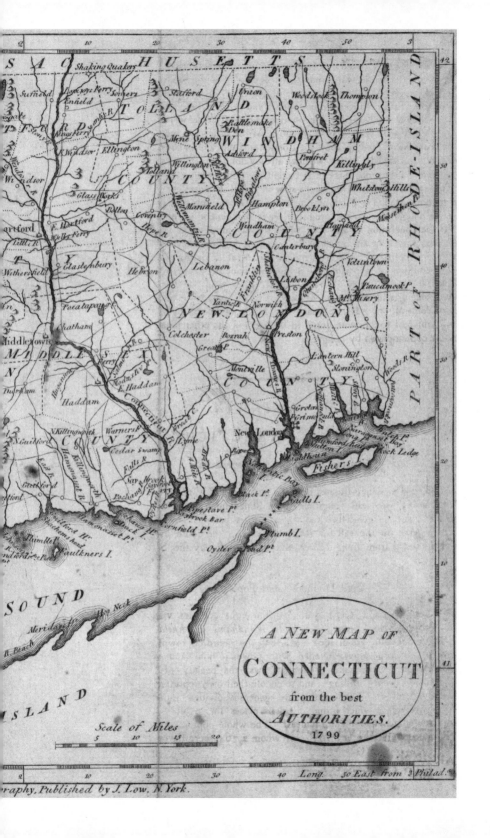

A NEW MAP OF
CONNECTICUT
from the best
AUTHORITIES.
1799

Scale of Miles

Preface

$\mathscr{I}$ first learned of Prince Mortimer in Richard Phelps's *Newgate of Connecticut: Its Origin and Early History,* a classic account of Connecticut's famous Newgate Prison, a colonial copper mine converted in 1773 into the country's first state prison and later used as a dungeon to confine Tories during the revolution. Writing in 1844, Phelps gave a brief account of the life of this Connecticut slave:

> Prince Mortimer, a prisoner, lived to a very advanced age. He died at the prison in Wethersfield, in 1834, supposed to be 110 years old; he commonly went by the name of Guinea, which was probably given to him on account of his native country. His complexion did not in the least belie his name, for surely he was the personification of "darkness visible." His life was a tale of misfortunes, and his fate won the commiseration of all who knew him. He was captured on the coast of Guinea by a slaver when a boy; was transported in a filthy slave-ship to Connecticut, then a slave colony, and was sold to one of the Mortimer family in Middletown. He was a servant to different officers in the Revolutionary War; had been sent on errands by George Washington, and said he had "straddled many a cannon when fired by the Americans at the British troops." For the alleged crime of poisoning his master he was doomed to Newgate prison, in 1811, for life. He appeared a harmless, clever old man, and as his age and infirmities rendered him a burden to the keepers, they frequently tried to induce him to quit the prison. Once he took his departure, and after rambling around in search of some one he formerly knew, like the aged prisoner released from the Bastille, he returned to the gates of the prison, and begged to be re-admitted to his dungeon home, and in prison ended his unhappy years.

Frankly, this passage did not make any particular impression on me at this first reading; the appeal of Prince's story struck me only after I reflected over the dates that Phelps mentions: Prince died in 1834, at the stated age of 110. (Some have questioned the accuracy of that figure, but I have found nothing that disproves it or even suggests a lesser age.) Since he was sentenced to life imprisonment in 1811, that meant, of course, that Prince's life as a prisoner began when he was 87. That also meant that Prince spent the next 23 years as an inmate, most of them within the stone-walled enclosures of Newgate, reputedly then the worst prison in America.

It was at that point that I became irretrievably drawn into the story of Prince Mortimer, prompting me to embark on a five-year course of investigation to learn more about his life. Prince had spent eight decades as a slave before going to prison. What had he done during all that time? Who was this master that Prince despised so much, and what could have prompted him to engage in such an ill-conceived criminal act? How could such a sick, elderly man survive in prison for so long a time, especially in such a notorious place as Newgate?

These were the questions that I needed to explore, but I soon learned how naïve I was in believing that the answers were readily available to anyone with a modicum of research ability. As it turned out, the Phelps passage constitutes the only secondary-source reference to Prince Mortimer to be found anywhere. But for this passage, in the 17 decades since Prince's death no one has deemed fit to write another word about him.

For eleven long and arduous decades, however, Prince Mortimer lived. Certainly there had to be some evidence of that fact, but where to look? Perhaps there were newspaper reports of his trial, or perhaps his death? Nothing. Connecticut's newspapers in 1834 were content to print column after column relating minute details of the most recent agricultural fair, but the death of a man at the age of 110 was apparently not worthy of their attention. The same held true for Prince's trial and conviction.

I suppose this should not have come as a surprise, since throughout his life Prince Mortimer subsisted in the lowest echelons of society, first as a slave and then as a prisoner. Short of inciting a rebellion, no one from either of those stations would be likely to catch the attention of many others—certainly not the press. Ultimately, I would come to discover that the sum and substance of every shred of available direct information on the life of Prince Mortimer would not fill a single page.

That would prove to be enough, however, to provide me with clues to the people and events that shaped the life of Prince Mortimer, and this book is the result of that inquiry. I am reluctant to refer to this story as a biography; usually that term is reserved for a work that explores the achievements of a person of some renown. Despite the obvious fact that Prince does not even begin to qualify under that definition, there remains something compelling about his life, something that certainly drew me to learn more, and something that I hope will prompt readers to do likewise through this book.

There may be some who will question the value of a study based on so little empirical information. To those persons, I would note two points. First, although little is known about the particulars of Prince's life in prison, a considerable amount has been written about the difficult conditions he and other inmates endured in that environment. To learn about those conditions is to learn about Prince Mortimer, because the essence of his story *is* suffering and endurance. Second, Prince's story does not derive its meaning from a series of defining events; quite to the contrary, its meaning lies in their absence. This is a story of perseverance, of a man who lived on in the face of a neverending series of indistinguishable days, each one filled with yet another dose of yesterday's privations and suffering. Viewed from that perspective, *A Century in Captivity* stands for the proposition that even the lowliest of men can lead lives that are worthy of note and from which all men can derive meaningful lessons.

Acknowledgments

$\mathcal{A}$ number of helpful people, any one of whom is more knowledgeable about Connecticut history than I ever expect to be, were of immense assistance in keeping me on track as I trudged along, trying to piece together the few known facts about Prince Mortimer. Dione Longley, director of the Middlesex County Historical Society, helped me get through the early stages of my research, providing a wealth of information about Middletown's early years, especially its maritime and slave history. A few miles up the Connecticut River, Brenda Milkofsky, then the director of Wethersfield's historical society, provided similar assistance in connection with the life of Martin Welles, as well as with the early years of Wethersfield State Prison. Karin Peterson, of the Connecticut Commission on Culture and Tourism, graciously shared her knowledge of Newgate Prison, opened her files to allow me to locate some of the late nineteen-century prison photos that accompany the text, and made some valuable suggestions on the manuscript. Nancy Finley, curator of graphics at the Connecticut Historical Society, assisted in locating some highly appropriate contemporaneous artwork that will be immensely helpful, I believe, in providing readers with visual depictions of the locations where Prince lived out his years of servitude and incarceration.

Library archive staffs are a special breed, combining their specialized knowledge with an eagerness to share that knowledge and their entrusted treasures with anyone in need of their services. I was immensely fortunate to benefit from the assistance of two such groups: the staffs of the Connecticut Historical Society Museum and the Archives Section of the Connecticut State Library. Prince's story never would have seen the light of day but for the help they provided in locating court and probate records, as well as a wide range of additional topics.

Certain areas of study were not directly connected with Connecticut history but were nonetheless critical in my ability to do justice to Prince's story. In particular, I am indebted to Dr. Ernest Kohorn, professor of obstetrics and gynecology at the Yale Medical School and an avid student of the history of medicine, for his guidance and suggestions regarding the material dealing with yaws. I also must express a special note of thanks to Kathleen Connick, director of the Lloyd Library and Museum, Cincinnati, for her prompt and immensely helpful assistance in locating contemporaneous information regarding *acidum arseniosum.*

Although only one name appears on the cover of this book, I view its production very much as a collaborative effort. Prince Mortimer lived his remarkable life in obscurity; *A Century in Captivity* sheds new light on that life only because of my good fortune in making the acquaintance of those to whom I am pleased to extend this acknowledgment.

A Century in Captivity

• 1 •

The Trial

"*A*ll rise."

The handful of men assembled in the small courtroom of Connecticut's Middlesex County Superior Court dutifully complied with Sheriff Parsons's command. The judge entered the courtroom through the door behind his raised bench, and the nod of his head gave Parsons the only signal he needed. The sheriff opened the door to admit the jury of twelve men, who proceeded in single file to the jury box and took their seats as soon as the judge had seated himself.

Prince was probably not surprised to see the jury returning so soon with its verdict. Only yesterday, he had been summoned to the courthouse from the county jail on Middletown's Washington Street green, his home during the four months since the August 1811 incident. Considering the seriousness of the charges levelled against Prince, the trial had been remarkably brief. It had begun with John Fisk, the clerk of the Superior Court, directing Prince to stand and face the jury. Fisk had then addressed the twelve men, reading from the information:[1]

> Gentlemen, look upon the prisoner, you that are sworn, and hearken to his charge. Prince Negro stands informed against by S. Titus Hosmer, Attorney for the State of Connecticut within the County of Middlesex, who complaint makes and information exhibits, that Prince a negro man of Middletown in said County, the servant of George Starr of said Middletown, a person of wicked mind and disposition, maliciously intending to poison and murder the said George Starr, in the fifth day of August last past at Middletown aforesaid, did knowingly and wilfully and maliciously buy or procure a large quantity of arsenic or ratsbane, being a deadly poison, and did put the same into a bowl filled with chocolate which had been

prepared for the breakfast of said George Starr, and soon after the same was by the said Prince delivered to the said George Starr to drink; and the said George Starr, not knowing the said arsenic or ratsbane to be in the said chocolate, took a small quantity thereof in a spoon to drink the same but by the appearance of the said chocolate, and of small particles of the said arsenic adhering to the said spoon, was deterred; all which doing was to his great damage and the extreme peril of his life, to the evil example of others in like manner offending, and against the peace and dignity of the State of Connecticut; therefore said attorney prays due process against the said Prince in the premises.

"On this information," the clerk had continued, "he hath been arraigned, upon his arraignment he hath plead not guilty, and for trial hath put himself upon his country, which country you are, so that your charge is to enquire whether he stands informed against. If you find him guilty, you are to say so and say no more. If you find him not guilty you are to say so and say no more. And now, gentlemen, hearken to the evidence."

There is no record of the trial itself, but the allegations of the information would suggest that the testimony proceeded rapidly and in a matter-of-fact manner. George Starr certainly testified in support of the facts alleged in the information, and Hosmer probably also saw fit to present testimony from a physician to confirm the presence of the arsenic. It is also most likely that Prince presented no defense; this trial was taking place long before the development of a public defender system, and any attorney who might have volunteered his services was not likely to expend a considerable amount of time formulating a defense to what appeared to be and open-and-shut case.

In that vein, closing arguments would have been extremely brief, with Hosmer reviewing the evidence and asserting to the jury that he had proven all requisite elements for a verdict of guilty. Similarly, the judge's charge to the jury was no doubt succinct; he would have reviewed the elements of the alleged crime, intent to commit the criminal act of poisoning, coupled with an overt act in furtherance of that intent. The judge then would have advised the group of twelve men that, if they believed the evidence as presented through the testimony of the witnesses, the state would have proven the elements of the crime and they had no choice but to return a verdict of guilty to the offense as charged.

In keeping with the brevity of every aspect of the trial to that point, it is also likely that the jury's deliberation was anything but prolonged. With the jury now back in its box, the clerk turned to them and inquired, "Gentlemen, have you agreed on a verdict?"

Together, they answered, "We have."

"Will you say by yourselves or by your foreman?"

One juror replied, "By our foreman." The foreman rose to his feet.

The clerk turned to Prince and commanded, "Prince, hold up your right hand." Prince complied, raising his right hand to shoulder level. Standing at the defense table, and despite his age and infirmities, Prince probably was still as tall as most of the men in the courtroom.

The only known description of Prince's physical characteristics occurs in one of the Newgate prisoner lists, which places him at five feet, ten inches. He may well have been taller in his earlier years. Quite likely, his stature was not unlike that of many slaves hailing from Guinea. In *A Narrative of the Life & Adventures of Venture, A Native of Africa, But Resident Above Sixty Years in the United States of America*, first published in 1798, Venture describes his African ancestors in this manner: "I descended from a very large, tall and stout race of beings, much larger than the generality of people in other parts of the globe, being commonly considerable above six feet in height, and every way well proportioned."

Lean and erect in posture, Prince's physique probably still retained strong evidence of a life of hard physical activity. His complexion was reportedly the blackest of any slave to be found in Middletown, a fact of which he had been proud throughout his life.

Another less commanding aspect of Prince's physical appearance, however, was the effect of his life-long battle with yaws, a tropical disease presenting symptoms similar in some respects to leprosy. Assuming the disease had run its normal course, what the jurors saw before them was a man whose face probably elicited repulsion more than pity. Most of Prince's face was quite likely covered with a combination of hard walnut-sized nodules and scar tissue left behind from old receded nodules. Additionally, considering his advanced age, Prince may well have suffered from the common symptom of deteriorating nose cartilage. In severe cases, the nose would simply collapse, leaving the victim with nothing but a hole in the center of his face.

The specifics of Prince's arrival and early years in Middletown are unrecorded, but it is highly likely that he contracted yaws during his sea voyage from Africa some eighty years earlier, as a child of six or seven. A bacteriological disease that was then rampant throughout most, if not all, tropical areas of the world, yaws was also known to the French as "pian" and to the Germans and Dutch as "framboesia." This latter term was derived from the French word "framboise," meaning "raspberry," an understandable derivation in light of the elevated papules characteristic of the early stages of the disease.[2] The crowded unsanitary conditions beneath the decks of the slaver would have formed an ideal breeding ground for the bacterium, and blisters from the shackles would have been similarly well suited to introduce that bacterium into its victims.

The first symptom probably manifested itself during the last couple of weeks at sea, with a single lesion appearing near the point of infection, perhaps just above the shackle on Prince's ankle. Although initially painless, this "mother yaw" would soon ulcerate, developing a punched-out center that quickly became covered with a yellow crust. The ulcer eventually became swollen and tender, a situation aggravated, no doubt, by the constant rubbing of the leg shackle.

Although the mother yaw would be Prince's sole indication of infection at the time of his arrival in Middletown, it would not be long before the next stage of the illness would appear. Within a few months, secondary oozing papules, equally painful, likely began to appear on Prince's face, arms, legs, and buttocks.

These manifestations were characteristic of what modern medicine has denoted as "early" yaws, and they would be expected to last about five years. It is only during this early period that the disease is contagious. Then would come a period of latency, when the symptoms subsided and the only evidence of prior infection would be some scarring left by the earlier papules. Although the uninitiated might be misled by this apparent remission, those familiar with the course of the disease were well aware that worse was yet to come.

By the time Prince was in his early twenties, he was exhibiting symptoms of "late" yaws: deep ulcerated nodules, about an inch or two in diameter, that imbed themselves well into all layers of the dermis, and eventually into cartilage and even bone. These are most evident on the victim's face, where the nodules can overpower the eye sockets and the mouth, seemingly making them disappear from view. As the nodules subside, they destroy tissue and leave thick scars in their place. In the severest cases, the destruction is so extensive as to involve the nose and entire palate, so that the mouth and nose become a single space.

As gruesome as this description may sound, perhaps the disease's greatest physical cruelty is that it is not inherently fatal, since it does not appear to affect the cardiovascular or central nervous systems. As demonstrated in Prince's case, a victim is doomed to an existence that is not only painful but also prolonged. Today, yaws is generally controlled through the use of antibiotics, but even now such treatment does not always effect a cure.

There was another aspect to Prince's illness, however, that may have been more distressing to him than its physical manifestations. Many of the slaves in Middletown had been permitted to marry and raise families, and it is likely that Prince also would have been afforded that opportunity. If he did marry and have children, there is no record to that effect. The more probable situation, however, was that Prince's affliction made him an unlikely candidate for marriage or, for that matter, even an occasional romantic interlude. Few prospective mates could ever look beyond the disfiguring lesions to appreciate the man behind that face, and none were ever willing to accept the risk of infection that they believed would come with intimacy.

This, then, is the likely sight that the jurors were forced to gaze upon as the clerk commanded, "Look upon the prisoner, you that are sworn. What say you, is he guilty of the crime wherewith he stands charged, or not guilty?"

At some point, a person's grotesque appearance crosses the line from arousing pity or sympathy to inciting fear and repulsion. Although the evidence must have appeared more than sufficient to support Prince's conviction, it is difficult to dismiss altogether the possibility that the jurors may have been swayed by the appearance of the defendant standing before them.

Showing Prince the first acknowledgment of his presence since the trial's beginning, the foreman looked directly at him and, without hesitation or emotion, answered the clerk's inquiry: "Guilty."

"So say you all?" asked the clerk.

The jury panel stated in unison, "We do."

The clerk sat and made a brief notation on the jacket of the court file: "December term, 1811—Guilty." He rose again and spoke: "Gentlemen, attend to your verdict as recorded." Once again, he asked the jury, "You on your oaths do say that the prisoner at the bar is guilty of the crime wherewith he stands charged?"

"We do," stated the foreman.

"So say you all?"

"We do."

The judicial system of 1811 did not waste time with such niceties as modern presentencing investigations. In all probability, Prince's case proceeded to sentencing immediately after the verdict. In conformity with the prevailing practice, the court pronounced sentence in a manner as succinct as the trial that had preceded it: "Prince, in this court you have been tried and found guilty of the offense as charged in the information. Accordingly, it is the sentence of this court that you be remanded to the custody of the sheriff, to be delivered by him to the Warden of New-Gate Prison, where you are to be incarcerated for the remainder of your natural life."

The brevity of Prince's trial, especially when coupled with the strong evidence of his guilt, belied the complex legal issues lurking beneath the veneer of this apparently straightforward prosecution. The very charges under which Prince was prosecuted reflected a bitter political struggle being waged in Connecticut at the beginning of its fourth decade as a state.

The state's attorney had seen fit to initiate Prince's prosecution by means of an "information," charging him with a crime at common law rather than a violation of a statutory provision. The information is a document by which prosecutors throughout the state, even today, commonly initiate a criminal prosecution. Its name is derived from the fact that the state's attorney has the right, and some would say the obligation, to inform the court of his belief that a crime has been committed.

Hosmer was certainly fully aware of the statute, enacted some years earlier by the Connecticut General Assembly, creating the crime of assaulting or poisoning with an intent to murder. That statute not only defined the crime but also mandated the punishment of a person convicted of that crime. Hosmer's information, however, simply ignored the statute, alleging instead a violation of a common law crime. Common law crimes were not crimes defined by statute; rather, they were activities that judges, over many years and through the precedent of many cases, had determined should be criminal in nature.

The distinction between common law and statutory crimes was rooted in the essential nature of government as it existed in Connecticut in 1811.[3] Although three decades had passed since the War for Independence, Connecticut had not yet seen fit to adopt a new state constitution, as had all the other states. These new constitutions followed the federal pattern of a separation of power among three branches of government: the executive, the legislative, and the judicial. Connecticut continued essentially to labor under its original "Fundamental Orders," adopted in 1638. Although the intervening years had seen some modifications to that document, the basic fact remained that the legislative and judicial functions were intertwined in the power of the General Court, later to be called the General Assembly. That body created the courts, appointed the judges, and, until it created a Supreme Court in 1784, was the court of last resort in the state. It was thus quite natural, most thought, that judges be afforded the ability to modify the law as they saw fit in pursuance of the desired goal of achieving justice.

But not everyone shared this view of the desirability of a judiciary essentially making the law it would then enforce. A vocal minority was beginning to advocate the need for a constitutional convention, which they hoped would culminate in a new state constitution following the federal pattern. Until that occurred, the state would continue to wallow in its hybrid system, where the rights, and perhaps even the fate, of the defendant often were decided long before his trial, simply by the prosecutor's decision as to which body of law he would use.

Those who defended the existing system argued that the original settlers had brought with them the accumulated body of English common law, which they then adopted as their own. For nearly two centuries, Connecticut's courts had been interpreting that common law and thus had made their own substantial contribution to that body of law. How could anyone realistically suggest, the proponents of the status quo would ask, that all of this law be simply tossed aside and replaced with only those provisions specifically addressed by the legislature? Indeed, the argument continued, how could the legislature ever codify every possible crime, let alone prescribe its punishment? The task was not merely daunting; it was impossible.

Connecticut's constitutional history, however, suggested that the colony's original settlers did not intend to simply pick up where the English courts had left off. Advocates for a constitutional convention would point to this provision in 1672 revisions to the Fundamental Orders:

> No man's life shall be taken away; no man's honour and good name shall be stained; no man's person shall be arrested, restrained, banished, dismembered, nor any ways punished; no man shall be deprived of his wife or children; no man's goods or estate shall be taken away from him, nor any ways endamaged; under colour of law, or countenance of authority unless it be by virtue or equity of some express law established by the general court.

At the time of Prince's trial, there was on the books a statutory provision establishing as a crime the act of administering poison with intent to murder. Hosmer's allegations clearly fell within the acts proscribed by the statute, so the casual observer might ask why anyone should have a problem with Prince's trial and conviction. Admittedly, as far as the elements of the crime were concerned, the critics would be hard pressed to fashion a strong argument against Prince's prosecution under the common law.

The elements of the crime, however, constituted only the first half of the statute. The second half prescribed the punishment: "imprisonment in the New-Gate prison during life, or for any time not less than ten years." Again, the casual observer might wonder where the problem lay, since Prince was sentenced to a term wholly consistent with the statute.

The problem lay not with the statute, however, but with the consequences of its provision for life imprisonment. Another Connecticut statute, also in effect at the time of Prince's trial, required that any person charged with a crime for which the punishment was either death or life imprisonment be presented to the grand jury. The general assembly had mandated that these serious offenses could be prosecuted only after a grand jury had made a determination that there was cause to believe that the defendant had committed the crime and had issued an indictment in the form of a "true bill."

There was no indictment in Prince's case, because there was no grand jury. Had Hosmer charged Prince under the statute, rather than with a common law crime, he would have been compelled to present the case to a grand jury. Was Hosmer worried that the grand jury might not return a true bill? That hardly seems likely, especially with such compelling evidence to support the prosecution. Was he laboring under time constraints that are not apparent on the record? That, too, seems unlikely, since the incident occurred in early

August and Prince was tried in the middle of December, only four months later. Court dockets in 1811 certainly were not as crowded as they would become two centuries later.

Unfortunately, answers to these questions are not to be found in the record of Prince's case, since the entire record consists of the single page of the information.[4] No other trial documents, if indeed there were any, appear to have survived. There was no appeal from Prince's conviction; had such an appeal been taken, a better record certainly would have been created to assist in the historical evaluation of Prince's case. Consequently, we are left with very little to assist us in discovering why Hosmer proceeded as he did.

It is likely that politics also figured heavily in the manner of Prince's prosecution. The vast majority of those in power throughout this time were Federalists, staunchly devoted to preserving their wealth and their property holdings. They strongly, even vituperatively, opposed the efforts of the egalitarian Jeffersonians, whose agenda was primarily devoted to mobilizing the poor to wrest power from the established order. Common law prosecutions such as Prince's would have served the Federalists well, in demonstrating that the existing judiciary was fully capable of safeguarding the population from criminal elements and that the Jeffersonian calls for a revolutionary change in the structure of state government were misguided.

Almost certainly, Hosmer was a Federalist and thus a staunch advocate of the common law; he may well have seen Prince's prosecution as an opportunity to demonstrate to constitutional reformists that the existing system worked perfectly well. That possibility has some support in the fact that, in the decade preceding Prince's conviction, at least four other persons had been tried, convicted, and sentenced to life imprisonment without benefit of the grand jury, under informations charging common law crimes.

Far more puzzling than Hosmer's motivations, however, are those of Prince. At the time of his conviction, Prince was eighty-seven years of age. What would prompt a sick, elderly slave, with apparently no prior indication of criminal propensity, to engage in a plot that he must have known had little likelihood of success and in which his complicity would certainly be discovered?

Prince was no doubt oblivious to the constitutional issues or political machinations that may have surrounded his trial and conviction. He alone knew what events had driven him to his desperate act, and now the time had come for him to face its consequences. Quite likely, then, as Prince heard the verdict and listened to the judge's sentence, his only concern was with the fate that awaited him: life imprisonment in the dungeon that was Newgate prison.

· 2 ·

The Early Years

$\mathcal{A}$lthough Prince was convicted on December 21, 1811, he would not be transported to Newgate for another seven days. His departure was delayed by the Christmas blizzard of 1811, forever immortalized in Whittier's *Snowbound.*[1] For Prince, this meant that he would spend his final week in Middletown as the solitary occupant of the county jail, a one-room wooden structure situated on the Washington Street green, in the center of the town's business and commercial district.

Indeed, winter had come early to Connecticut in 1811. The first nor'easter struck in late October, abruptly denying the oaks and maples their autumnal glory. By early November the ponds had frozen over, and the lakes would soon follow. During that entire month, the temperature would briefly rise above freezing only twice, but each time only to allow another storm to work its way up the coast and add to the winter's already substantial snowfall.

It was a pattern that had begun in 1807 and was intensifying with each passing year.[2] The Connecticut River, flowing only a single block to the east of the county jail, had been freezing each year since the beginning of this harsh weather pattern, and by this time the ice floes were getting increasingly larger and more numerous; in a matter of days the river would become frozen solid and impassable. To be stuck in port over the winter was an invitation to disaster, both economic and physical. Not only would the loss of a season's voyage threaten financial disaster for a ship's owners, but the masses of ice pressing against the hull throughout the entire winter almost certainly would wreak havoc on the vessel itself.

A frozen Connecticut River would have a serious adverse effect on Middletown's economy, but not nearly as disastrous as it would have had in an earlier era, for the Middletown of 1811 was but a shadow of its former maritime

9

self. Throughout the eighteenth century, and especially around the time of the War for Independence, Middletown had enjoyed a status and prosperity unique among its sister towns in Connecticut.[3]

For more than eighty years, Prince had lived and toiled in the midst of this activity, but he certainly had not been among those privileged to share in the town's prosperity. Rather, his was a life spent in the service of others and for others' benefit. From the moment he had stepped off the slaver onto the Middletown docks as a child of six or seven, Prince had known not a day when he could call his life his own. He probably spent his early slave years as a farm hand, tending to crops and farm animals. Some thirty years later, Prince was acquired by Philip Mortimer and labored at least another forty years as a spinner in Mortimer's ropewalk. In all, Prince could look back on more than eight decades spent at the service of a series of masters, some more benevolent than others, but all masters nonetheless.

As a spinner, Prince possessed a skilled trade that would have assured him a good income, and thus a good life, had he been a free man. His status as a slave, however, meant that his years of service would be rewarded, at best, with the basic necessities and little more. His long life near the Connecticut had enriched him, however, with an intimate knowledge of the river and its importance to his town. Although in winters past Prince had seen a hard freeze on the river, it was an uncommon occurrence. In recent years, however, the freeze-over had become an annual event, and an unwelcome one at that. Although Middletown's days of maritime glory were on the wane, that part of its history was not yet totally defunct. Prince, along with most of the town's population, was acutely aware of the extent to which Middletown's fortunes remained tied to the river, and the economic threat posed by its frozen waters, particularly when they arrived so early in the winter season.

The Connecticut is not a majestic river, offering neither the tremendous breadth and magnificent palisades of the Hudson nor the exciting white-capped rapids of the Penobscot. Rather, it derives its appeal from the manner in which its calmly flowing waters blend with the surrounding countryside to form a cohesive landscape. The longest river in New England, it rises from two lakes, appropriately named the Connecticut Lakes, situated in northernmost New Hampshire, near the Canadian border. From there, the river flows in a southerly direction, forming most of the border between New Hampshire and Vermont; it then continues through western Massachusetts and central Connecticut, emptying into Long Island Sound, a total distance of 360 miles from its headwaters.[4]

The river is navigable for most of its distance through Connecticut. Although a Dutch explorer, Adriaen Block, first explored the river in 1614, it would be left to the Puritans to settle it some twenty years later. That first settlement, Windsor, lies some forty-five miles inland from the mouth of the Connecticut. Middletown, so named because of its location at the approximate halfway point between Windsor and the Sound, was first settled around 1650. Although the river flows southerly throughout Connecticut, in Middletown it takes a sharp turn to the east and continues in that direction for a few miles before resuming its southerly flow. That sudden change in direction has caused the river to widen somewhat at the elbow of the curve and to form a natural harbor, a fact that was fundamental to the subsequent development of Middletown as a maritime community.

Shipbuilding began in Middletown as early as 1676, and by the 1750s the river port had developed a substantial trade with both England and the West Indies. Middletown played a particularly significant role in the war effort during the revolution, since enemy vessels were not inclined to venture this far up the river. Distance was not the only factor contributing to Middletown's safety; some two and a half miles south of Middletown harbor, the Connecticut River narrows to fewer than 500 feet, causing the flow to increase significantly. A captain attempting to sail against this force finds that piloting skill is not the only factor involved in a successful run up the straits—a favorable southerly wind is also essential. If the wind is not there when the ship arrives, then there is no alternative but to wait it out, hardly a plan conducive to a successful surprise attack on Middletown.

Thus, the town's shipbuilding contribution continued unhampered throughout the war. The *Bourbon,* the *Trumbull,* and the *Connecticut*—all were warships that could claim Middletown as their place of birth. Prince had walked each of their decks, and those of many others, delivering miles of line for the ships' rigging.

Shipbuilding, as well as maritime trading, remained strong even after independence had been achieved, so that Middletown was designated a United States Customs port, quite a rarity for a town so far removed from the coast. This degree of activity ensured Middletown's continued growth into the 1790s, when the town's population reached over 5,000 inhabitants, making it the largest community in the state.

Politics, however, was destined to reverse the town's century of growth and good fortune. In 1807, President Jefferson persuaded Congress to adopt the Embargo Act to curtail the seizing of American ships by the English and the French, who were then at war. Both countries were freely seizing goods and impressing American crews into their own navies. Madison's Non-Intercourse Act of 1809 continued the embargo. While achieving their goal of protecting American property and crews, these acts also had an incidental disastrous effect on the economy of trade-reliant towns such as Middletown. For nearly four years now, ships had remained in port, cutting off access to

Middletown Harbor, 1799–1801. Watercolor by Miss M. Russell. (The Connecticut Historical Society Museum)

foreign and even national markets for produce and locally manufactured goods.

So began the decline of Middletown. Although newly developing manufacturing activity had begun to take up the slack of the declining maritime economy, it could not compensate entirely for that loss. Prominent local families, recognizing the direction in which the town appeared to be heading, moved westward to New York and Ohio, where a number of them had been granted land holdings as a reward for their service in the War for Independence.

Prince had ample time during the week following his conviction to look back on a life that already had spanned nearly nine decades, more than eight of which had seen him held in bondage. Although northerners preferred the term "servant," the harsh reality was that Prince had been a slave for nearly all of his long life, since the day he had disembarked from the slaver onto the docks of Middletown. If he had any memories of his early life in Guinea, on the west coast of Africa, or of his abduction from his Susu village at the age of six or seven, he is not known to have spoken of it in later years.

Prince's recollection of the sea voyage was at best vague, not only because of the passage of time but also because of the illness that had consumed him during the trip. No man, however, would want to remember that voyage, forced to lie with the others, shackled on wooden bunks, with little food and no choice but to void in place, with human waste dripping continually onto the person on the bunk below, all constantly adding to the unbearable stench and bacteria-infested environment.

When Prince's slaver arrived in Middletown, it was almost certainly greeted by the town's two slave dealers, Dr. Walker and Captain Gleason, whose businesses were situated at nearly opposite ends of Main Street.

As disruptive as the symptoms of Prince's yaws may have been, it is unlikely that his chronic illness was an obstacle to his masters' determination to make full use of his productivity.[5] In all probability, Prince was first acquired by a farming family, spending his youth and young adulthood tending to farm animals and helping with the planting and harvesting of crops. Documented histories of Connecticut slavery suggest that Prince and others like him were not made to work any harder than their masters' families, who generally labored alongside their slaves in the field. Prince would not have been denied the basic necessities of life—adequate food, appropriate clothing, and shelter from the elements—nor would he have wanted for the limited palliative care for his yaws that eighteenth-century medicine could offer.[6]

Prince's experience would have been typical of the manner in which slavery had developed in Connecticut throughout the seventeenth century and the first half of the eighteenth.[7] The Puritans who settled Connecticut accepted slavery as part of the natural order in which they lived. If necessary, they could

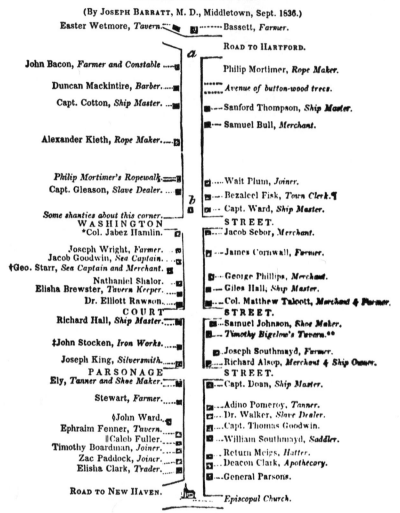

PLAN OF MAIN STREET, MIDDLETOWN, SHOWING THE BUILDINGS AND OCCUPANTS, FROM ABOUT 1770 TO 1775.

(By Joseph Barratt, M. D., Middletown, Sept. 1836.)

Easter Wetmore, *Tavern.* ......Bassett, *Farmer.*

ROAD TO HARTFORD.

John Bacon, *Farmer and Constable* ....

Philip Mortimer, *Rope Maker.*

Duncan Mackintire, *Barber.*....

Avenue of button-wood trees.

Capt. Cotton, *Ship Master.* ...

...Sanford Thompson, *Ship Master.*

— Samuel Bull, *Merchant.*

Alexander Kieth, *Rope Maker.*....

Philip Mortimer's *Ropewalk.*==

Capt. Gleason, *Slave Dealer.* ...

....Wait Plum, *Joiner.*

— Bezaleel Fisk, *Town Clerk.*¶

-- Capt. Ward, *Ship Master.*

Some shanties about this corner.

WASHINGTON   STREET.

*Col. Jabez Hamlin.

....Jacob Sebor, *Merchant.*

Joseph Wright, *Farmer.*

Jacob Goodwin, *Sea Captain.*

--James Cornwall, *Farmer.*

†Geo. Starr, *Sea Captain and Merchant.*

Nathaniel Shalor.

Elisha Brewster, *Tavern Keeper.*....

--George Phillips, *Merchant.*

--Giles Hall, *Ship Master.*

--Col. Matthew Talcott, *Merchant & Farmer.*

Dr. Elliott Rawson.

COURT   STREET.

Richard Hall, *Ship Master.*

--Samuel Johnson, *Shoe Maker.*

-- Timothy Bigelow's *Tavern.***

‡John Stocken, *Iron Works.*....

.Joseph Southmayd, *Farmer.*

Joseph King, *Silversmith.*

..Richard Alsop, *Merchant & Ship Owner.*

PARSONAGE   STREET.

Ely, *Tanner and Shoe Maker.*

--Capt. Doan, *Ship Master.*

Stewart, *Farmer.*

...Adino Pomeroy, *Tanner.*

◊John Ward.

...Dr. Walker, *Slave Dealer.*

Ephraim Fenner, *Tavern.*

...Capt. Thomas Goodwin.

‖Caleb Fuller.

...William Southmayd, *Saddler.*

Timothy Boardman, *Joiner.*

.Return Meigs, *Hatter.*

Zac Paddock, *Joiner.*

..Deacon Clark, *Apothecary.*

Elisha Clark, *Trader.*

--General Parsons.

ROAD TO NEW HAVEN.

Episcopal Church.

Plan of Main Street, Middletown, 1790 to 1800, by Dr. Joseph Barratt, drawn 1836.

look to the Bible for its justification, where Hebrew law permitted the enslavement of captured heathens. Further, the settlers readily accepted as natural the division of society into a number of distinct classes: the relationships of man to god, subject to ruler, child to parent, and servant to master—all seemed valid testament to the proper order of society as ordained by God.

Slavery first arose in Connecticut as a result of wars between the settlers and native tribes, first the Narragansetts and later the Pequots. Captive Indians, however, proved to be unsatisfactory slaves. They were far from docile, and the fact that many were native to the area facilitated their frequent escape. Had the Indian population remained as the sole supply source for slaves, the institution would have disappeared in Connecticut by the early 1700s. But the importation of blacks began in earnest at about the same time, ensuring that human bondage would continue to be part of the colony's social and economic experience for yet some time.

Prince's arrival in Connecticut around 1730 came at a time when the black slave population was on the increase, although much more rapid growth would occur during the twenty years preceding the Revolution. Slave trading was active in Middletown throughout this time, eventually rivaling the intensity that occurred in Newport, Rhode Island, the North's primary slave center, which supplied slaves for distribution throughout the region.

Historically, it was always believed that northern plantation farming was limited to Rhode Island and that slaves sold to plantation farmers in the Newport area faced a fate not unlike that of their counterparts in the southern states. The prevailing belief was that such large-scale plantation farming never developed in Connecticut and that, as a result, most Connecticut slaves found themselves utilized as house servants or as hands on small family-owned farms. Recent archaeological work in the area of Salem, Connecticut, however, has uncovered evidence that a number of plantations, some much larger than anything in Rhode Island, were prospering in parts of eastern Connecticut in the early and mid-eighteenth century.[8]

Although the experience of Connecticut plantation slaves may have been somewhat different, for the most part the relationship between master and servant in the state, and generally throughout the North, was dictated by the religious and moral code that governed most other aspects of colonial life. Slaves were generally considered members of the household. The relationship was similar to that of children whose care and protection was entrusted to the master. The master was also expected to assume the responsibility for Christianizing his servants and having their children baptized. Many of the clergy owned one or two servants; these men of the cloth saw this relationship as fully in accord with God's will. By taking these poor wretches from a heathen land and converting them to Christianity, they saw themselves as assisting in the salvation of their souls.

In the late 1750s, Prince was acquired by Philip Mortimer, a man whose visions and decisions would prove to have a profound impact on the remainder of Prince's life.

Philip Mortimer had arrived in Middletown from Ireland only one year earlier, by way of a short stay in Boston. Then in his late forties, he was already a man of wealth. Apparently, sensing a growing need for ropewalks to provide line for the burgeoning shipbuilding industry, Mortimer had been scouring the New England colonies in search of an appropriate location to build such a facility. Although Boston enjoyed an active shipbuilding industry, the presence of a number of ropewalks in the city suggested that competition for business would be an obstacle to success. The same circumstance likely proved to be the case in all the New England coastal cities involved in shipbuilding.

Mortimer no doubt saw opportunity in Middletown immediately upon his arrival. Although the town's shipbuilding industry was well established, Mortimer must have recognized that it had not yet reached its peak. And, as good fortune would have it, the town did not have a ropewalk. The local shipbuilders were compelled to buy all of their rigging from rope makers in New London or even as far away as New York or Boston, which added to costs and put the local builders at a competitive disadvantage. A few conversations at the local taverns with the more prominent townsfolk soon convinced Mortimer that this was the location he had been seeking. In a matter of months, the Irishman had acquired a parcel of land on Main Street, just one block from the harbor, and construction of Middletown's very own ropewalk was underway.

Eighteenth-century sailing vessels consumed an incredible amount of rope, or line. Fully rigged ships hoisted at least fifteen sails, each of which was edged with boltrope around its perimeter. There were halyards for raising and lowering the yardarms, tacks, bowlines, buntlines, clewlines, and leechlines. Then there was the running rigging for raising and lowering the sails, all of which had to be long enough to run up and down the entire length of the masts. Ratlines provided the means for sailors to get about the rigging while under sail. All in all, this complicated labyrinth of ropes constituted the nerves and tendons giving life to the ship's skeleton of hull and masts.

Not only was a ship's rigging extensive, but many of the lines also had to be long and unbroken. Every ship required a number of anchor lines at least 120 fathoms in length. Manufacturing ropes of that length required a special structure, and eighteenth-century ropewalks could trace their heritage back to the days of the Egyptians.

Townspeople who had never seen a ropewalk must have marveled at the unusual structure they saw being erected. Beginning on the westerly side of Main Street at the northerly end of the town green, the single-story building was about one thousand feet in length and about twenty-five feet wide.[9] Within the building would take place all but the first of the several distinct procedures involved in rope making.

Hemp harvested in Asia or the western and southern territories would be stored in large bales outside the ropewalk. Workers would use a hatchel, a special tool resembling an oversized hairbrush, to comb out the hemp fiber and remove knots and dirt. The hackled hemp would then be brought into the ropewalk to be spun into yarn.

Spinning was a skilled trade, and master spinners could achieve that status only after serving a long apprenticeship. A spinner would begin by securing a bundle of hackled hemp around his waist. He would attach a few fibers of the hemp to a spinning wheel, located at the very end of the ropewalk. On one side of the wheel was a crankcase handle, usually operated by a boy whose only concern was turning the wheel at a uniform rate. The wheel was attached by a pulley system to a series of six whorls, each of which was connected to the main wheel by its own thin line. This pulley system enabled three spinners, working together, to spin as many as a half dozen yarns simultaneously. A master spinner was able to spin two yarns at a time, letting out hemp with each hand and teasing it between his thumb and fingers as the wheel's turning imparted the necessary twist. The spinner would walk backwards from the wheel as he spun, stopping only to take on more hemp as needed. Eventually, the spinner would end up at the far end of the ropewalk with two yarns about a thousand feet in length.

Being a natural fiber, hemp was susceptible to deterioration from the weather and salt air. To delay this process, workers would then gather up the yarn to be tarred and seasoned.

Next, a number of tarred yarns would be laid out on the forming ground of the ropewalk. They were compressed together by being pulled through holes in a rack and would then be spun, in the opposite direction from the yarns, to form a strand. Finally, the rope would be made from three or more strands, depending on the desired thickness of the rope, twisted together in the opposite direction from that of the strands.

The length of the ropewalk was dictated by the fact that each step in the process reduced the length of the final product. Since ships required ropes of at least 100-fathoms (600 feet), it was necessary to start out with yarns of a thousand feet, and thus that was the length of the ropewalk.

Another necessary ingredient in the rope-making process was manpower. Although Middletown was the largest community in the state, counting nearly six thousand souls at about this time, the population was fully employed. Further, the work being offered at the ropewalk was not likely to be appealing to men accustomed to working outdoors in the lumber and shipbuilding trades. The one certain source for such labor was the slave population of the town and beyond. At the time, Middletown's black slave population was the third largest in Connecticut, counting approximately 225 men, women, and children servants.

Mortimer set out to acquire the twenty or so men he would need to work the ropewalk. His first efforts were probably directed at the town's free white population, but he must not have met with much success, prompting him to supplement his hired force with slave labor. By offering generous payment to local slave owners, he may well have been able to obtain the remainder of the necessary work force. These slaves, being already versed in English, would have been far preferable to the new arrivals he might have procured from the slave dealers.

No doubt Mortimer was able to lure a few spinners from other New England ropewalks to help train the rest of the work force and oversee the beginning of production. The ropewalk appears to have been an immediate success. At the time, Prince was in his late thirties, and he probably began his career performing the more menial jobs, such a hackling. Eventually, he apprenticed as a spinner, and it appears that he became quite proficient at the trade, since Mortimer's will, drafted some thirty years later, makes specific reference to Prince being "kept at spinning."

Prince's illness must have presented him with a challenge. Dexterity was a necessary attribute for a competent spinner, and the combination of scar tissue and new nodules covering his hands and fingers must have required Prince to make constant adjustments in the way he held the yarn. His subsequent long career as a spinner, however, confirms that he was successful at working around his handicap.

A line used on any part of a ship had to be strong and reliable, qualities present only to the degree that the underlying spinning of the yarn and strands was properly done, and Prince's developing status as a master spinner must have made him increasingly valuable to Mortimer. At the beginning of the War for Independence, Prince had been at the ropewalk for about fifteen years. Despite his enhanced status in the ropewalk, however, Prince's status in society did not, and could not, follow suit.

As much as Philip Mortimer may have appreciated Prince's efforts at the ropewalk, it probably never occurred to him to show that gratitude to any great degree. Although Prince never wanted for adequate food and clothing and was given reasonable opportunity for relaxation on evenings and Sundays, the fact remained that each night his head still rested on the same cot in the ropewalk bunkroom as he had first occupied nearly two decades before.

Prince may have been accepting of his physical lot, but he was also well aware of the rising emancipation movement that was gathering strength. Abolition sentiment was particularly strong in Rhode Island, which had a substantial antislavery Quaker population, but it also had its advocates in Connecticut, and the colony's newspapers were regularly reporting the debate over the continuance of slavery as an institution. Now in his early fifties, Prince had been laboring as a servant for more than four decades, and what he heard of the growing abolition movement must have filled his head with dreams of living out the remainder of his life as a free man.

But this was 1774, and more pressing issues were occupying the minds of Connecticut's citizenry, so the fight for abolition would have to yield to a more immediate struggle. John Locke's theories of natural right were being preached from pulpits throughout the colonies as justification for separation from an autocratic monarchy. What was not then appreciated by the colonists, but in its time would become painfully clear, was that Locke's theories were equally applicable to the institution of slavery. The time for that debate, however, had not yet arrived.

· 3 ·

The Will to Be Free

*D*uring the first few years of the revolution, Middletown's protected position some twenty miles inland enabled the port to function unhampered in its shipbuilding industry,[1] and Philip Mortimer's ropewalk was hard-pressed to produce all of the rigging demanded by these new vessels. Long days, with only minimal periods of rest, were the norm.

The burden that fell so hard on Prince and the other workers and servants in the ropewalk did not arise because of any opportunistic greed on the part of Mortimer. Rather, the principal factor was the severe shortage of labor, since Middletown had responded with patriotic fervor to the call to arms. As a result, a substantial percentage of the town's prime work force was away at war, and the remaining population was simply inadequate to meet the demand, not only for Mortimer but for the other trades as well.

Mortimer himself was fervently patriotic. He never took for granted the opportunities that his adopted country had afforded him, and he may well have regretted that his advancing age kept him from assuming a more direct role in the war effort. However much he recognized that his ropewalk served an important role in that effort, Mortimer probably believed his contribution inadequate and was determined to do more.

By 1780, the war was not going well. September 1777 saw the Continentals suffer the loss of over 1,000 troops at Brandywine, a defeat that enabled the British to take control of Philadelphia. Only a month later, Washington's failed attempt to recapture the city was made all the more frustrating by the fact that the Patriot failure at the battle of Germantown was due in part to American flanks firing on each other in dense fog.

The ordeal of the Continental Army at Valley Forge during the winter of 1777–1778 did nothing to inspire confidence in the Americans' likelihood of success; estimates of losses during that encampment range as high as 2,500 soldiers. American spirits continued to be dampened when they suffered heavy casualties in the South. An attempt in October 1779 to regain Savannah saw another substantial American defeat, followed the next summer by an equally disastrous rout in Camden, South Carolina. In light of such defeats, even some supporters of the cause had begun to say openly that they believed the colonies might lose the war.

These circumstances must have spelled especially bad news for Prince. As a slave, he knew full well that his fortunes were dependent on the success of the war for independence. Slave trade was an integral element of British commerce, and an English victory would guarantee the absence in the foreseeable future of any change in Prince's lot or, for that matter, that of any other American slave.

The American forces were becoming increasingly depleted, and Congress had put out a plea to all of the states for more men. The call extended not only to freemen but to slaves as well. Throughout the colonies, slaveholders were being implored to commit their servants to the cause, and Mortimer's patriotism prompted him to respond immediately to the opportunity. What his age prevented him from doing directly, he would accomplish vicariously through his servants.

So Prince, quite probably accompanied by some of Mortimer's other male slaves, was off to war. In all likelihood, this was not a terribly distressing situation for him. He certainly shared the abolishionists' belief that their movement had only been slowed down, and not completely thwarted, by the war. Also, Prince was aware that many Connecticut slaves had been promised their freedom as a reward for serving in the Continental Army. Such a reward, it was common knowledge, had even been promised to Southern slaves from Virginia. So Prince went off to serve in the Continental Army harboring the likely hope, if not the expectation, that his service in the war would become his means of attaining freedom.

The only known record of the extent of Prince's service in the war is revealed in a short passage in Phelps' *Newgate of Connecticut, Its Origin and Early History*, written in 1844. Phelps writes of Prince that "[h]e was a servant to different officers in the Revolutionary War; had been sent on errands by General Washington, and said he had 'straddled many a cannon when fired by the Americans at the British troops.'"

Colonial records are inconclusive in verifying the nature of Prince's service record, but regardless of the extent to which he actually participated in the war, it is reasonable to assume that he returned from service harboring the same hopes shared by most of the other returning slaves. For many, not only in the North but even in the South, those hopes would indeed become reality, as their masters honored their promises and emancipated them for service in the cause of American independence.

But Prince's lot was not to follow that course. After the war, he returned to his work as a spinner in Mortimer's ropewalk, and life for Prince was probably no different from what it had been when Connecticut was but an English colony. It is easy to imagine Prince's frustration, perhaps even resentment, at seeing fellow slaves, men with whom he had fought shoulder to shoulder, rewarded with freedom while he himself was denied that recognition.

Prince's heightened desire for freedom would not have been purely subjective. All around him were indications that slavery as a social and economic institution in Connecticut was in decline. The humanitarian idealism that had fueled the revolution could no longer deny the inconsistency of its philosophical tenets with the institution of slavery. Further, it was becoming increasingly apparent that slavery was unprofitable and a threat to free white labor, especially now that the white work force was being rapidly augmented by an army of returning men.

The Connecticut legislature never demanded of masters that they free slaves who served in the war. In 1777, however, it did encourage that result by releasing masters of financial responsibility for slaves freed because of military service.

The citizenry of Connecticut was probably reconciled to the eventual abolition of slavery, but this fundamentally conservative state was not about to overturn instantaneously an institution with roots going back a century and a half. In 1784, the General Assembly passed an act intended to begin the process of deinstitutionalizing slavery in the state. It provided:

> Whereas sound policy requires that abolition of slavery should be effected as soon as may be, consistent with the right of individuals, and the public safety and welfare. Therefore, Be it enacted, that no negro or molatto child, that shall after the first day of March, one thousand seven hundred and eighty-four, be born within this State, shall be held in servitude, longer than until they arrive to the age of twenty-five years, notwithstanding the mother or parent of such child was held in servitude at the time of its birth; but such child, at the age aforesaid, shall be free: any law, usage, or custom to the contrary notwithstanding.

In this way, Connecticut sought to achieve its goal of complete emancipation, albeit on an attrition basis, while at the same time preserving the property interests of slaveholders. The stain of slavery would eventually be eradicated from the state, although the process would take several decades. Part of the law's efficacy, however, probably was to encourage slave owners to free their slaves voluntarily without waiting for the time limits of the statute to take effect.

Despite the fact that no slaves were immediately freed by the Act of 1784, its passage must have served to intensify both Prince's frustration as well as his desire for freedom. Now turning sixty, Prince may well have been wondering whether he would ever become a free man. He may have begun to believe that he was destined to live out his remaining years in servitude, no less a slave than he had become some fifty-three years ago, as a young boy shackled to a wooden bunk in the rank bowels of a slave ship.

Middletown's status as a maritime community was at its height as it prepared to enter the final decade of the eighteenth century. These were indeed Middletown's golden years. There was one element of these times, however, that was dampening Philip Mortimer's ability to appreciate fully the fruits of thirty years of labor in creating his prosperous enterprise: He was growing old.

Now in his early eighties, Mortimer was increasingly aware of the reality that his time on earth was growing short. No doubt, fewer days were being spent at the ropewalk and more at his mansion. His stately home was situated off the northern end of Main Street, on a private lane that the town residents knew as the "Avenue of the Buttonwood Trees," a tribute to the sycamores that lined the route to the mansion. The site lay on a gently sloping grade, covered with grassy lawns that made their way down to the riverbank. Mortimer enjoyed the role of gracious host; he caused benches to be placed along the walkway, an open invitation to the local citizenry to sit a spell and enjoy the view. It was probably the most pleasant site in all of Middletown, and during the war many American and French officers had partaken of Philip Mortimer's hospitality, reportedly on several occasions dancing the summer evenings away beneath the sycamores.

Now those days were but an ever-receding memory. From his front porch, Mortimer could still look south and enjoy his unobstructed view of the river bend and the Middletown docks. While he might savor his moments of reminiscence, however, Mortimer was too much the seasoned businessman to be content to live in the past and not plan for the future. It was probably on that very porch, then, that Philip Mortimer began to plan his last will and testament.

Mortimer's "family" stretched the definition of that term, even by today's broad standards. His wife, Martha, had died in 1773, leaving him no children. Mortimer's only blood relative in America was his niece, Ann Carnall, who had come from Ireland in the mid-1760s, when she was in her early twenties, to live with her uncle. In 1775, at the age of thirty, Ann married George Starr, a prominent Middletown merchant. Starr would later distinguish himself during the war as the state's quartermaster, a position of some responsibility, since each state bore the burden of outfitting and sustaining its own troops.

George and Ann were blessed with two children. Martha was born in 1777, to be followed after the war, in 1783, by her brother, Philip Mortimer Starr. Mortimer's will would make reference to his having previously adopted Ann as his daughter, but there is no independent evidence that he ever legally did so. Consequently, Martha and Philip were in actuality Mortimer's grandniece and grandnephew, but that technicality did not prevent him from becoming their de facto grandfather nor them from becoming the focal point of the old man's later years.

Since their births, Mortimer had been partial to his two "adopted" grandchildren, and his retirement offered the aging gentleman ample opportunity to form an even tighter bond with the children, especially with Philip. Although Mortimer's will makes it clear that he harbored a great fondness for Martha, it was Philip who totally captured his heart. It is easy to visualize the two of them looking out upon the harbor, whiling away endless summer hours in conversation on the veranda.

As Mortimer's will confirms, the two were inseparable. This relationship must have prompted great consternation, and perhaps even resentment, on the part of George Starr, Philip's father. He may well have come even to resent his son's name—Philip Mortimer Starr—obviously given to him as a tribute to the elder Mortimer.

The other part of Mortimer's "family" consisted of his numerous slaves, which he referred to as "servants." Since he never remarried after Martha's death some twenty years earlier, Mortimer continued to occupy his mansion, the "Mortimer Lodge," with his staff of about sixteen servants. Mortimer very much saw his servants as an extension of his family and as appropriate beneficiaries of his bounty.

Philip Mortimer had accumulated extensive land holdings, as well as substantial liquid assets and a wide range of personal property, ranging from valuable jewelry, through household goods and furniture, and down to his servants. Disposing of all of these divers assets in an orderly manner would have been a daunting task for even an "ordinary" will, if such a thing exists, but Mortimer's mind had fashioned bequests that were anything but ordinary.

What emerged is a document that, at the time, was undoubtedly the most complex testamentary disposition to see the light of day in Middletown and perhaps in all of Connecticut. It must have taken weeks, if not months, for Mortimer to fashion the various dispositions in his own mind, and then maybe just as long to commit them to paper. From an historical perspective, it was certainly a worthwhile effort, since the resulting six manuscript pages comprise a document that is truly magnificent; it speaks volumes about the man who was Philip Mortimer, of the men and women with whom he interacted, and of the times in which they lived.

Mortimer's will begins in the typical manner of the day (he also followed the custom of capitalizing all nouns and adjectives):

> In the name of God, Amen. I, Philip Mortimer of Middletown in the County of Middlesex and State of Connecticut in New England in America—being advanced in Years, but through the Goodness of God in Perfect Health and of Sound Mind and Memory, calling to Mind the Frailties of my Nature and that my Life if spared to Old Age is verging fast towards its Last Period in this Stage of Existence, that the Remainder of Life which it shall please God to allot me, be it Longer or Shorter, should be all (as far as may be) devoted to a Nearer Contemplation of and Due Preparation for that Final State of Existence which with Me must shortly commence, and to disencumber Myself as much as possible of Earthly Cares and Concerns upon the Approach, and upon the Hour of Death, do for the Letters of my Temporal Affairs make and ordain this my Last Will and Testament.

Mortimer then directs his interment in his tomb alongside his wife, in the cemetery he had previously given the town. Next, he devises additional land to be used for cemetery purposes "for any Person or Persons that may hereafter have Occasion to build Tombs."[2]

Mortimer also devises another parcel, also adjacent to the cemetery, to the Citizens of the City of Middletown "for a building Spott to Erect a Granary House after the following Dimensions for the Use of the Inhabitants of said City." The dimensions are set out with considerable specificity: The house is to be built of brick, forty feet square and two stories, each story to be twelve feet in height. Each story is to have four rooms, each of which is to be lighted by four windows, and the entry is to be eight feet in width, running through the length of the house. To finance the cost of construction, Mortimer bequeaths the City the sum of £600.[3]

In addition, Mortimer bequeaths to the same citizens of the City of Middletown the sum of £400

> for the purpose of purchasing One Thousand Bushells of Wheat, five hundred Bushells Rye and five hundred Bushells Indian Corn, always to be and remain as a Stock to supply the Necessities of those that may stand in Need, and to be always understood to be under the Management and Inspection of the Mayor and Aldermen of the City of Middletown for the Time being.

Mortimer then mentions his belief that he had previously adopted his niece Ann as his daughter, but he now takes pains to reiterate that intent in his will. That recital is very much relevant to Mortimer's next disposition, his bequest to Ann. Although Mortimer certainly harbored the love of a father towards Ann, and even more so for her son Philip, his feelings for her husband George apparently were hardly of the same caliber.

Mortimer apparently was grappling with the problem of determining how to provide properly for Ann and her children, but at the same time keeping his fortune outside of George's control. This was a difficult task, particularly in light of the status of the law of husband and wife as it then existed. Connecticut's law was consistent with the English common law, and that of the other states as well, in treating the relationship as a "marital unity." Upon their marriage, a man and a woman were considered in the law as a single entity, and for the most part that entity was personified in the husband. In most respects, particularly having to do with property rights, the law recognized no separate legal existence in the wife. Her status during the marriage was known as coverture; any property she brought to the altar, and any property she acquired during the marriage, automatically came within the unfettered control of the husband. It was a rule of law that would remain in effect in the state for many more years; not until 1877 would the Married Women's Act finally provide that "all property hereafter acquired by any married woman shall be held by her to her sole and separate use."

Mortimer's bequest to Ann initially gives the appearance of an absolute disposition; it begins:

> I give, devise and bequeath to my Niece Ann Starr, whom I have adopted as my Daughter, Mortimer Lodge, that is to say my Mansion House (so called), with the Lands, Buildings, Orchards and Gardens thereunto belonging ... also my Wife's Diamond and Emerald Rings ...

Immediately following that disposition Mortimer adds the brief phrase "for and During her Natural Life." The effect of those six words was to place all of his bequests to Ann substantially out of the reach of George. To be sure, although Ann's life estate would also come within the control of the law of coverture, George's rights in the property were significantly limited. George's interest would be only usufructuary. Literally, the term means that the husband had the right to "use the fruit" of the property. If the property was a bank account, the husband was entitled to its "fruit"—the accruing interest. If the property was real estate, the husband could claim the crops, and even rents, but he could not sell the property out from under the wife.

The grant of a life estate to Ann meant that she would receive all of the practical benefits of ownership of the mansion and the use of the jewelry, but they were not hers absolutely. Upon Ann's death they would not become part of her estate and thus would not pass to George if he were to survive her. Rather, the remainder interest in the mansion would pass immediately and absolutely to Ann's son, Philip. In addition, Mortimer then directs that the remainder interest in the jewelry, except for his wife's diamond ring, pass absolutely to Ann's daughter, Martha.

Although Mortimer had more bequests to make regarding Philip, he put those aside temporarily to address another group for whom he had particular concern: his servants. Mortimer then owned about seventeen slaves. Only two of them, Prince and Peter, worked in the ropewalk; since the death of his wife, however, he had come to rely heavily on his other servants to run the homestead. This reliance certainly peaked in the old man's later years, and his will makes it clear that he valued not only the benefit but also the comfort of their continuous presence in his home.

There is no indication that Mortimer ever freed any of his slaves during his lifetime. He had to be aware of the growing sentiments in the state for the abolition of slavery, yet like slave owners before and after him, he may well have believed that his entire staff, without exception, was completely devoted to him and to his home and quite content with their lot. After all, he could tell himself, did they not enjoy the run of his substantial house, with all the amenities it offered? Probably he earnestly believed that his bond with his staff was such that they would never wish to abandon their lifestyle for the uncertainty that would come with emancipation.

Such obtuseness did not mean that Mortimer was indifferent, much less hostile, to the idea of abolition. He probably merely believed that his situation was outside the general experience of the community when it came to the issue of slavery.

Even with the provision for Ann to enjoy life use of the mansion, Mortimer knew that his servants would come under the indirect control of Starr, and that was an outcome he apparently wished to avoid. Accordingly, Mortimer next turns his attention to these servants:

> I give unto my Negro Man Bristol after my Decease his Freedom. I also give him and his Wife Tamer the Garden Spot and House thereon as it is now fenced for and during their natural Lives.
>
> I give my Negro Woman Hagar and her Daughter their Freedom. I also give unto Hagar Five Pounds to buy her Mourning.
>
> I give unto the three Sons of my Negro Woman Sophy named Lester, Dick, and John in equal Parts one and three-quarters Acres Land adjoining Joseph Starr's Lot, forever reserving to my Negro Woman Sophy and her Husband Jack the Use and Improvement during their natural Lives. I also give Sophy and Jack their Freedom.
>
> I give unto my Negro Woman Amarillas her Freedom. I also give unto her and her Children one Rood Land at the west End of the Lot adjoining Joseph Starr's forever.

I give to my Negro Woman Silvy her Freedom directly after my Decease.

I give to my Negro Girl Peg when she shall arrive at the Age of Twenty-six her Freedom during which Time she shall live with and serve Elihu Starr.

The three young Children of Sophy named Lester, Dick, and John I would have brought up by their Mother Sophy and kept to School until they arrive to the age of Fourteen Years then put to Apprentice by my Executors, the two Eldest to be put to House Joiners until they arrive to the Age of Twenty-one Years and then give them their Freedom.

All of these servants worked and lived in the Mortimer mansion, and Mortimer's bequests were specifically directed at their particular needs, apparently on the basis of their ages. The younger servants, Mortimer must have believed, would be able to provide for themselves more easily than those, such as Jack and Sophy, who were older and who were also in need of providing for their family.

Prince and Peter, the servants working at the ropewalk, are the next to be given Mortimer's attention. Although Mortimer seems to have fully intended to grant both of them their eventual freedom, he also must have been concerned with the continuing viability of the ropewalk, perhaps as a source of income for Ann and her children. Prince and Peter were senior spinners and would be difficult, if not impossible, to replace. Mortimer was apparently convinced that their departure would seriously jeopardize the success of the ropewalk. Torn between these conflicting desires, Mortimer comes up with the best compromise that he could fashion: "I give to my Negro Peter three Years after my Decease his Freedom, which three Years he's to live with and serve Capt. George Starr." He makes the same bequest as to Prince, and then concludes, "My Will is that Peter and Prince both be kept at spinning."

After putting his mind at ease regarding his servants, Mortimer turns his attention back to his grandson. He clearly intended Philip to be the prime beneficiary of his will. He begins by reaffirming his adoption of Philip as his son, an incongruous act in view of the fact that he had also adopted Ann, Philip's mother, as his daughter. Mortimer appears not at all to have been troubled by the curious result of mother and son having been transformed into adoptive brother and sister; clearly, his chief goal was to legitimize the testamentary disposition that was to follow.

Having already given Philip the remainder interest in Mortimer Lodge, Mortimer goes on to devise to him the ropewalk and several additional parcels of land, including a wharf lot with a store, some city lots, and several large meadow tracts.

It must have always been a serious disappointment to Mortimer that he had had no male children to carry on the Mortimer name. Adopting Philip as his son was the first step, Mortimer certainly believed, towards remedying that circumstance. Although Mortimer did love Philip dearly, he appears also to have had an unabashed ulterior motive in making Philip his primary beneficiary and bestowing upon him one of the largest fortunes in the state.

That motive becomes immediately apparent when Mortimer continues penning his will. All of the bequests and devises to Philip are made

> under the following Limitations and Conditions, viz. that in Case the aforesaid Philip Mortimer Starr shall take the Name of Mortimer for his Sir Name and cause the same to be Confirmed and Established to him and his Descendants by the General Assembly of this State, then my Will is that all the Parcels of Real Estate together with the Appurtenances herein before Devised to George Starr and Ann Starr for the Term of their naturals Lives shall revert to the said Mortimer and his Heirs bearing the same Name forever and I do Give, Devise and Bequeath the Same to him and his Heirs Bearing the same Name accordingly.

In the event that Philip refuses to honor the condition, Martha is given life use of the property, and the remainder is to pass to her eldest son, provided he, too, agrees to adopt the Mortimer family name.

The only remaining business was the appointment of Mortimer's executors. Although the will itself says a great deal about Mortimer's less-than-favorable feelings for George Starr, Mortimer appears not to have been above rubbing some salt in the wound, and he did so by appointing George as one of his coexecutors. He also appointed two of his close friends, Elihu Starr and George Phillips, as additional coexecutors of the will. As Mortimer certainly knew quite well, no single coexecutor could act alone as to any of the duties or prerogatives that might arise in connection with probating the estate. By denying George the status of sole executor, he diminished Starr's power even more; Mortimer must have taken no small amount of delight in dwelling for a few moments on the frustration his niece's husband would experience because of that situation.

The final step lay in formalizing the will. It was not enough that he merely sign it. Connecticut law was similar to that of all the states; all had adopted the English common law rules regarding the requirements for a valid will. Not only did the will have to be signed, but the act of signing had to take place before three witnesses. Further, the testator was required to "publish and declare" the will before the witnesses. That is, the testator had to inform the witnesses that he was about to execute his last will and testament; they did not have to read it, nor be in any way familiar with its contents. They would sign the will as witnesses, in the presence of the testator and in the presence of each other. But their status was not merely passive. Witnesses to a will were charged with the burden of evaluating the testator's state of mind, at least to the extent of being satisfied that he was of sound disposing mind and memory, aware of his surroundings, and under no apparent improper influence or duress. In the event the will were ever to be challenged in court, the witnesses would be required to testify in court as to such matters.

On the morning of July 9, 1792, Mortimer summoned to his mansion the three men he wished to serve as witnesses. Although the terms of the will may have been extraordinary, there would be nothing unusual about the way in which the will would be executed. Without doubt, Mortimer followed the prescribed formalities for the proper execution of a last will and testament.

"I, Philip Mortimer," he would have begun, making eye contact with each witness as he spoke, "of the City of Middletown, County of Middlesex and State of Connecticut, publish and declare this document to be my last will and testament." He would have lifted the first page of the will so that it faced the witnesses, and held the page briefly before each witness, just long enough for them to read the first line, in which his name appeared.

"I further declare," Mortimer would have continued, "that I make this last will and testament of my own free will, that I am not acting under duress or under any improper influence or restraint. I have asked each of you to witness the execution of this instrument in my presence, and in the presence of each other."

With that, Mortimer lifted his quill pen, dipped the tip in the adjacent inkwell, and subscribed his name to the will. He then took the lit candle stationed in the corner of his desk and, holding it horizontally, allowed a few drops of wax to fall upon the paper, immediately to the right of his signature. Finally, he removed his silver seal from its special container and pressed firmly into the still-soft wax.

Mortimer's work was done. He handed the last page of the will to Timothy Starr, who also accepted Mortimer's pen and inscribed to the left of Mortimer's signature, "Signed, Sealed, Published & Declared in the Presence of—."

Beneath that phrase, Timothy subscribed his signature. He passed the page and the pen to Joseph Sage, who did likewise. Elihu Starr signed as the third witness, and the will was complete.

· 4 ·

The Codicils

$\mathcal{C}$onsidering the time involved in producing such a complex will, the house servants were quite probably aware of its existence, and perhaps even of its terms relating to their fate. So also might Prince have been aware of the less-than-ideal disposition Mortimer was making as to him and Peter. Although the house servants were to be freed immediately, the two spinners would be forced to continue working, under the control of George Starr, for three more years following Mortimer's passing. It was now 1792; although Mortimer, at eighty-two, may well have begun to show signs of advancing age, there was no reason to believe that he would not be around for quite some time. Prince was now about sixty-eight, and the prospect of continuing to live in servitude for another decade, or possibly even longer, must have been disheartening. Also, he must also have been galling to be less generously treated than the house servants. Certainly his life at the ropewalk had been harder than what the house servants were experiencing, working and living in the mansion. And now they were being granted their immediate freedom, while he was forced to wait.

If Mortimer was indeed favoring the house servants over Prince and Peter, so also was he partial to certain of those house servants over the others. The will granted to Sophy and her husband Jack not only their freedom but also life use in a house and lot on Main Street. Additionally, upon the death of Sophy and Jack, ownership of that property was to pass to their three sons, Lester, Dick, and John. In the 1790s, for a black family to own a house outright was uncommon enough, but for that house to be set on a valuable property lying in the heart of the town's business district made this bequest extraordinary, if not unique.

Mortimer's beneficence to Sophy's family did not end with the devise of the house and lot. He specifically directed that Sophy's three boys be kept in school until they were fourteen, and then the older two were to be apprenticed as joiners, a skilled and lucrative trade. And some fifteen months after the execution of the will, Mortimer took it upon himself to draft a codicil, or amendment, to his will. On a single sheet of paper, and in his own hand, he wrote:

> Middletown, October 8, 1793
>
> In addition to my last will which this cover Dated the 9th Day of July, 1792, I, Philip Mortimer do will & bequeath unto my Negro woman Sophy my chest which I had made at the beginning of the late War, also my wash kettle which contains about twenty four or five gallons, also one small kettle which contains about eight gallons, also so much of the furniture as either two of my executors shall see fitt to give her in part to furnish her for House Keeping.
>
> In order to enable my Negro Man Jack and his Wife Sophy to bring up their Children, my will is that they use and enjoy the Interest I have in a Fishing Place in Chatham Nearly opposite the House in which Reuben Plum and others are concerned, during their Natural Lives, and I give and bequeath unto Lester, Dick and John, Children of Jack and Sophy, my Right and Interest in the above said fishing place, after Jack and Sophy die, forever.

Chatham, most of which is now known as East Hampton, was located about ten miles east of Middletown, and was home to a small lake that was already well established as a fishing and hunting destination. No doubt, Lake Pocotapaug had offered Mortimer many years of good fishing; it was a pleasure, as the codicil suggests, that he was happy to share with his servants. It is easy to imagine Mortimer taking delight in the antics of Sophy's young boys, as they made their way back to the cabin with a mess of bass for Sophy to fry for her family and her master.

It is also easy to speculate that Mortimer may have had another motivation in making this additional devise: it would place yet another property outside of George Starr's control.

THE WINTER OF 1793–1794 must have been particularly difficult for both master and servant. Prince was likely still upset over his treatment in Mortimer's will, delaying yet again dreams of emancipation that had been filling his mind for decades. It was a dream fueled not only by his own natural desire for freedom but also by public opinion.

That public opinion does not appear to have troubled Mortimer, but he must have followed with interest newspaper reports of the formation of the Connecticut Anti-Slavery Society in 1790. Mortimer was certainly aware of the fervent preaching of a New Haven pastor, Jonathan Edwards Jr., who had

addressed the Society in 1791 at its Hartford conference. The *Courant* had reprinted the speech in its entirety. "To hold a man in a state of slavery who had
a right to his liberty," Edwards had said, "is to be every day guilty of robbing
him of his liberty, or of man-stealing, and is a greater sin in the sight of God
than concubinage or fornication."

Although the Puritans had joined with the Quakers in adopting the
Society's abolitionist agenda, the Episcopalian pulpit had not been nearly as
assertive in denouncing slavery. Indeed, since it can safely be presumed that
Mortimer's slaves routinely accompanied him to church, it is difficult to con-
jure up the image of a pastor, in the presence of those very slaves, lecturing one
of the town's most prominent citizens on the evils of slavery.

In any event, Philip Mortimer greeted the early spring of 1794 from what
was soon to be his deathbed. There is no indication of what malady caused his
abrupt physical deterioration; perhaps it was pneumonia, brought on by a flu,
or perhaps a stroke. Whatever the cause, Mortimer's energy was sapped.

Despite that limitation, the dying man was determined to effect some
additional changes to his will. In early March, he summoned to the mansion
his longtime friend Elihu Starr, probably a cousin of George Starr. If Elihu
had not seen his friend for a while, he must have been shaken by the emaciated
appearance of the old man lying before him—a man, as it turns out, who was
suffering through his last few days of life.

The purpose of the summons, as Mortimer disclosed, was not merely
social; Mortimer wished to rewrite his will, executed less than two years earlier. The changes to the will were relatively simple, though not insubstantial,
and easily could have been implemented through the use of a brief codicil.
Nonetheless, Mortimer was intent on having these changes incorporated into
a complete rewrite of the entire document. This was a task not easily accomplished; the will consisted of several tightly scripted legal-length pages. Too
weak to transcribe the will by himself, Mortimer had called on his friend to be
his hands for the project.

It must have been a slow and tedious process, no doubt made all the
more difficult by Mortimer's weakened state of health. At first, Elihu may
well have been doubting his friend's state of mind, since it was not until they
had reached the sixth page of the will that Mortimer finally dictated a change.
His earlier disposition as to Prince and Peter gave them their freedom three
years after his decease, during which time they were to continue working for
George Starr as spinners. Mortimer now dictated his new disposition regarding these two servants. He instructed Elihu to delete that prior provision and
to insert the following in its stead: "I give unto my Negro Peter his Freedom.
I give unto my Negro Prince his Freedom."

As it turned out, that simple provision constituted the only substantive the same Annually with the Judge of Probate for the time being, whome I appoint to superintend the same

Item   I Give and bequeath unto Lois the wife of Daniel Osborn of Stratford Fifty pounds Lawfull mony — I also Give and bequeath unto her oldest Son as a memorial of me Ten pounds Lawfull mony

Item   I Give and bequeath unto the Revᵈ Mr Abraham Jarvis Ten pounds Lawfull mony

Item   I Give and bequeath unto my Niece Ann Starr my Tomb for a burying place for them and their family this forever, also my pew in the Church which I Occupy

Item   my wearing apparel I Give to my Negros to be Equally Divided and disposed of amongst them as my Executors shall see fit

And I make and Ordain my Nephew George Starr and my respectable Friends Elihu Starr & George Phillips my Executors, to Each of which I Give five pounds Lawfull mony as a Token of my Esteem and in Case any of the [...] my estate that the [...] be supplied by the Judge of probate, in Testimony whereof I have hereunto set my hand And Seal in Middletown this 10 Day of March A.D. 1794

Signed Sealed published &
Declared in presence of us   Philip Mortimer

At a Court of Probate held in Middletown in and for the District of Middletown on the 25ᵗʰ day of Augᵗ A.D. 1794

Then this instrument was Exhibited in Court as a Codicil to the Last Will & Testament of Philip Mortimer Esqʳ late of Middletown Decᵈ was accepted & ordered to be Recorded in the Registry of this Court

Test Bezaleel Fisk Clerk

change to the entire will. Viewed from the perspective of all of the substantial devises and bequests found in the will as a whole, it was a minor amendment. Viewed, however, from the perspective of the two men whose lives would be affected by those eight short words, it held unchallenged promise as the most significant event of their lives.

The last paragraph concluded, "In Testimony whereof I have hereunto set my Hand and Seal in Middletown this 10th day of March A.D. 1794." Beneath that final line, Elihu Starr wrote:

> Signed, Sealed, Published &
> Declared in Presence of us

Elihu then carried the will to Mortimer, likely propping it up on the cover of a book so that the old man could review the will and sign it. Too weak to reread the entire document, Mortimer simply instructed Starr to turn to the last page. Elihu did so, and handed it to Mortimer; he then retrieved a pen from the desk and presented it to his dying friend. Summoning what little strength remained, Mortimer slowly signed his name to the will. But his hand was shaky, and each unsteady, wavering, letter of his signature certainly confirmed to Elihu that this was among the final acts of a man whose time on earth was rapidly coming to its close.

History has not recorded the definitive reason for Mortimer's change of heart. For many slave owners, economics was as much a factor as charity in their decisions to free their slaves, since Connecticut law made slave owners responsible for the continuing support of slaves that they emancipated. Mortimer's wealth suggests that such factors were not at work in this instance. A more plausible reason may lie in Mortimer's deep religious convictions, and it may be that the admonitions of abolitionists such as Jonathan Edwards had finally made their impression on a man preparing to stand face to face with his Redeemer. Perhaps Mortimer was struck by a sense of shame in not sooner having granted emancipation to his servants. Perhaps he was repentant for having attempted to fool himself with justifications, such as his poor health and chronic need for assistance in running the mansion. He may have come to believe that there was no longer any time for such duplicity, and he was resolved to leave this life honest to both himself and his Maker.

• 5 •

Probate

*W*ithin two days of his meeting with Elihu, Mortimer was dead. Although a number of people would be affected by his demise, its impact would prove to be greatest on two men, Prince and George Starr. Until Mortimer's death, these two inhabitants of Middletown had coexisted in relative indifference to each other, but Mortimer's will would change that forever. Having lived for decades at opposite ends of the social hierarchy, quite likely for the first time in their lives they now found themselves sharing something in common—the terms of Mortimer's will.

But their respective interests in the will were hardly compatible. For Prince, Mortimer's final bequest was, quite literally, a dream come true. After almost seventy years of servitude, his freedom was nearly at hand. The frustrations and disappointments of the past—not being freed for his service in the war, not being freed under the terms of Mortimer's first will—were now history. Certainly, Prince was saddened by his master's death. For over thirty years, he had labored for Mortimer at the ropewalk, and the benevolent terms of the will suggest that he was a fair-minded and responsible master. But whatever sorrow Prince felt over Mortimer's death had to be eclipsed by his sublime joy at the prospect of finally being emancipated.

George Starr was also acutely interested in the will, but in quite a different way. As much as Prince must have been surprised to learn of the second codicil, Starr also must have been not merely surprised but enraged to learn of the extent to which Mortimer had seen fit to disinherit him. No doubt Starr had long ago set his designs on his wife's inheritance; he fully realized that the rules of coverture would give him, in effect, nearly absolute control over the Mortimer fortune. He was not about to let that fortune slip between his fingers.

And so the battle lines were drawn. Of course, neither Prince nor any of the other slaves was equipped to defend the will on their own, but they would not have to. Many others shared their interest in having the will approved, since the entire town stood to gain from its admission into probate. Additionally, the coexecutors, by the very nature of their appointment, were charged with the duty of administering and defending the will.

But first there was the matter of the funeral.

Philip Mortimer's funeral was among the grandest that Middletown had seen to date. The Episcopalian church was situated at the southerly terminus of Main Street, where the street takes an abrupt turn to the west, and had been constructed on land that Mortimer had donated to the congregation. From the steps of that church, one could look north along the entire length of the flat, straight street, all the way to the Avenue of the Buttonwoods, a distance of perhaps a mile and a half.

The gathering that came together to bid Mortimer farewell ran the gamut of Middletown society. Even the Congregationalists swallowed their pride and entered the ordinarily forbidden domain of the rival Episcopalians. Politicians, businessman, tradesmen, and finally Mortimer's own slaves—all were assembled to beseech their God, in a single egalitarian voice, to welcome one of their own into His realm.

The eulogy has not survived, but it is fair to speculate on its contents, likely extolling Mortimer's many virtues, his generosity to his community, and his Christian concern for the servants under his patronage. Perhaps, now that Mortimer was no longer in the congregation, the preacher dared to bring up the subject of slavery and praise Mortimer for his Christian charity in emancipating, through his will, so many of Middletown's servants.

The procession made its way up most of the length of Main Street, toward Mortimer Cemetery, another of his gifts to the town. Mortimer's hearse rolled past the shops and homes of friends and acquaintances who, if they were not already walking in the procession, lined the street on both sides to pay their respects.

In view of Middletown's prominence at the time as Connecticut's largest community, it is somewhat surprising that only a very few colonial-era maps of the town have survived. The most famous is a small sketch drawn by John Warner Barber as part of his *Connecticut Historical Collections,* showing Main Street shortly before the Revolution.[1] The cemetery was located, and remains to this day, just north of the site of Mortimer's ropewalk on the west side of Main Street.

The funeral procession passed directly in front of Dr. Walker's building. For many decades, Walker had been one of the town's two slave dealers. This small, barnlike structure had been the port-of-entry for thousands of slaves, certainly including some of Mortimer's servants now marching in the procession. Now vacant for several years, the building would soon be demolished, a fact that Prince and the others saw as a milestone in the abolition campaign. Dr. Walker's had closed shortly after slave trading was abolished by the Act of 1774, which provided that "no Indian, Negro, or Molatto Slave, shall, at any Time hereafter be brought or imported into this Colony, by Sea or Land, from any Place or places whatsoever, to be disposed of, left, or sold within this Colony."

Although Prince had passed Dr. Walker's countless times since he had first arrived in Middletown some sixty-four years ago, it may well have occurred to him that this time was different, not only for him but also for the others marching with him. This would be the last time he would do so as a slave.

At the cemetery, Mortimer was laid to rest next to his wife, Martha, who had left him a widower some twenty years earlier. The gravestone was made of brownstone, quarried across the river in the part of Middletown known as Portland. About four feet square, it lay unpretentiously flat upon the ground. Mortimer himself had written the brief epitaph that filled the upper quarter of the stone:

> Friends
> Envy us not this little spot
> Nor move our bones from hence.
> Since this is all we claim.
> Let our dust lie still,
> For that's the will
> Of Him that built the same.

Well before the funeral, George Starr knew he was facing a dilemma. As one of the coexecutors of Mortimer's last will and testament, he was charged with the duty of administering that will and defending it against challenges. The problem, of course, lay in the fact that he was the very person intent on presenting the challenge.

Starr had good reason, he must have believed, to seek to have the will and its codicils set aside. From a financial perspective, the will placed the bulk of the Mortimer fortune outside of his control. After twenty years of marriage to Mortimer's niece, the old man's only living relative on this side of the Atlantic, Starr may well have seen himself as having vested rights to that inheritance. Clearly, he was not about to simply accede to Mortimer's testamentary desires and walk away from Middletown's most substantial fortune.

As compelling as were the financial aspects of a challenge to the will, Starr may well have been driven by an even greater motive. By now, the terms of Mortimer's will no doubt had been informally spread about town, and even beyond. It must have been quite humiliating for Starr to have everyone think that Mortimer believed Starr's relationship with his young son to be so superficial, so tenuous, that the boy could be bought off with promises of a substantial inheritance. All that the ten-year-old had to do was disavow the Starr name and adopt Mortimer's surname as his own.

There was much work to be done before the will could be submitted for probate. Primarily, the executors would have to prepare an accurate inventory of all of Mortimer's assets as of the time of death and then place a value on each item. This included not only the principal and easily discovered assets, such as real estate, but also such things as receivables, promissory notes, and all items of personal property, beginning with the furniture and down to every silver spoon and linen napkin.

Another category of property to be inventoried was the slaves themselves. Slaves constituted valuable property, a fact that proved problematic as states, even in the North, wrestled with their desire to eradicate the institution of slavery. Mortimer's inventory, however, belies that supposition, and suggests that factors other than profit were at play in the ropemaker's slave ownership. Submitted two years after Mortimer's death, the inventory lists nearly all of the slaves mentioned in his will and codicils. It reads:

1	Negro	man	60 years old	named Briston		£0
1	do.[ditto]	do.		Jack		£10
1	do.	do.		Dublin		£0
1	do.	do.		Prince sick with the yaws		£0
1	do.	do.		Peter on board man of war and likely dead		£0
1	Negro	girl		named Sophy	100 shillings	
1	do.	do.		do. Silvy	20 shillings	
1	do.	do.		do. Peg	20 shillings	
Lester					100 shillings	
Dick					100 shillings	
John					100 shillings	
1	girl	child		named Rachel		£0

The entire slave inventory constituted only a small fraction of Mortimer's estate, valued at £4980. It is quite obvious that Philip Mortimer did not see his slaves as a work force for the production of wealth. These nominal values, even for Jack at £10, suggest rather that Mortimer viewed his servants as an extension of his family; this conclusion is further supported by his generous testamentary dispositions to these persons, granting them not only emancipation but generous bequests of various types of property.

By mid-August, the inventory was complete, and the will was ready to be submitted for approval. At the hearing of August 25, 1794, the first order of business was George Starr's statement to the court that he was refusing to accept the appointment as coexecutor. Since the court had no power to compel Starr to serve, that matter was disposed of quite expeditiously.

The next matter was the executors' petition to have the will duly admitted into probate. The procedure, in Mortimer's day as well as now, involved "proving" the will. The executors were required to prove several matters to the court: that the will was duly executed by the testator, that it was duly witnessed by three witnesses, that the testator signed, published, and declared the will in the presence of the three witnesses, and that, at the time of execution, the testator appeared to be of sound mind and under no improper influence.

The task was likely satisfied by the cryptic testimony of Timothy Starr, Joseph Sage, and Elihu Starr, confirming that all of the requirements for a valid will were in fact present at the time of execution. Based on such testimony, all that remained was for the court to accept the will.

That approval, however, did not mark the conclusion of the hearing. Next, the executors sought the acceptance of the two codicils. Although the record clearly confirms that the probate court did in fact accept both of these instruments, those approvals could not possibly have gone as smoothly as did the approval of the will itself.

The first codicil was the one-page document, dated October 1, 1793, in which Mortimer left the wash kettles and the fishing shack to Sophy's family. The threshold problem with this codicil was that it was neither signed nor witnessed. Since the requirements for a valid codicil were identical to those for a valid will, it is difficult indeed to discern how the probate court was able to overlook these defects and still approve the codicil. The only plausible reason is that the executors were able to convince the court that they were familiar with the handwriting of Philip Mortimer and they could confirm that the first codicil was in Mortimer's hand.

Even if the executors could get past that issue on that rather weak argument, the absence of witnesses should have been fatal to the approval of the codicil. The record discloses, however, that it was approved despite such a glaring defect. It can be safely assumed that George Starr objected strongly to the approval of this codicil and that he raised the absence of both a signature and witnesses as the grounds for his objection. In view of that likelihood, the judge's ignorance of the law can be discounted in our attempt to rationalize the court's ruling. The likely reason for the approval, it becomes increasingly apparent, is that the probate judge was determined to admit the Mortimer will and codicils regardless of their dubious validity and regardless of the strength of any arguments advanced by George Starr. To phrase it in a more contemporary idiom, the fix was in.

The second codicil, written only a few days before Mortimer's death, should have fared no better. Although it did display a signature that Elihu Starr might well have sworn to be Mortimer's, the absence of witnesses should have been fatal to the document's approval. Again, despite such a fundamental flaw, and despite the certain objections of George Starr, the probate court accepted the second codicil as it had the first.

And so concluded the probate hearing of August 25, 1794. The various parties certainly exhibited widely divergent emotions as to its outcome: George Starr, no doubt, saw the hearing as a farce and probably had to content himself with the expectation that he would be vindicated through the appeal he was planning.

Elihu Starr and George Phillips, the remaining coexecutors, probably viewed the day as having produced mixed results. They could not have genuinely believed that the court would have accepted the codicils, as defective as they were, and may well have expected that Starr would prevail on his appeal as to those documents. But they also probably felt that the acceptance of the original will was quite safe from being overturned, since it clearly had been executed with all of the requisite formalities. Additionally, there could be no doubt as to Mortimer's soundness of mind at the time of execution of that will, some two years prior to his death.

Of course, the final group to have a highly vested interest in the day's proceedings was the slaves, since Mortimer's will held the key to their freedom. It is doubtful that the servants were present at the hearing, but perhaps they received an encouraging report from the executors. Encouraging, that is, for all save Prince and Peter, whose real hopes for freedom hinged on the second codicil. Although not educated in the law, the slaves would reasonably be expected to have acquired a rudimentary knowledge of probate by virtue of their interest in the Mortimer estate, and we have to believe that the executors briefed them on the likely outcome of the probate appeal.

Once again, Prince must have felt the frustration of having his freedom tossed about like a reed upon the wind. First, he was denied his freedom for so many years since the war; then, he was to be free after three years; then again, he was to be free immediately; and now it looked like he would probably be back to the three-year provision. Now in his seventies, Prince must have felt that his life would be over before he would ever walk the streets of Middletown as a free man. For him, he feared, freedom delayed would indeed be freedom denied.

· 6 ·

The Appeal

On the last Tuesday of December 1795, George and Anne Starr filed their appeal in Haddam Superior Court, as the Middletown Probate Court had directed. The appeal asserted four distinct grounds for seeking a reversal of the acceptance of the will and its codicils:

1. "That Timothy Starr, Elihu Starr, and Joseph Sage (whose names are subscribed as witnesses to the writing bearing date the 9th day of July 1792 and approved by said Court of Probate as aforesaid as being the last will and testament of said deceased at the date aforesaid) were and ever since have been and now are inhabitants of said town and citizens of said city of Middletown, and that, as such, being interested in the devises and bequests mentioned in said writing, they neither are nor ever were legal witnesses in the premises;"

2. "That the writings aforesaid were drawn up by and are in the handwriting of Elihu Starr, one of the persons who have undertaken the trust of executor. Consequently, Elihu Starr is also an interested person, entitled to certain benefits and bequests therein, and therefore the said Elihu Starr is further and particularly interested under said writings, and as such, neither is nor ever was a legal witness;"

3. "That the writings aforesaid which were by said court accepted as codicils and ordered to be kept on file as aforesaid are not witnessed by any persons whatever; and the said writing, bearing date the 10th day of March, 1794 was never subscribed or published by the said Philip Mortimer, Esquire;"

4. "That at the dates aforesaid the said Philip Mortimer, Esquire was not of sound and disposing mind and memory."

George Starr was certainly aware of the resentment his appeal must have created amongst the servants. Of course, in Starr's mind the servants' plight was only an incidental aspect of the appeal. His real goal was to gain control of the Mortimer fortune, and the fact that the servants' freedom also hung in the balance was probably not of any great concern to him. Just as Mortimer in his last months had apparently come to rethink the question of abolition, so also was George Starr undoubtedly very much aware of the political climate of the day regarding slavery. He, too, recognized that the institution was on its last legs, at least in the northern states. That prospect was not likely to disturb him, however, since he had never become dependent on slavery for his business enterprises.

Were the appeal to be successful, Starr would incidentally gain control over Mortimer's servants. In truth, he probably saw that as more of a burden than a benefit. Economically, Starr may well have realized that slavery was unworkable and thus doomed to eventual extinction. But if he had any plans of emancipating most of the servants anyway, it would not have been on humanitarian grounds; rather, he would have seen such emancipation as a way of easing the financial burden their maintenance placed on the estate. It would be considerably less expensive to hire necessary help than it was to house, feed, and clothe a houseful of servants.

For reasons not set out anywhere in the public record, at some point the appeal was transferred from Haddam to Middletown Superior Court. Perhaps George Starr felt particularly comfortable in the recently constructed Middletown courthouse. As was common practice at the time, the construction had been financed through subscription. Three dozen of Middletown's most prominent citizens had pledged contributions in varying amounts to finance the £600 cost of construction. Starr had been one of the most generous contributors, pledging £40 to the project, twice what Philip Mortimer had pledged. Perhaps he felt himself advantaged by having the appeal heard in "his" courthouse.

An appeal from probate is heard de novo; that is, unlike most appeals, in which the appellate court simply reviews the correctness of a lower court's decision, a probate appeal is not so limited. Instead, the matter is heard entirely anew — de novo — with the court taking its own testimony and rendering its decision without regard to what occurred in the probate court.

The evidence on Mortimer's soundness of mind must have been highly charged. George Starr's most conspicuous evidence was the will itself, along with the codicils. What man in his proper mind, he must have argued, would essentially ignore the proper object of his bounty, his own niece, and instead make a series of highly unusual bequests to unrelated persons and entities? Valuable land in the center on town, to be used for a municipal cemetery; more valuable land, and considerable monies, to be used for a granary; bequests and devises to common slaves—do not any and all of these unusual dispositions suggest that the man was no longer in full command of his faculties?

Of course, Starr certainly argued, the most glaring evidence of Mortimer's unsound state of mind would be his ridiculous disposition to Starr's own son, a mere ten-year-old, trying to entice him to abandon his family name in return for inheriting the bulk of the Mortimer fortune. How could anyone in his right mind have fashioned such a heinous dilemma for an innocent adolescent, also no doubt seeking in the process to alienate son from father?

As compelling as such an argument may have sounded, the executors were able to introduce equally compelling evidence to establish Mortimer's mental competency. First and foremost, the original will was in fact witnessed by three persons, each of whom must have testified that Mortimer was in complete command of his senses at the time. Elihu Starr would be able to establish that same fact as recently as a few days before Mortimer's death, when Elihu spent several hours with the dying man as he dictated the revisions to his will.

Of course, the mere fact that Mortimer saw fit to make his unusual dispositions did not by itself establish that he was of unsound mind. George Starr would have had a stronger argument if Mortimer had completely ignored Anne and her children. He could then have argued a well-established legal precept: That it is natural for a testator to recognize the natural object of his bounty, his family, and to provide for them in his final testament. The failure of a will to make such provision, while leaving the estate to others, is frequently indicative of a person who lacks testamentary capacity.

Except for the one factual issue regarding Mortimer's soundness of mind, the rest of the appeal rested primarily on legal arguments. It was indeed ironic that perhaps the most intricate, complicated will to appear in a Connecticut probate court was being challenged on the simplest of possible grounds: the absence or the qualifications of witnesses. More specifically, the two codicils were being challenged for their failure to have any witnesses at all, while the challenge to the original will was based on a claim that the witnesses were not competent.

Consistent with the law of other states, Connecticut law regarding codicils was, and continues to be, that they must be executed with the same formalities as the will itself. The reason for such a requirement is obvious. Since the codicil seeks to amend the will, it must be equally free of the risk of forgery or fraud. Mortimer's first codicil was not even signed. That fact alone should have served to disallow its admission. But, in addition to that most glaring defect, the executors were also confronted with the fact that the codicil was not witnessed.

Thus, the court's hands were tied regarding the first codicil: with no signature and no witnesses, the court had absolutely no basis for concluding that the document represented the testamentary intent of Philip Mortimer. Quite simply, it could have been written by anyone. The second codicil would not fare much better. Even if the court were to allow Elihu to qualify as a witness, the second codicil was still two witnesses short. Of course, even that possibility begged the question of the first two grounds of appeal, both of which challenged Elihu's competence as a witness.

George Starr's argument regarding the original will was founded on the statute then in effect regarding the requirements for a valid will. The applicable Connecticut statute provided that a will had to be signed by the testator and witnessed by three men, who were required to subscribe their names in the presence of the testator. Further, the statute required that the witnesses be competent to act as such.

The law recognized a variety of reasons why a person might be incompetent to act as a witness. He might be intellectually deficient and lacking a due sense of the obligations of an oath. Or he might be a convicted felon. Finally, and most relevant in this case, he might have a pecuniary interest in the will.

Starr must have argued that the law did not fix any specific level of financial interest that would disqualify the witness. It did not say the witness was incompetent if the will contained a bequest to him in excess of £1 or in excess of £20. The amount was irrelevant. Any interest, however slight, would serve to render the witness incompetent. And it follows that, once deemed incompetent, a person could not be counted among the three witnesses the law required for a valid will.

In this case, Starr's argument would have continued, all three witnesses were disqualified because of their status as citizens of Middletown. Philip Mortimer's will left substantial land and money to the citizens of Middletown. There was land to be used to expand the cemetery, land to be used as a site for a town granary, and funds to be used to finance the construction and get the granary operational. There could be no doubt but that the three gentlemen who acted as witnesses to the original will of Philip Mortimer would derive some benefit from these dispositions. In view of these circumstances, Starr's argument would continue, the court could reach no other conclusion but that the witnesses, each and every one of them, were incompetent. And without competent witnesses, the will was doomed to fail.

The second claim of Starr's appeal was related to the first, in that it advanced an additional reason for the disqualification of Elihu Starr as a witness. Mortimer's will made a bequest of £5 to each of the executors. That bequest, Starr contended, served to further disqualify Elihu Starr as a witness.

The executors were not without some persuasive law in support of their own position. Obviously, they had to acknowledge the existence of the statute requiring competent witnesses. They probably argued, however, that the case offered the court an opportunity to apply well-recognized equitable principles to achieve a result that was both just and, more important, consistent with the clear intent of the testator, Philip Mortimer.

The executors may well have reminded the court that the law strongly favors the descent of estates by means of a will rather than by intestate succession. People should be free to determine to whom they wish to leave their property upon death, and the law assists in effectuating that policy whenever possible. It is only when a person dies without a will, or when a will is inconsistent, incomprehensible, or suspected as unauthentic, that the law steps in to disallow the will and instead order distribution to the decedent's heirs.

The statutory requirement of competent witnesses, Elihu and Phillips likely continued, does not mark the end of the inquiry; it merely denotes the beginning. Competency is not, as George Starr suggests, something to be determined only by statutory definition. It is a matter appropriately left to the courts to determine, based on the relevant factors made known to that court.

It would have been altogether appropriate for the executors to criticize George Starr's claim as producing a harsh, and rather absurd, result. What if, instead of making the devises to the citizens of Middletown, Mortimer had made the same disposition in favor of the citizens of the State of Connecticut? Could the appellants then argue that every citizen of the entire state would be incompetent to act as a witness to such a will? Would the laws of this state force the testator to travel to New York, or Providence, or Boston to make such a devise, or, alternatively, to bring in nonresidents to witness the will? It was a preposterous conclusion and served to demonstrate the appropriateness of the court rejecting a literal reading of the statute in favor of a reasonable interpretation to reach an equitable result.

Mortimer's witnesses were only three persons in a city populated by some 6,000 souls. On a per-capita basis, their individual interest was something in the order of one sixtieth of 1 per cent. By anybody's reckoning, that was a miniscule number, hardly likely to influence the independence of successful businessmen. Further, there was no basis for presuming that these persons would avail themselves of any of the bequests. The witnesses were all men of means and would have little or no need to make use of a town granary. Similarly, they all owned family plots in the existing cemetery and thus would not have need for the new cemetery contemplated by Philip Mortimer's will.

This was a will that was obviously drafted over a substantial period of time, with a great deal of thought having gone into its provisions. It would constitute a grave injustice if all this effort, and its beneficial intent, were to be frustrated by the court setting aside the will, especially on such a dubious ground.

Such were the arguments that most likely were advanced by the parties. Clearly, both codicils were on shaky ground, but the executors probably did not really care if those documents were disallowed because of their relatively minor dispositions. Without doubt, their greater concern lay with the challenge to the original will, where they had raised worthwhile defenses and had a reasonable basis for expecting that the will would be sustained.

But that was not to be. The court's decree upheld the executors on only one issue: Mortimer's competence to make a will. The court concluded that Philip Mortimer was of sound mind during the entire period at issue, from the time of the original will through the second codicil, only days before his death. Ironically, winning on this ground was probably more disheartening to the executors, and to the beneficiaries, than if the court had determined Mortimer to be of unsound mind. At least then, they would have had the comfort of knowing that there was nothing at all that could have been done to save the will. For the court to find Mortimer competent, and then to set aside the will and codicils on the basis of the incompetence of the witnesses, meant that the documents would have prevailed, if only more attention had been paid to the formalities.

As the executors no doubt expected, the court set aside both codicils. Elihu must have been particularly disappointed in the disallowance of the second codicil and may well have felt some degree of responsibility for that result, since he had played such an important role in its creation. If only he had been more attentive to detail, he may have thought, by procuring competent witnesses and seeing to it that there was compliance with the formalities of the execution of his friend's revised will, the executors would not now be in this position.

The issue of the original will may well have been quite difficult for the court to decide, and that difficulty may account for the lapse of several months from the time of trial to the date of the court' decree. True, the statute required three competent witnesses, but it was left to the court to interpret just what constituted competence. Judges of the time, however, generally were not prone to creative interpretations of the law. There was a certain degree of safety in basing one's rulings on the strict letter of the law.

The executors' equitable arguments may well have been sound, but in the end they were not persuasive. The court ruled in favor of George Starr, concluding that the witnesses were indeed incompetent because of their status as citizens of Middletown and that Elihu was doubly incompetent because of his status as a coexecutor.

So it was that, on January 25, 1796, the last will and testament of Philip Mortimer, and its codicils as well, became relegated to oblivion, as ineffective as if they had never been written. All of the thought and effort that Mortimer put into his bequests, all of his desires to benefit the community that had been so accepting of this Irish immigrant, and perhaps most important, all of the hopes for freedom that had no doubt sustained Mortimer's slaves—all of it was gone. The cryptic one-page decree, devoid of any statement of the court's rationale in reaching its conclusions, dashed forever these hopes and these dreams and substituted for them the very different desires and aspirations of a single man: George Starr.

• 7 •

The Conviction Revisited

$\mathcal{S}$tarr's successful appeal certainly did not mark the end of the probate process. Now that the will had been declared void, Philip Mortimer's estate would have to be probated as though he had died without a will, that is, intestate. In such cases, the first order of business for the probate court was the appointment of an administrator.

The duties of an administrator of an intestate estate are essentially the same as those of an executor in a testate estate. Once appointed, the administrator is charged with a variety of duties. First, he has to determine the identity of all of the decedent's heirs; then comes the filing of an inventory of all of the assets of the estate. Next, the administrator has to settle all claims against the estate, and finally, he oversees the distribution of the assets to those heirs whom the court determines to be entitled to inherit.

Within weeks of concluding the appeal, George Starr was appearing before the Middletown Probate Court securing his appointment as administrator. Elihu Starr and George Phillips had already accomplished the bulk of the work involved in assembling the vast estate inventory, but there was still much to be done, and Starr probably wasted no time in enlisting the help of the servants to finish the job as quickly as possible.

Eventually, the task was accomplished, and upon submission of the inventory, the probate court entered an order distributing the entire estate to Mortimer's niece, Anne. Of greater importance to George Starr was the fact that, by virtue of the laws of coverture, he became entitled to enjoy the benefits of all of Anne's newly acquired fortune.

No doubt, none of Mortimer's servants shared in that joy, since Starr's victory meant that they were to be denied the freedom that Mortimer had granted them in his will and probably had promised them during his later years.

The greater likelihood, however, is that Starr saw their continuing servitude as more of a burden than a benefit. The eventual demise of slavery in Connecticut was generally accepted as fact. America's first census in 1790 recorded that free blacks in Connecticut outnumbered their enslaved brethren: there were 2,759 slaves in the state, compared with 2,801 free blacks. Clearly, that trend was destined to continue in the years to come.

Although public sentiment was generally sympathetic to the demise of slavery as an institution, there were practical impediments to mass emancipation of Connecticut's slave population. Slave owners desiring to free their slaves were not always motivated by the noblest of sentiments; many were simply seeking to free themselves from a financial burden. Unfortunately, a freed slave with little or no skills would find it difficult, if not impossible, to sustain himself or herself independently.

These circumstances gave rise to one of the sublime ironies of this era: slave owners in the 1790s were not free to free their slaves. There were rigid rules limiting the conditions under which an owner could grant manumission to one of his slaves. Such rules had been in place for most of the eighteenth century, and the one in effect in the 1790s was a somewhat modified version of its predecessor. The earlier rule had placed control of manumission in the hands of the town selectmen; they were charged with the task of issuing manumission permits only upon a determination of the slave's ability to support himself or herself in a "Good and Peaceable Life and Conversation."

The town's interest in a freed slave's sustenance was hardly humanitarian, since the burden of caring for impoverished sick and elderly former slaves would ultimately fall on the town, although it did have the right to seek reimbursement from the slave's former owner. A manumission permit, however, was a mutually beneficial document; it freed not only the slave but the master as well, since it "forever discharged" him from the obligation of support.

In 1792, the General Assembly tightened the manumission statute by permitting only slaves between the ages of 25 and 45 to be manumitted and also requiring manumission certificates to be filed in the town records. In later years, this second requirement would prove beneficial in helping genealogists track slave histories. As to the fourteen slaves listed in Philip Mortimer's will, however, only one such manumission certificate appears of record, relating to Amaryllis. It reads:

> This may certify that Amaryllis, the Wife of James Gunn, as we are informed & verily believe is in good health—that she is not of greater age than forty five years nor less than twenty five years of age & that we are convinced from information & proof that she is desirous of being made free, that the said Amaryllis was formerly the servant of Philip Mortimer, Esq. late deceased & married by the Rev'd Abn Jarvis, Rector of Christ

Church in Middletown Connecticut Dec. 23rd 1790 to said James Gunn as appears from his certificate in Middletown. Dec. 3rd AD 1800.

Elijah Hubbard }

Justices of the Peace

S. Titus Hosmer}

Be it known that I, George Starr of Middletown, Admr of the Estate of Philip Mortimer, Esq. late deceased do by these presents emancipate & set free Amaryllis—the Wife of James Gunn named in the above certificate.

Middletown Dec. 3rd 1800

The fact that only this one certificate found its way to the town clerk's records might initially suggest that George Starr simply continued to hold the Mortimer slaves for his own use, except for the solitary manumission of Amaryllis. Circumstances, however, suggest otherwise. The census of 1810 discloses that George Starr owned no slaves as of that year; likewise, no slave holdings are reported with respect to Anne Starr. Further, George Starr's estate inventory, prepared some ten years later, shows no slave holdings.

These facts suggest that the manumission ordinances were largely being ignored in the first decades of the nineteenth century. This is understandable in view of the status of slavery in the state at that time. The importation of slaves into the state had been illegal for nearly twenty years, and the Act of 1774 had decreed that all slaves born after that date would be free upon their twenty-fifth birthday, with that requirement reduced to twenty-one years in 1794. Consequently, by 1811, the year of Prince's conviction, the slave population was both aging and diminishing rapidly.

One conspicuous bystander to these events was Prince. The period between 1794, the year of Mortimer's death, and 1811, the year of Prince's conviction, is devoid of any documentation by which we can establish with any certainty what was taking place in Prince's life. The land records, however, do disclose that Starr sold the ropewalk in 1806 to two brothers from New Hampshire. Along with the deed, there is recorded a document evidencing the sale of ropemaking tools, suggesting that the purchasers were intent on continuing the business for some period of time. Since Prince was a skilled spinner, it is reasonable to suppose that he continued working at his trade for some time after Mortimer's death, perhaps even as late as the time of sale of the ropewalk.[1]

At that time, Prince would have been eighty-two years of age, so it is also reasonable to suppose that by then Starr may well have retired him from the ropewalk and transferred him to work as a servant at the Starr residence. Whether in 1811 he was Starr's sole servant is not known, but the 1810 census states that Starr owned no slaves at that time. The information charging Prince with Starr's attempted murder identifies him as Starr's servant, so it is apparent that the prior year's census was inaccurate, at least as to Prince's status.

The possible inaccuracy of that census becomes significant in trying to discover a motivation for Prince's crime. Were there other Mortimer servants left off the 1810 census? That seems unlikely; after all, the census takers were probably local residents familiar with the town population. They certainly would be expected to be especially familiar with one of the town's more prominent families. Of course, that familiarity raises questions as to how Prince was missed in the first place, but the fact of his omission is undeniable. If, of all of Mortimer's servants, Prince was the only one still not emancipated, a motive begins to suggest itself.

For decades, circumstances had been operating to frustrate Prince in his undeniable quest for freedom. He had seen several of his fellow slaves set free as a reward for service in the war, but he himself had been denied that recognition. After another dozen years of faithful service, he was tantalized by Mortimer's will, offering him the promise of freedom after three more years of service. Freedom seemed even closer when Mortimer's second codicil granted Prince his immediate emancipation. Those hopes, too, were promptly dashed by George Starr's successful appeal. To add to that already substantial list of disappointments, it appears from the census records that, by 1811, Starr had emancipated most, if not all, of Mortimer's other slaves. Given such a long and frustrating history, with George Starr the ubiquitous nemesis in Prince's quest for freedom, is it not possible that the old slave's frustration, after nearly nine decades of servitude, may have finally driven him over the edge?

Considering also Prince's age and ill health, he may well have been indifferent to the consequences of his attempt on Starr's life. He could not have had any doubt that his complicity would be discovered, regardless of whether or not his plan succeeded. Despite his affliction with yaws, he had already lived well beyond the life expectancy of a black male born in the early eighteenth century. Most, if not all, of his lifelong friends and acquaintances were long-since deceased, and he may well have considered himself overdue to join them in their well-deserved final rest.

Had Prince succeeded in poisoning Starr, his certain punishment would have been death by hanging, a fate he probably foresaw with little trepidation and perhaps even some degree of relief. Failure, he also certainly knew, would doom him to imprisonment at Newgate. The conditions at that prison were common knowledge throughout the state, and Prince probably expected that his life in that dungeon might be difficult, but mercifully short.

Even if Prince was simply tired of living, especially the life of a slave, obviously there were other easier ways of resolving those feelings besides an attempt on his master's life. Certainly, Prince could well have been motivated by an intense, even passionate, desire to exact vengeance on the man who, since Philip Mortimer's death some seventeen years earlier, had been constantly frustrating Prince's desire for freedom.

But, as compelling as all of these reasons may seem in resolving the question of what was behind Prince's actions, they do not tell the whole story. One of the unresolved mysteries surrounding Prince's attempted poisoning of George Starr is whether he acted alone. Buried deep in the state archives is a document strongly suggesting that he did not. For nearly two hundred years, resting in its aging, musty archives box alongside Prince's file, is an innocuous single sheet of paper, folded twice upon itself and tied with a ribbon to form a file. The jacket simply reads "State vs. Jack Mortimer Dec. 1811." Written upon the inside of that sheet is the following:

Middlesex County Sup. Court
Dec. Term 1811

S. Titus Hosmer, Attorney for the State of Connecticut within the County of Middlesex, complaint makes and information exhibits—

That Jack, a Negro man of Middletown aforesaid, commonly called Jack Mortimer, a person of wicked mind & disposition, maliciously intending to poison & murder George Starr of said Middletown on or about the 5th day of August last past; did unlawfully & wickedly, solicit, instigate, advise, persuade, & procure Prince, a Negro of said Middletown, servant of the said George Starr, to give & administer a quantity of Arsenic or Ratsbane, being a deadly poison, to the said George & for this purpose aforesaid did buy, obtain, & to the sd Prince deliver a large quantity of the said Arsenic or Ratsbane; & the said Prince, then & there in pursuance of said solicitation, instigation, advice, persuasion & procurement, having received the said Arsenic or Ratsbane of the said Jack, did put the same into a bowl filled with Chocolate which had been prepared for the breakfast of the said George Starr, & soon after the same was by the said Prince delivered to the said George Starr to drink, & the said George Starr, not knowing the said Arsenic or Ratsbane to be in the sd Chocolate took a small quantity thereof in a spoon to drink the same but by the unusual appearance of the said Chocolate & of small particles of the said Arsenic adhering to the said spoon was deterred; all which doings were to his great damage, & the extreme peril of his life, to the evil example of others in like manner offending, & against the peace & dignity of the State of Connecticut; therefore the said attorney prays due process against the sd Jack, commonly called Jack Mortimer, in the premises.

S. Titus Hosmer

The allegations of this information are quite similar to the one by which Prince was charged, except in two significant respects. First, although Prince is conspicuously set out in Jack's information as a coperpetrator, the reverse does not hold true: No mention of Jack's involvement occurs in the Prince information.

The significance of such a variation is enormous. Since Prince is asserted as a necessary actor in Jack's information, it would be difficult, if not impossible, for Jack to be convicted independently of Prince. Without a conviction in Prince's case, or an acquittal based on insanity, there was no case to be made against Jack. In Prince's case, however, Jack does not figure at all; as a consequence, it would be possible to convict Prince completely independently of proving, or even mentioning, Jack's involvement in the crime.

This first observation leads to the more significant second variation: Although charged, Jack was never prosecuted. The jacket of Prince's file cryptically recites the outcome: "guilty—New Gate for life—[undecipherable, possibly a judge's name]—Dec. 21, 1811." The jacket of Jack's file, however, is completely blank. Nonetheless, that silence says much about what happened in Jack's case. It confirms that Jack was not even tried on the charges against him. Had he been tried and convicted, the jacket would read identically to Prince's. Had he been tried and acquitted, the jacket equally certainly would have indicated that acquittal. Instead, the absence of a disposition is a clear indication that Hosmer, the state's attorney, simply chose not to prosecute Jack Mortimer.

Prosecuting attorneys, in 1811 as well as in modern times, are not generally in the habit of initiating criminal prosecutions in the absence of strong evidence of guilt. Certainly, Hosmer believed there existed some factual basis for charging Jack. Unfortunately, no other records, even of a secondary nature, exist by which to discover the reasons for Jack's involvement or Hosmer's decision not to prosecute.

Who was Jack Mortimer? The information describes him as "a Negro," but says nothing of him being a servant. The additional fact that he is attributed a family name also strongly suggests that he was not then a slave. It was common practice for freed blacks to take on the surname of their former masters. The distinction is starkly manifested in Prince's information, in which he is repeatedly referred to only by his given name and as a servant.

Mortimer's will clearly establishes Jack as one of Mortimer's slaves. He is further described as Sophy's husband and the father of three sons, Lester, Dick, and John, also slaves of Philip Mortimer. As with all of Mortimer's slaves, he was supposed to have been granted his freedom by virtue of the will. Although Jack was also denied his freedom by virtue of Starr's successful appeal, by 1811 his situation had apparently changed dramatically from Prince's, since Jack was then a free man. Jack was also considerably younger than Prince, so Jack was not likely to share Prince's perspective of a man whose life was clearly in its twilight.

Certainly these facts, taken alone, are difficult to reconcile with the allegations made against Jack. Jack would have no reason to share in Prince's likely bitterness over his denial of freedom. Freedom, however, was not the only benefit that Mortimer's will had sought to confer upon Jack and his family. First, there was this provision:

> I give unto the three Sons of my Negro Woman Sophy named Lester, Dick, and John in equal Parts one and three-quarters Acres Land adjoining Joseph Starr's Lot, forever reserving to my Negro Woman Sophy and her Husband Jack the Use and Improvement during their natural Lives. I also give Sophy and Jack their Freedom.

After three other dispositions to other slaves, the will continued:

> The three young Children of Sophy named Lester, Dick, and John I would have brought up by their Mother Sophy and kept to School until they arrive to the age of Fourteen Years then put to Apprentice by my Executors, the two Eldest to be put to House Joiners until they arrive to the Age of Twenty-one Years and then give them their Freedom.

It is obvious that Philip Mortimer held Sophy and Jack's sons in unusually high regard; these bequests, being made to a family of former slaves, were hardly typical, since they were providing Jack's family with property and benefits exceeding those available even to many white families. But Mortimer had desired to benefit this favored family even beyond the provisions of his original will. His first codicil had provided:

> In order to enable my Negro Man Jack and his Wife Sophy to bring up their Children, my will is that they use and enjoy the Interest I have in a Fishing Place in Chatham Nearly opposite the House in which Reuben Plum and others are concerned, during their Natural Lives, and I give and bequeath unto Lester, Dick and John, Children of Jack and Sophy, my Right and Interest in the above said fishing place, after Jack and Sophy die, forever.

All of these bequests, of course, became the stuff of dreams when Starr's appeal succeeded in having the will and its codicils set aside. The 1810 census confirms that Jack and his family had obtained their freedom by then. It is highly doubtful, however, that their lot was as bountiful as it otherwise would have been, were it not for George Starr.

Was there enough lingering bitterness over these losses to prompt Jack, some seventeen years after Mortimer's death, to conspire with Prince to do away with a mutual enemy? Was Prince not even the primary instigator in the plot against Starr? Was he perhaps simply an sickly old slave, by now disfigured

Superior Court Jacket: State vs. Prince Negro, detail. (Connecticut State Library, State Archives Record Group No. 3, Middlesex County, Superior Court, Judgments and Defaults, 1798–1904)

Superior Court Jacket: State vs. Jack Mortimer, detail. (Connecticut State Library, State Archives Record Group No. 3, Middlesex County, Superior Court, Judgments and Defaults, 1798–1904) by yaws to the point of repulsion, being manipulated by a man seeking revenge for a fortune lost? Was the case against Jack so weak that Hosmer thought it not worth his while even to attempt a prosecution? Or did Hosmer see in Jack an opportunity to ensure, by his testimony, at least one conviction in this crime perpetrated against one of Middletown's most prominent citizens?

Answers to such questions lie buried with the bones of the participants. There is one additional fact, however, that helps bridge the gap between history and conjecture and suggests that Jack Mortimer was not a benign or passive character in the events leading to Prince's conviction: Some eleven years later, in 1822, Jack Mortimer was tried and convicted of arson and sentenced to five years' imprisonment in Newgate. He had burned to the ground a house belonging to Martha Mortimer Lewis, the married daughter of George Starr.

So perhaps, on the night of December 21, 1811, Prince should not have been the one spending his first night in jail as a convicted felon, or at least as the sole convicted felon. But that is where he, alone, spent that cold winter's night. The small wooden jailhouse, set conspicuously in the center of the Washington Street Green, probably went unguarded that night as its solitary occupant, aged fourscore and seven, pondered his future at Newgate, Connecticut's dreaded dungeon.

· 8 ·

To Newgate

$\mathcal{A}$lthough Prince was convicted on December 21, 1811, Newgate Prison records disclose that Sheriff Parsons did not deliver him there until December 28. The delay was attributable to the great Christmas blizzard that struck the northeast that year. The storm had begun innocently enough during the early afternoon hours of the 23rd, with an increasingly cloudy sky crowding out a cheerless mid-day sun.[1] The first snowflakes arrived in the early-morning hours of Christmas Eve, and by daybreak the storm had intensified to blizzard conditions—gale-force winds blowing a thick heavy snow, and near-zero temperatures. The storm's ferocity would remain constant for a full twenty-four hours, finally departing on Christmas morning. It left in its wake, however, enough snow to cause mail delivery to be suspended for four days in the cities, and much longer in the outlying areas.

Throughout the storm and its aftermath, Prince remained in the local jailhouse. Despite its prominent placement in the center of the town green, the small building remained all but abandoned as Middletown at first battened down for, and then slowly began to reemerge from, the worst storm anyone under the age of thirty had ever witnessed.

Although the trip to Newgate involved a distance of only about twenty-eight miles, this was not a journey to be undertaken lightly, especially in an open sleigh in the dead of winter, and even more especially in deference to the notoriously poor conditions of many Connecticut roads at that time.

Throughout the colonial period, Connecticut had suffered the ignominy of having the worst roads in all of the colonies.[2] To some extent, this situation was attributable to the geography of the state; although Connecticut's east-west distance is only about eighty-five miles, within that breadth are to be found about a half dozen tidal rivers of varying width as well as many smaller rivers fed by innumerable streams and brooks. For millennia, all of these riparian waterways had been chiseling their paths into the countryside, in many instances resulting in chasms or gorges, and all were intent on emptying their flow southerly into Long Island Sound. Since most travelers were heading either east to Providence and Boston, or west to New York, it was impossible for them to avoid the challenge presented by these formidable watery obstacles.

The wider rivers could be traversed by ferries, but these bore little resemblance to the image that term inspires in a twenty-first century mind. For the most part, these ferries were nothing more than small rowboats or rafts tethered to a rope straddling the river. Often, the rope would become detached or broken, resulting in a heavily laden craft fighting a losing battle against a strong current. The hapless travelers, upon finally making it across the river, could find themselves and their possessions stranded several miles from their intended destination across the river. Occasionally, the aggravated conditions of the spring thaw or heavy downpours would cause the ferry to take on water and sink, with loss of property or livestock and sometimes even human life.

The smaller streams presented a somewhat safer but no less daunting challenge. Bridges, if they existed at all, were primitive. These structures offered horses less-than-ideal footing, and the odds were quite good that either the steed or the horseman would end up in the water. Quite often, the bridges were not even wide enough to accommodate wagons, so travelers might find their trip interrupted by the need to fabricate their own additions to whatever inadequate bridge structure they might encounter.

Of course, all of that presumed that the bridge was there in the first place. Storms and thaws did not limit their mischief to the rivers, and it was a common occurrence for a traveler to come upon a stream where the bridge had been completely washed out. Depending on the depth of the water, the traveler had to choose between wading through the stream and turning around in search of a different route.

Conditions on dry land were not much better. Five distinct mountain ridges run generally north-south through Connecticut's landscape. The resulting topography is marked by an endless variety of deep, narrow valleys and jutting cliffs. All of these were covered by a forest of evergreens and oaks with trunks often measuring five feet in diameter. The ground between the trees was not barren but covered by thick underbrush that made foot travel difficult, and the use of horses nearly impossible. It was not a wilderness conducive to the building of roads of any sort, let alone the kind of comfortable passway to which, by the time of the revolution, most travelers had become accustomed in other regions of the country.

Even the Post roads, by far the most famous road system in Connecticut at the time, were not immune from these symptoms. Except for a short stretch from Hartford to Windsor, the capital city's immediate neighbor to the north, the Post roads were as poor and difficult to traverse as any others in the state.[3]

By the time Prince was about to undertake his journey to Newgate, these conditions had not improved to any appreciable degree. The Anderson map of 1799, reproduced in this volume, shows quite clearly which routes Prince's journey must have taken. The first lap, heading north from Middletown, through Wethersfield, and on to Hartford, was probably the most heavily traveled and consequently the best maintained. It was also an easy, level stretch, following for the most part the westerly bank of the Connecticut River, inland just enough to protect the road from the damaging spring floods. A small portion of this leg, from Wethersfield to Hartford, formed part of the Upper Post Road and was probably the best section of roadway that Prince would encounter.

From Hartford, the journey then proceeded west along the road to Albany, generally considered the worst road in the state. Compounding the poor condition of the roadway was the fact that it crossed a mountain range some ten miles west of Hartford. Although the range is not particularly high, it is steep enough to discourage a straight route directly over the top, so that a traveler would be slowed by the added distance of the road's serpentine route up and over the range. The heavy snow of the recent storm must have served to make even more difficult what was a tedious stretch of road even in the best of conditions.

The final leg of the trip offered Sheriff Parsons a choice. Two routes, running parallel to each other and about five miles apart, led north from the Albany road towards Granby, Newgate's host community. Although the first road was somewhat more direct, it ran along the base of a mountain range for most of the distance to Newgate, perhaps ten miles. No doubt it was a difficult route, offering a rough terrain aggravated by the challenge of the Christmas snows.

Parsons probably found the more western route to Granby more appealing; its more level terrain, well distant from any troublesome ranges, certainly facilitated much of the final portion of his late-December travel. But even this route was not free from the challenges of a mountainous road. Newgate, after all, was built atop an old copper mine dug from the side of the mountain. To get to Newgate, you had to climb the mountain; there was simply no way of avoiding it.

Retracing Prince's route in a modern automobile involves less than an hour's travel time. In 1811, however, the trip posed a considerably more formidable challenge, especially after heavy snows. Snow plows did not exist; along some of the more heavily traveled roads, the snow would be compressed by large wooden rollers, about six feet in diameter and just as wide, drawn by a team of horses. Although this process left a good base for sleigh travel, the large size of the roller limited its use to the wider roads, such as the one from Middletown to Hartford. The rest of Prince's journey, however, for the most part was not conducive to the use of snow rollers, except perhaps near the centers of some of the outlying towns, such as Simsbury and Granby.

Sleighs were designed to glide over deep snow, but the horses that pulled them were not always able to get through heavy drifts. Time then became the traveler's only ally; a little sunshine could go a long way in shrinking the drifts down to a manageable depth to permit horses to handle them. Weather histories report that the storm was followed by a series of sunny but seasonably cold days that may have helped a little in making the roads more passable.

A twenty-eight-mile trip across poor and occasionally mountainous roads, with an eighty-seven-year-old passenger on board, was bound to be difficult under the best of circumstances, and the dead of winter certainly did not offer these travelers anything close to ideal travel conditions. If Parsons had any intent of completing the trip in a single day, they would have started out well before daylight and not arrived at Newgate until late in the evening.

As tedious a trip as this may have been for Parsons, it must have been torturous for Prince. It is doubtful that Parsons viewed Prince as a flight threat, so he probably spared the old man from shackles or other like restraints. Such a consideration, however, would not have afforded Prince much relief from the other miseries he had to endure in an open sleigh during the long journey: hour after hour of bitter cold aggravated by strong north winds, tempered perhaps only by a couple of old blankets, while he sat constantly jostled about the sleigh's hard wooden bench. Anyone would have found such a journey intensely difficult; Prince's age and infirmities must have aggravated these conditions to the limits of old man's endurance.

William Stuart, a counterfeiter who spent five years in Newgate, beginning in 1820, in his later years saw fit to write his autobiography.[4] Some nine years after Prince's journey, Stuart himself experienced a similar sleigh ride as he was transported to Newgate from Bridgeport, a considerably longer journey than Prince's had been. From his account, we can only hope that Sheriff Parsons was gentler to his prisoner than was Gen. Foote, the deputy sheriff who had charge of Stuart during his trip. The following passage reveals tremendous detail about the transportation of prisoners in the early 1800s; equally interesting, if perhaps not as significant, is the example it provides of Stuart's ever-present wit. He writes:

> Gen. Foote, of Bridgeport, a deputy sheriff, took a sleigh to carry me to the mines in Simsbury. I was double ironed, handcuffs about my wrists, close

and tight as the skin, a clasp about each ancle [*sic*] about the size of the wagon tire, fastened to an iron bar about eighteen inches in length. Besides this, a circular bar about my body, fastened by a lock in front, and on each side a chain was hanging from holes through this circular bar down to my feet, and its lower ends locked into staples in the bottom timber work of the vehicle.

Thus caparisoned, I was placed in the bottom of the sleigh, the general sitting on one side of me and the driver on the other, and I was thus confined between their feet. The general and his aid carried a demi-john of brandy, from which they drank often and treated me to all I could drink. Thus arrayed in irons, I was as helpless as an infant, yet the old general displayed all the courage of Knickerbocker's Swedish governor. In each hand he carried a double charged and cocked pistol, ready to shoot me if I should take the sleigh to which I was chained, together with the horses, and the loading all on my back, to run away. I laughed at this wondrous specimen of courage in a general who had rode triumphantly for five years at the head of his regiments, with every gun divested of cartridges and flints. In case our country should be invaded by an army of Lilliputians, such men would acquire laurels which would rebound to the honor and glory of our distinguished epauleted chieftains.

Prince's trip to Newgate, although perhaps not as harsh as Stuart's, may well have been difficult enough to cause him to look forward to his arrival at the infamous prison, despite his certain familiarity with its reputation as a place of immense degradation and suffering. It is also quite possible that the combination of Prince's age, ill health, and a waning will to live caused him to be less intimidated by what lay ahead than would have been the case for a younger inmate.

Prince was also old enough to know, perhaps from bitter personal experience, that the concept of incarceration as a mode of punishment was a relatively recent development in human history. Of course, many crimes in the colonial period, and even for several decades thereafter, were capital offenses; incarceration in those cases was only incidental to the ultimate punishment. Most other offenses, however, whether major or minor, were not punished by terms in prison or jail; rather, the preferred method of dealing with antisocial activity was corporal punishment.

It was a tradition whose roots are to be found, possibly without exception, in every ancient civilization. The code of Hammurabi, based on the notion of "an eye for an eye," is familiar to everyone who has ever taken a course in world history. There is also extensive support for corporal punishment in both testaments of the bible. With such a heritage as its most formidable credential, it is not at all surprising that various forms of corporal punishment were still very much in vogue, even in America and even into the final decade of the eighteenth century.

Without doubt, the most widely used method of corporal punishment was flogging. Its popularity was probably due to the fact that its variable intensity made it appealing not only as a means of redressing criminal acts but also as a persuasive disciplinary device in the family, at school, and in the military. The British were especially adept at flogging; sometime around the seventeenth century, they introduced the "cat-o'-nine-tails," so named because of its construction: nine thongs of rawhide, knotted at the ends, and attached to a handle. The design was specifically intended to permit the scourger to inflict maximum pain with each flog as it dug deeply into the victim's flesh. Frequently, a defendant sentenced to such a flogging found it unofficially transformed into a death sentence, as his body proved incapable of recovering from the punishment inflicted at the whipping post.

The "cat" was not unknown on this side of the Atlantic and continued to be used until the 1840s as one of the navy's chief disciplinary tools.[5] Even though Newgate had been set up as Connecticut's state prison three years before the war, the General Assembly was hardly quick to adopt incarceration as the punishment of choice for offenses both great and small. The state's first comprehensive statutory code was adopted in 1784; although a number of crimes were statutorily defined, and their punishment denoted as well, a review of those laws confirms that the idea of incarceration as punishment had not yet taken hold in the state. The following table lists some of the crimes addressed in the 1784 statutes, along with their prescribed punishment:

CORPORAL PUNISHMENT IN CONNECTICUT, 1784

The Crime	*The Punishment*	*Other Comments*
Adultery	"They shall be severely punished, by whipping on the naked body, and stigmatized, or burnt on the forehead with the letter *A*, on a hot iron; and each of them shall wear a halter about their necks, on the outside of their garments, during their abode in this State..."	If the criminal was ever found without the halter, a justice of the peace could order him/her "whipt, not exceeding thirty stripes."
Counterfeiting	Whipped twenty stripes, a fine of 100£, and 10 years at hard labor	Second offense: thirty stripes, and life imprisonment

(continued)

The Crime	*The Punishment*	*Other Comments*
Defamation	10£ fine	"If any Negro, Indian, or Molatto slave shall utter, publish or speak such words of or concerning any other person that would by law be actionable if uttered, published or spoken by any free person, . . . such Negro, Indian, or Molatto . . . shall be punished by whipping on the naked body . . . not exceeding forty stripes, and . . . shall be sold or disposed of to defray all charges arising thereupon . . ."
Drunkenness	8-shilling fine, and "the offender shall be set in the stocks, there to remain not exceeding three hours, nor less than one hour."	
Fornication	33-shilling fine, or "corporally punished by whipping, not exceeding ten stripes"	
Manslaughter	"shall forfeit to the public treasury of this State, all the goods and chattel to him or her belonging . . . and be further punished by whipping on the naked body, and be stigmatized, or burnt on the hand with the letter *M*, on a hot iron . . ."	
Breaking the peace	Pay "such fine as . . . the judge shall determine"	"if any Indian, Negro or Molatto servant or slave, shall disturb the peace, as aforesaid, or shall offer to strike any white person, and be thereof convicted, such servant or slave shall be punished by whipping . . . not exceeding thirty stripes."
Perjury	Forfeit 20£, and "imprisonment by the space of six months"	"And if it happen the said offender . . . have not any goods or chattels to the value of twenty

The Crime	*The Punishment*	*Other Comments*
		pounds, that then he or they shall be set in the pillory by the space of one whole hour, in some county town where the offense was committed, and to have both his ears nailed."
Theft	Pay victim treble value, fine, and whipping, not exceeding ten stripes	
Horse stealing	Pay owner treble value, fine, "and be further punished by being publicly whipped on the naked body not exceeding fifteen stripes, and be confined in a work-house or house of correction not exceeding three months, there to be kept at hard labour, and be further whipped on the first Monday of each month, not exceeding ten stripes each time, and shall be set astride on a wooden horse before each whipping as aforesaid, not exceeding two hours."	

This list is in accord with the types of punishment prescribed in most of the other states around this time. It is apparent that ideas of reform or societal protection were not at the forefront of legislators' minds when they were fabricating these laws. Rather, the clear intent involved a mix of punishment, humiliation, and deterrence, since the sentences were invariably carried out in public view.

The legislature did not merely *desire* a public element in the punishment—they *demanded* it. Another of the 1784 laws mandated that "every town in this state shall make and maintain at their own charge, a good pair of stocks, with a lock and a key, sufficient to hold and secure such offenders as shall be sentenced to be set therein." A town failing to maintain its stocks was subject to a fine of six shillings for each month it was in breach of this requirement. Middletown's whipping post stood in the center of the south green, just opposite the Episcopal church. The last reported whipping, for a misdemeanor, took place around 1805. Subsequently, the whipping post gradually became transformed into a signpost and was eventually taken down around 1815.

Although the winds of change were beginning to stir in the post-war decades of the eighteenth century, they were calm in Connecticut. Rather, it was in Pennsylvania, with its strong Quaker influence, that the new republic would commence the process of renouncing corporal punishment, and its underlying precepts, in favor of a more humane system of criminal justice.

As the country's capital after the war, Philadelphia was the political, social, and intellectual center of the new country. European thought, especially French egalitarian ideas developed from its own revolution, strongly influenced such men as Franklin and Jefferson, who had spent much time in that country. The barbarism of European justice systems made the American forms of corporal punishment seem tame by comparison. In England, for instance, no fewer than 222 crimes, even as minor as petty theft, were capital offenses. Throughout the entire continent, prisons were notorious for the squalor in which the prisoners subsisted and the acts of torture that took place behind their walls.

Prominent political voices, such as Jeremy Bentham and Thomas Paine in England and Voltaire and Montesquieu in France, had been protesting their countries' penal codes even before the time of the American revolution. It was an Italian, however, who was destined to produce a work that, even today, is universally acknowledged as having laid the foundation for modern concepts of penology. Cesare Beccaria's *Trattato dei delitti e delle pene* (Essay on Crimes and Punishments), published in 1764, espoused a system strongly influenced by the French and English rationalists; it was imbued with novel ideas regarding both men's relationships to one another and the proper means of dealing with crime and punishment in an ordered society.

Beccaria's ideas, for the most part, are quite consistent with modern thought, but they challenged notions that were fundamentally ingrained in the minds of seventeenth-century Europeans. He began with a view of society that Bentham called *eudaemonics*: that the basis of all social action should be to achieve the greatest good for the greatest number. Crime, in any form, is an injury to society, and the only measure of a crime's severity is the extent of its injury to society. The punishment of crime is not as important as its prevention, and the first element in the prevention of crime is to have in place a well-considered and fully published criminal code, so that members of society can at all times remain aware of which behavior is forbidden in that society. Secret accusations and torture are not consistent with such a society and must be abolished, to be replaced by speedy public trials, where the accused is afforded every opportunity to bring forth evidence on his own behalf.

Punishment, Beccaria continued, is intended only to deter other persons from committing crime, not for the purpose of exacting social revenge. Therefore, the severity of the punishment is not as important as its certainty and its expeditious execution. Offenses against property should be punished only by fines; imprisonment should be imposed only when the accused is unable to pay the fine.

Capital punishment, Beccaria maintained, should be abolished. Noting that England's 222 capital offenses had done little to deter crime in that country, he asserted that life imprisonment would be a much more compelling deterrent. Further, the finality of capital punishment made no allowance for mistake.

Finally, and most significantly, Beccaria argued that imprisonment should be more widely utilized instead of corporal punishment. The physical conditions in prisons, however, had to be significantly improved, and provisions made to segregate prisoners on the basis of age, sex, and degree of criminality.

Beccaria's essay had a profound effect on many European heads of state, such as Russia's Catherine the Great and Austria's Maria Theresa, and resulted in the repeal of much of the barbarous criminal codes that had prevailed throughout the continent. His influence, however, was not limited to Europe; even as America's war for independence was just beginning, the colonial legislatures had begun to re-examine their penal codes and their prison systems.

Tangible evidence of change occurred even as the first shots of the war were being fired. On September 28, 1776, the Pennsylvania legislature adopted a new constitution that included several aspects of penal reform premised on Beccaria's ideas. It directed that:

> To deter more effectually from the commission of crimes, by continued visible punishment of long duration, and to make sanguinary punishments less necessary; houses ought to be provided for punishing by hard labor, those who shall be convicted of crimes not capital; wherein the criminals shall be employed for the benefit of the public, or for reparation of injuries done to private persons. And all persons at proper times shall be admitted to see the prisoners at their labor.

The war delayed implementation of these reforms for a full decade, but in 1786 the process began in earnest with Pennsylvania's enactment of a law repealing the death penalty for robbery, burglary, and sodomy and substituting a prison term not to exceed ten years. The new law also provided that any noncapital crime previously punishable by "burning in the hand, cutting off the ears, nailing the ear or ears to the pillory, placing in or upon the pillory, whipping or imprisonment for life" would thereafter be punishable by imprisonment at hard labor for not more than two years. Additional reforms followed quickly, the most significant being the repeal of capital punishment for all crimes except premeditated murder.

All of these revisions came at a price, however; since so many crimes would now be punishable by imprisonment, it quickly became necessary to establish a formal prison system in place of the colonial jails and workhouses. By 1790, Philadelphia's Walnut Street Jail had been converted to the state's first prison structured consistently with the penal reforms that the Pennsylvania legislature had enacted in prior years. The principal goal was to segregate the inmates according to the severity of their crimes—the worst offenders would be held in separate cells, while the lesser criminals were held in larger dormitory-type rooms.

Although initially the system appeared to work, it quickly became apparent that the prison was destined to failure. Overcrowding was the culprit; so many new convicts were being sentenced to the prison that the congregate cells were bursting at the seams, and the plan to harbor the worst felons in solitary confinement had to be abandoned. Within a decade, it was painfully obvious that this first attempt in America at scientific penology was a dismal flop.

New York, having also modernized its criminal code, was facing similar problems. In 1797, Newgate Prison opened in Greenwich Village. Built exclusively on a congregate housing plan, it, too, rapidly became overcrowded, frustrating reformists in the same manner as was occurring in Pennsylvania.

These were the circumstances existing in Pennsylvania and New York in 1811 as Prince was making his way to Connecticut's Newgate. It was no coincidence that two prisons shared the same name; both were named after London's notorious Newgate Prison, a medieval dungeon whose reputation alone reputedly served as a strong deterrent to criminal conduct. New York's Newgate was probably so named in an effort to capitalize on the original's infamy, although that was the only characteristic it shared with its English namesake. In contrast, Connecticut's Newgate had much more in common with the original—first and foremost, it too was a dungeon. A spent colonial copper mine now given new life as a place of punishment, Connecticut's Newgate may not have been subjecting its inmates to the medieval tortures practiced by its English namesake, but it was not without its own brand of misery to inflict on its unfortunate occupants.

By this time, Connecticut had also joined the ranks of states that had made significant revisions to their penal codes. Prince's own sentence of life imprisonment for attempted murder was in keeping with the new code; had he been convicted of the same crime some fifteen years earlier, his punishment would have been death, either expressly imposed at the gallows or indirectly at the whipping post.

Although Connecticut had joined the reform movement with respect to its penal code, it was in no rush to pursue a program of prison reform to accompany the new code. Opened as the first state prison in the country in 1773,

Newgate in 1811 offered its inmates accommodations that were only slightly improved from its earliest days, coupled with a system of punishment that was totally indifferent to the ideas of Beccaria and the Pennsylvania and New York reformists.

The only interruption in Newgate's twelve-foot stone perimeter wall was a double-door arched gateway along the prison's easterly presentation that ran along the road. Chiseled into the arch's massive keystone were the words "Newgate Prison—1802." Sheriff Parsons banged on the gate to draw the attention of the guard posted within. The guard swung open one of the two heavy wooden doors, and Newgate Prison welcomed into its fold the man who was at once its newest, and its oldest, inmate.

· 9 ·

Early Newgate

*W*hatever shock Prince may have experienced at his first sight of New-gate, even obscured by the dark of a cold winter night, easily must have been eclipsed by the prison keepers' shock at the appearance of their newest arrival. Knowing full well the rigors that their little prison on the hill imposed on its occupants, these guards must have seriously doubted that the man standing before them would last the winter. Weary and cold from a long winter day's travel, Prince's aged and yaws-ravaged body must have presented them with an image resembling a walking corpse. They also recognized that the prison lacked facilities to care for a man of such age and condition. But Prince was their charge now, and they would have to deal with him as best they could.

For his part, Prince's nighttime arrival at the prison offered him only a shadowy glimpse of the guardhouse, but that alone was probably enough to verify his worst fears about this place. The term "guardhouse" was somewhat of a misnomer, however, since this small building served a variety of functions in addition to housing the guards. Built in 1802, the brick guardhouse was merely the tip of the iceberg, presenting to the world only a minute part of what was Newgate prison. For beneath this nondescript building lay the prison's ominous feature that was both its great glory but its even greater shame—its caverns.

In 1705, more than a century before Prince came to call Newgate home, the presence of copper was discovered in the eastern hills of the town of Simsbury.[1] The town appointed a committee to investigate the feasibility of exploiting this fortuitous discovery. At that time, the area of the find was in the hinterlands, considerably removed from the center of town, and its use was limited to hunting grounds for both the town inhabitants and roving Indians. Since no one owned the land, it came under the control of the association of the town's proprietors, essentially all of the community's population of sixty or so souls. After some discussion, the association appointed the town's three clergymen to undertake the first efforts at mining and smelting the ore.

These three gentlemen, having had the benefit of a formal education in England, were generally regarded as the most likely to be able to acquire the knowledge needed for this new undertaking. Their academic achievements, however, did not translate to business acumen; during the first four years, the new mine had proven itself quite unprofitable, to the extent that the proprietors were considering suing the clergymen for their mismanagement. The company of proprietors persevered, however, principally by leasing out the mining rights to a series of entrepreneurs, who would continue to extract copper ore from the mines for another sixty years.

These endeavors were not limited to a single mine. A number of other shafts were dug all along the ridge, but none would prove as rich as the one that would eventually become Newgate. At that site, two separate vertical shafts were chiseled through solid rock, one being about thirty-five feet in depth, and the other nearly eighty feet, and about two hundred feet apart. At that depth, the mines branched out horizontally, eventually resulting in a series of caverns extending over a hundred feet in all directions.

Since the mining was occurring in rock, the lack of adequate drainage presented the operation with a chronic problem. A method had to be devised to expel the rainwater that would percolate through the rock and flood the caverns. Until a separate drainage tunnel was dug some years later, the task was accomplished by the use of pumps. This proved to be quite an expensive proposition, since it occupied about thirty people on a full-time basis.

There was yet another factor negatively affecting the bottom line: the English Crown. In an effort to deter competition with the smelting operations in England, British law forbad the smelting of ore anywhere other than in the motherland; consequently, in the early years of the mine's operation the copper being extracted from the Simsbury mines first had to be carried overland to Hartford, a distance of fourteen miles, then loaded onto a ship for the trip down the Connecticut River and Long Island Sound to New York, and finally to England.

The mining companies soon determined that these prohibitive shipping expenses threatened their profitability, and around 1720 they started smelting their ore in a nearby secret location a few miles away. This illegal enterprise did not long remain undiscovered, however, and eventually the mine proprietors found themselves levied against by the Crown for their conduct. (Apparently, these penalties were not severe enough to deter subsequent efforts at local smelting; in 1737 through 1739 a certain enterprising Granby gentleman by the name of Higley actually began minting his own coins to substitute for the legal currency that was always in short supply.[2])

In addition to all these obstacles, there were also clear indications of theft by miners who took advantage of their absentee employers and diverted the best grade ore to their own buyers. Nonetheless, over the following decades various partnerships, including one led by Jonathan Belcher, the colonial governor of Massachusetts, continued to seek their fortunes in the Simsbury mining operations. Such efforts continued until 1772, when the chronic financial losses of the mines finally forced their closing.

By that time, Connecticut had finally begun to abandon some, but certainly not all, of its old colonial corporal punishments in favor of jail terms, and the colony was beginning to feel the need for more facilities, beyond its local and county jails, to incarcerate its growing convict population. In 1773, the general assembly appointed a three-man commission to evaluate the feasibility of converting the main abandoned cavern into a prison.

After examining the site, the committee made its favorable report that the mine could be utilized as a prison at very little expense — £60 to buy out the remaining nineteen years on a lease, £17 to construct wooden bunks in the main cavern, and £20 for an iron door to secure the access shaft. Thus, for the meager sum of £97, Newgate, America's first state prison, was born.[3]

The facility, of course, was as meager as the funds used to acquire it and convert it to a prison. At ground level, the prison was effectively invisible to the passerby, since there were no improvements at all above ground. In the early years, there were not even any guards posted at the gate during the daytime. The prisoners were permanent residents of their communal underground cell; the only light of day ever to grace their faces was the small patch of daylight, some sixty feet distant, they might see if they stood directly beneath the longer shaft. From above, only upon approaching the access shaft would a visitor observe that there was more to this scene than initially met the eye, for a glance down that shaft would disclose the iron gate, anchored some six feet below the surface, serving to keep Connecticut's citizenry safe from its most dangerous and pernicious criminals.[4]

The prison that existed on the other side of that gate was unlike any other on the continent. The shaft itself was only three feet in diameter; access was had by a wooden ladder affixed to the wall. Beyond the gate, the shaft continued vertically some twenty more feet until it reached the cavern. At the base of the ladder was an enclosed area of about eight feet square, connected by another iron gate to the main cavern. In truth, to call this opening a cavern would be doing injustice to the term, for the area certainly did not resemble the many vast natural caverns found in many parts of the world. Rather, this was an opening carved by men from solid rock. Apparently, these miners were not inclined to dig any more than they absolutely had to, so the cavern was only about five feet in height. In their excavation, the miners followed the natural inclination of the strata; consequently, most of the main cavern is not level, but rather slopes downward to the east at an angle of about 23 degrees.

The main cavern varied from 80 to 100 feet in width and had a linear distance of perhaps 165 feet.[5] The outside weather would determine the dampness of the cave, as rainwater would eventually percolate through rock fissures into the opening. Since the cavern's floor was at a considerable slope, the nearly constant dampness made for slippery movement. The dampness was also not very compatible with the hay that the prisoners would use as mattresses on the rough bunks built along the cavern walls; throughout Newgate's history, the prisoners would be complaining that the damp hay was an ideal breeding ground for fleas.

Dark and damp, the cavern presented anything but a comfortable environment to its occupants; further adding to the discomfort was the fact that most men, being of normal height, could find no place within the entire cavern where they could even stand fully erect. Except for the fleas, insects apparently were not a problem, since the absence of any organic material denied them any reason to cohabitate with the prisoners.

As any modern visitor to this place can attest, however, the most eerie and unnatural feature of the cavern is the effect its solid-rock walls have on the human voice. Sound waves bounce haphazardly throughout the room, imparting on the spoken word an alien metallic timbre not easily duplicated.

There is one area in particular, at the end of a shaft, which narrows to only a few feet. A heavy wooden door, built only twenty feet or so from the end of that shaft, served to create a small cell for solitary confinement of unruly prisoners. Any convict unfortunate enough to be committed to this cell, sitting or lying for hours on end in total darkness on a wet stone floor, found himself as close to being buried alive as could be imagined. That degree of punishment, however, apparently was still deemed insufficient, since the prisoner would also be chained to the floor at his ankle. Quite possibly, the men subjected to this ordeal may well have yearned for the good old days of the whipping post.

That may well have been the case for William Stuart, who devotes a few lines in his autobiography to his time in this dreadful place.[6] Having refused to confess to the warden about his involvement in an uprising, Stuart was punished by being place in solitary confinement. This is how he describes the ordeal:

> In a few days I was sent to the dungeon, and as the Captain supposed, kept on bread and water. This dungeon was about twenty feet square, cold and damp, rock above rock all around, and the middle of the rock was a little elevated, so that the dripping water passed about the edge of this cavern. Upon the center of this rock, I was chained by one leg to an iron bolt. Occasionally some of the men came down into the adjoining room,

and supplied me with additional clothing, more food, and plenty of liquor. Tuller sentenced me to this place for twenty days; but in about twelve he liberated me, and I was brought into day-light again.

Stuart's autobiography confirms him as a man who was intelligent and extremely self-assured. His strong personality certainly was an asset in helping him emerge unscathed from his time in the dungeon. Others, no doubt, did not fare as well.

The road winding by Newgate Prison was hardly more than a cart path, and directly across that road from the old copper mine stood the home and tavern of Captain John Viets. Since the house stood immediately adjacent to the road, the distance between Viets' home and the access shaft was perhaps no more than 200 feet. That fact alone, apart from any other qualifications he may have had, made the captain an ideal candidate to assume the position of keeper of the new prison, since it spared the colony the expense of erecting a suitable structure for housing any other person the general assembly might have chosen as keeper.

It was not long at all before the prison welcomed John Hinson as its first occupant. Committed on December 2, 1773, Hinson spent only eighteen days in the dungeon before managing his escape. Apparently, in the dark of night his paramour dropped a rope down the ventilation shaft, and Hinson made his way up the seventy-foot shaft, never to be seen or heard from again. So much for the observation in the original commissioners' report that the mines could be so perfectly secured that "it would be next to impossible for any person to escape."

Within the following four months, it appears that four more prisoners would attempt an escape. Three of them did so by following an abandoned semivertical ore shaft that had been refilled with stones. In the process of removing the loose stones, they apparently caused a cave-in upon themselves. Although two of the men were believed to have been buried in the rubble, Viets was not so sure, and he ran an ad in the *Connecticut Courant* offering a reward for their capture and return. They were never found, however, and some believe that the remains of these two convicts lie still buried in the shaft.

After these attempts, the general assembly authorized funds to build a blockhouse, directly above the entrance shaft, in an attempt to strengthen the prison's security. The blockhouse was sturdily built from ten-inch timbers and contained two rooms, one for the guards and another to house the keeper, since by that time Viets had resigned the post and retreated across the road to the comfortable life of tavern keeper.

Newgate's infamy was already so renowned that General Washington sent several incorrigibles there, with this accompanying note:

Cambridge, Dec. 7th, 1775

Gentlemen:—The prisoners which will be delivered you with this, having been tried by a court martial and deemed to be such flagrant and atrocious villains, that they cannot by any means be set at large, or confined in any place near this camp, were sentenced to Simsbury, in Connecticut. You will therefore be pleased to have them secured in your jail, or in such other manner as to you shall seem necessary, so that they cannot possibly make their escape. The charges of their imprisonment will be at the Continental expense.

I am, &c.,

George Washington

The prison's reputation grew even broader when it became a convenient holding place for Tories during the war.[7] Every colony had its population of British supporters, and each dealt with their presence in its own way. No colony, however, was more callous than Connecticut in addressing the problem. Various towns, acting through their vigilance committees under such names as the "Committee of Safety" or the "Committee of Inspection," were charged with verifying the loyalty of the population. The process may not have been as brutal or oppressive as the Spanish Inquisition, but in some instances it was just as deadly. At least one British sympathizer was shot in Simsbury, and another was hanged in Hartford, his body allowed to remain in public view for several days as a means of intimidating like-minded Tories.

There were obviously sound reasons for identifying and containing Tories, since their opportunity for espionage and ability to relay information to the enemy represented a real threat to the American cause. If a man, upon inquiry of the committee, was thought to be indifferent to the cause, he could be confined to his own property. To venture beyond that permitted area was an invitation to much worse punishment, and even death. If, however, a man dared to voice ardent support for England, the committee would promptly dispatch him to Newgate. Initially, there were only a few such Tories confined at the prison, but in short order their numbers swelled to more than forty.

These men were not isolated from the general prison population, and they were treated in the same manner as were the convicts. Essentially, this meant that they remained in the caverns on a permanent basis, lending their forced labor to the efforts at mining that were still continuing on a half-hearted basis.

Under other circumstances, these Tories would have been quite different, in both temperament and disposition, from the career criminals who were now their fellow inmates. They may have been neophytes in their new world populated by swindlers, rapists, burglars, parasites and sycophants, but they were anything but placid and submissive in their captivity. In 1776, they attempted their first organized escape by setting fire to the blockhouse over the access shaft. Unfortunately, no one had given any thought to the fact that the fire would create dense smoke that eventually would fill the cavern. By the time the guards were able to extinguish the fire and get into the cavern, one prisoner had died and five others suffered severe smoke inhalation. Undeterred, the following year the Tories again set fire to an aboveground barracks built to house them, succeeding in burning it to the ground. Several managed their escape, but eventually all were recaptured and returned to their subterranean cell.

These events would prove to be minor, however, in comparison to the uprising that occurred in 1781. By that time, the war was being waged furiously, and the hatred engendered by the fighting was at its height. Newgate was hardly immune from these attitudes. Most of the thirty or so prisoners were Tories, more intent than ever to make good their escape, and they had willing accomplices in the non-Tory prisoners.

Their opportunity came on the night of May 21, when the wife of one of the prisoners came to visit her husband. Two Tories were lying in wait on the other side of the iron gate, just a few feet below ground level. As the two guards opened the gate to let her down, the prisoners rushed out, overcame the guards, and forced them down into the cavern. Most of the other prisoners climbed up the ladder to assist in the uprising.

This was not as benign an incident as the prior escape attempt. There were nearly as many guards as there were prisoners, all armed with muskets, bayonets, and knives. As the prisoners managed to overcome some of the guards and acquire their weapons, the fighting became increasingly ferocious. There were wounded on both sides, and the darkness caused such confusion that some prisoners were injured by their own comrades. When it was all over, one guard was dead, six others severely wounded, and as many prisoners so wounded that they were unable to make their escape.

Of those who did manage to escape, most were recaptured in due course and returned to the prison. Their experiences, however, had not tamed them in the least. In November of the following year, only eighteen months after the great uprising, the Tories again attempted to aid their escape by burning to the ground all of the prison's remaining wooden buildings. Their desire for freedom at that particular time is especially understandable, since some six months earlier Cornwallis had tendered his surrender. These Tories must have been especially distressed over their circumstances, since apparently the only reason they remained captive at Newgate was Congress's indecision on how to deal with the property interests of those who had supported the English side during the war.[8]

The departure of the Tories from Newgate marked the conclusion of an unfortunate, even deplorable, episode in both American and Connecticut history. Although the need to protect the patriots' cause from the potential threat of British sympathizers was justifiable, what may not have been as justifiable was the harsh manner by which that objective was accomplished. This country's history offers other examples of detention being imposed on suspect elements of its citizenry in times of war. As harsh as conditions may have been in those later instances, at least the Newgate solution was not followed, where the detainees were placed in a facility intended to house only the worst miscreants that the state of Connecticut had to offer. Housed in tight quarters with such wretches of society, they were also treated in like manner as the convicts, subjected to the same harsh conditions, and even forced to engage in hard labor.

Newgate's reputation as a place of terror was firmly established by the end of the war, but its worst years were yet to come. By the time Prince would walk beneath its arched entryway nearly three decades later, the prison had grown both in size and infamy. Its reputation, Prince would quickly learn, was well deserved.

• *10* •

Mortimer, Prince

*T*he Tories hardly would have recognized the prison that Prince was now entering. Gone were the wooden barracks that had occupied their arsonous attention in their several escape attempts. Also gone was the wooden fence that for decades had enclosed Newgate's original half-acre parcel. In its place rose a twelve-foot stone wall marking the expanded two-acre perimeter of the prison property. Within the grounds stood two new buildings, a guardhouse and a nail shop, both erected in 1790.[1]

The guardhouse was a two-story structure, having a footprint of only thirty × forty feet, built into the hillside. Its modest size, however, belied the massive nature of the materials that went into its construction. The lower level was fashioned from stones hewn to six to eight feet in length, and held together by iron cramps. The floor consisted of stones three feet square and about ten inches thick. There were two rooms at this level, separated as well by a stone wall: the larger room, known as the "jug," which first served as an infirmary and later as a sleeping room for a few of the less difficult prisoners, and the smaller "passage" room, which provided access to the shaft leading to the cavern.

Because of the slope of the land toward the west, the guardhouse's east-wardly facing second story also provided ground-level access. Built of brick, it contained four rooms, two of which were used as a residence by the keeper and his family and the other two serving the guards. The floor of one of the guards' rooms had a trap door and a ladder leading down to the passage room. Prisoners entering or leaving the cavern could only do so by means of the trap door. The narrowness of the door meant that only one prisoner at a time could enter the guard room, so the risk of a mass uprising or escape attempt was minimized. The Tories were long gone, but the design of this arrangement demonstrated that they were not forgotten.

Escape was constantly on the minds of not only the prisoners, but the keepers as well. As with the passage room, the only access to the infirmary was through another trap door leading down from the guards' room. Apparently, no prisoner was ever expected to be so sick as to be unable to climb a ladder.

Until the arrival of the Tories, the prisoners had been kept occupied by continuing to mine copper ore, but the exercise proved to be unproductive. Perhaps of greater concern was the fact that the mining process gave the prisoners easy access to tools to use as weapons or by which they might plan an escape. Consequently, the decision was made to put the prisoners at work making hand-wrought nails. A nail shop was built for that purpose in the northeast corner of the prison. The shop had only a single door and a few barred windows to let in a small amount of light. Inside were three forges and sufficient workstations to accommodate thirty-two prisoners.

A 1799 engraving made by Richard Brunton, a prisoner at Newgate at the turn of the century, presents an accurate and telling depiction many of the prison's features at the time of Prince's arrival, although some modifications would occur in the intervening dozen years. Along with the guardhouse and the nail shop are shown a small cooper's shack, used for making wooden barrels, a small wooden barracks, and a bake shop. Prominently featured in the center of the yard is a man strapped to the whipping post, and a guard is administering the expected punishment. Flogging was frequently used, not only as punishment for infractions but also to motivate prisoners who might otherwise be inclined to slack off on their nail production quotas.

A telling feature of Brunton's depiction is that he shows about twenty other persons engaged in a variety of other tasks about the yard, but not a one is showing any interest in the activity at the whipping post. Assuming that depiction to be accurate, and intentional on Brunton's part, such apparent indifference to a prisoner's suffering suggests a great deal about the level of misery that permeated daily life at Newgate.

No doubt Beccaria would have been appalled to learn that, nearly a half-century after his book had started Europe on the road to humane prison reform, inmates at Newgate were being routinely subjected to such tortures as flogging, solitary confinement on bread and water, hanging by the heels, and being made to bear the constant weight of double or triple sets of iron.

Ironically, the most dreaded torment at Newgate was never designed as a punishment at all. The stepping mill, introduced in the early 1820s, was primarily intended to provide profitable (for the state, of course, not for the prisoners) employment for those men whose terms of imprisonment were so short that there was not enough time to teach them one of the more permanent prison skills. The men provided the power for grinding grain by stepping in unison onto the rotating paddles of an elongated treadmill, wide enough

A Prospective View of Old Newgate, Connecticut's State Prison. Engraving by
Richard Brunton. (The Connecticut Historical Society Museum)

to accommodate ten men. The gears transferring their power to the actual
gristwheel beneath them were hardly a model of engineering efficiency, and
the men had to exert considerable effort with each step to keep the system
operating.

A prisoner's turn at the wheel was regulated by having the men move
slowly to the left as they worked. Eventually, a man would be forced off the
wheel at the far left end, and at the same time his replacement would climb
on at the opposite end. Depending on the number of men in a work detail,
they would average ten to fifteen minutes of rest every hour, but that was not
enough to prevent them from wholly despising this exhausting assignment.

Financial considerations were not the only ones leading to the introduction of the stepping mill at Newgate. Many saw it as an effective tool for maintaining discipline, since the men expended so much energy at the wheel that there was little left for mischief. Zephania Swift, Connecticut's leading jurist at the time, viewed the treadmill as perhaps "one of the most valuable improvements in criminal jurisprudence that ever has been made." His classic treatise, *Swift's Digest*, lavished considerable praise on this new device. "This, by hard and severe labor," he wrote, "unattended with cruelty or barbarity, causes such extreme fatigue that it is confidently believed, from the experiments which have been tried, it will prove a more appropriate and effectual punishment to restrain the commission of crimes of a certain description than any which has hitherto been devised."[2]

Swift was not alone in anticipating tremendous success for the stepping mill. The overseers' report for 1824 indicates that thirty prisoners were employed at the mill during the prior year. Sharing Swift's optimism, the report continues, "It is also confidently believed that the severity of the labour (although by no means cruel) will have a tendency ultimately to reduce the number of prisoners by operating as a 'terror to evil doers' and in that way render an essential service to the community."

Even the *Connecticut Courant* saw fit to extol the many benefits of the stepping mill. Its August 29, 1822, edition devoted two full columns to an article describing an English mill in considerable detail. The article claimed that the stepping mill was effective both in providing prison employment and in reducing recidivism, "as many prisoners have been known to declare that they would sooner undergo any species of fatigue, or suffer any deprivation, than return to the house of correction, when once released."

As it turned out, the high aspirations of Swift, the prison administration, and the *Courant* for the stepping mill's success were never realized; there was so much dissent among the prisoners that the plan was abandoned after only a couple of years.

A rather curious feature of Brunton's engraving is his decision to superimpose the official State of Connecticut emblem onto an empty area of the prison yard. The emblem reads "Qui transtulit sustinet," meaning "He who transplanted still sustains." The motto's origin is uncertain, but its use goes back to the earliest days of the colony. Its inspiration is no doubt found in the desire of the colonists to succeed in their new environment; Brunton may well have added the motto to his engraving as an expression of sarcasm, but perhaps he was also offering encouragement to the prisoners, who had all been transplanted from their familiar environment into this place of painful misery and gloom.

One of the great ironies of Prince's introduction to life at Newgate was

Wide east/west view showing the south elevation of Newgate Prison complex, and the façade of Viets Tavern. Photo circa 1890. (Historic Preservation & Museum Division of the Connecticut Commission on Culture & Tourism)

that, despite the many degradations it constantly imposed on all of its in-habitants, it did bestow on Prince one element of dignity that he had never known: it was here that Prince received, for the first time in his already long life, a surname. It may well have been done only for administrative purposes, but whatever the reason Prince was no longer to be known merely as "Prince Negro," as the information charging him with his crime had described him; he would forever be shown on the roles of Newgate as "Prince Mortimer," a fact that now made him an equal with each and every one of the other prisoners, be they white or black, free or slave. In this minor way, at least, Prince had finally acquired one small indicium of a free man.

The prison population fluctuated dramatically during the years of Prince's incarceration. A report prepared in January 1811, about a year before Prince's arrival, states that Newgate then housed 46 prisoners. That number would grow steadily over the next several years, to 116 in 1825. The following year, however, would see that number decrease to 95 and then grow again to see 129 prisoners transferred in 1827 when the prison was closed.

The racial composition of the prison does not appear to have fluctuated as much. The 1811 report indicates that 32 of the 46 prisoners (70%) were white, and the remaining prisoners were stated to be Negro, Indian, or mulatto. By 1825, 77 of the 116 inmates (66%) were white. Unfortunately, similar information is only partially available for the final transfer list. That list is divided into three sections, apparently in accord with the way the prisoners were transferred. Racial information, as well as other statistical information on the prisoners, apparently has been lost as to the third section. For the first and second sections, however, out of 81 prisoners, 47 (58%) were white.

The prison's population increase was not due merely to the fact that the courts were sending more men to Newgate; it also had to do with the fact that prisoners were required to remain at the prison far longer than their sentence, as imposed by the court, might suggest. A defendant, upon being convicted, found that his sentence consisted of two elements: the first, of course, was the term of incarceration. The second, however, was the court's order that the defendant repay the state for the cost of his incarceration. Thus, at the end of his sentence, a prisoner found that he had to remain in prison to work off this debt, at the rate of five dollars per month. A typical inmate, sentenced to five years' imprisonment, would find that his financial obligation was about $375; at the stated rate, he would have to remain in Newgate an additional six years to work off the debt.

A routine, begun at about the time the nail shop was constructed, most likely was still in effect by the time Prince arrived some twenty years later: The prisoners would be summoned from the cavern at daylight; in groups of three, they would emerge from the guard house wearing ankle irons and would then proceed to the nail shop, but always under the watchful eye of the accompanying guard. Since the chain connecting the shackles was quite short, it was impossible to walk at a normal stride, so most inmates elected to hop across the prison yard. The combination of the sound of their clanking chains and the grunts of their early morning exertions piercing the mist might well have called to mind a scene with which Dante would have been quite comfortable.

Once in the shop, the guards shackled each prisoner securely at the ankle to his workstation. Apparently fearing that even that degree of security was inadequate for some of the more recalcitrant prisoners, the guards would also shackle some of them by the neck to a wooden beam suspended above their work areas. In this manner, with hardly enough slack to allow them to move to the right or to the left, or even to lean forward when tired, these unfortunate souls would pass the next nine or ten hours turning out wrought nails, which the state hoped it could sell at a profit to help defray the expense of maintaining the prison.

After a few hours of work, the prisoners would receive their daily rations. Until about 1815, there was nothing at Newgate that functioned as a dining hall, so the allowances were distributed to the convicts where they worked. Each prisoner was given either a pound of beef or three-quarters of a pound of pork, a pound of bread, and some potatoes. Vegetables were added when they were in season and could be locally obtained. The convicts were on their own, however, as to how they prepared their rations. Some cooked in small kettles, but others simply threw their meat into the embers of the forges and transferred the finished product onto an anvil, where they devoured it without benefit of utensils. Whatever degree of dignity a prisoner may have had when he entered Newgate was significantly diminished by the time he left, as he was compelled to satisfy his most essential needs in a manner not much removed from animals in the wild.

Although the allotted portions might initially appear to be ample to sustain an adult male, the quality of the meat was usually quite poor, and much of it was either spoiled or so gristly as to be inedible. After the cattle were slaughtered, the warden and the guards would routinely help themselves to the best cuts, and only the bony remainders were left for the inmates.

Conditions had not improved some years later, when William Stuart came to serve his sentence. Stuart, a prisoner at Newgate from 1820 to 1825, devoted three chapters of his autobiography to the prison, and his observations certainly confirmed what was generally recognized about the quality of the food:

> Our food was insufficient, not more than one-third that my system required. It was chiefly huck bones, bulls' necks, and skins. If any marrow was in them it was bored out with large gimblets before it came to be cooked. When our scanty meals were taken from the pot, Capt. Tuller ordered the cook to skim off every particle of grease, and from the beef thus used in this prison he sold 3000 lbs. of tallow yearly. . . . I and my fellow prisoners have picked the bones bare for a meal, and often it would not be two table spoons-full.[3]

The presence of a bakeshop on the prison grounds might suggest that at least the convicts enjoyed reasonably good bread; the quality of the meal was so inferior, however, that even freshly baked loaves were hard and not easily consumed. As Stuart wrote, "Our bread was made of rye and corn ground together, without bolting, and was hard enough for gun flints."

Most likely, the saving grace in the lives of many of the prisoners lay in the fact that they were also allowed a daily pint of cider. (Apparently, at that time spirits were generally viewed as essential to sustain human life.) Since the prisoners were allowed to swap allowances, a number of convicts saw fit to trade their solid food for the liquid component of their neighbor's ration. It was not at all uncommon for prisoners to become so intoxicated that they were unable to work. Apparently, this was not considered a punishable offense, since these men eagerly repeated the process at every available opportunity.

Regardless of the season, work in the nail shop ended at 4:00 p.m., and the prisoners would be led back to the darkness of the cavern. Charles S. Miller, writing about the life of another prisoner at Newgate, gives this graphic account of the prisoners' nightly descent:

> At four in the p.m. the work of the day was finished. The handcuffs and shackles were replaced, the collars and fetters unlocked, and with slow walk

Interior of Newgate Prison yard facing south showing the east prison wall, ruins of chapel, and corner of guardhouse. **Photo circa 1890.** (Historic Preservation & Museum Division of the Connecticut Commission on Culture & Tourism)

and hobble the men, unless granted the indulgence of remaining for over-work, made their way back to the pit. As they passed the trap, a bit of candle an inch long was given to each. Holding up his shackles as best he could, each then backed slowly down the ladder to the regions below.[4]

Once back in the caverns, the inmates had to contend with living conditions that were nothing short of abominable. In their 1814 report, the overseers made no effort to hide their frustration from the legislature:

> The overseers have taken pains to keep the prison & the prisoners cleanly and have succeeded so far, at least, to prevent the formation & stagnation of noxious & pestilential vapor; but some of the prisoners appear to love filth, & are inclined never to put off their clothes for washing, or so much as to wash their face and hands. This tendency to wallow in filth arises out of their degraded condition and is no more than a natural expression of mental depravity. It requires a constant effort of the prison keeper to counteract it.

Since Prince's age made him an unlikely security risk, he was sometimes prevailed upon to make cider runs to the tavern across the road. He would eventually return, laden with two or three gallons, but having deducted his fee in kind from his delivery. Even though the distance from the tavern to the prison gate was less than a hundred feet, there were nights when Prince failed to negotiate the return trip on the same day he had started out, putting both the guards and the prisoners in great distress as to his whereabouts. Invariably, though, Prince had spent the night huddled against the prison wall, having made liberal use of his cargo to ward off the night chills.

Other aspects of Prince's life in Newgate were much less pleasant. Although his age and ill health certainly exempted him from work in the nail forge, no doubt he was made to take on some of the more menial tasks the prison had to offer. No aboveground cells would be built until 1815, so during the first four years of his imprisonment Prince spent most of his nights in the caverns along with the average complement of forty to fifty other inmates, although on occasion in the summers he may well have been afforded the relative comfort of the "jug."

Without doubt, during those years Prince had occasion to pull more than a few tours of duty as cullyman. The term was probably as uncommon in Prince's day as it is now, so a new prisoner being told he was to be appointed to this position may well have believed himself quite fortunate. That belief was short lived, however, once the responsibilities of the job became known to him, for the cullyman had the unenviable task of gathering the buckets of the prisoners' excrement from the caverns and carrying them up to the surface for disposal. It was certainly an appropriate name for a job given to neophyte prisoners, since the term "cully" generally is used to denote a dupe, one who is easily tricked or manipulated.

Years after Newgate's closing, stories of its hardships continued to captivate the public interest, to some degree because tales of some of its more colorful or notorious inmates had become quite embellished with the passage of time. Prince himself was the subject of one such story; Richard Phelps, in his classic *Newgate of Connecticut: Its Origin and Early History*, tells of an unnamed newspaper reporter who visited the caverns in the 1850s and later wrote of his adventures, fumbling in the dark through the damp and slippery passages after he had dropped his lantern into a puddle. Apparently, the reporter had heard of Prince and described a spot in the caverns "where old Prince the Negro, who had once been servant to an officer under Gen. Washington, died shackled to the wall, and rotted where he died. The old man was too decrepit to work, and was hence not looked after by the prison officials."[5]

Phelps relates another story, unfortunately not so inaccurate, about an inmate known only by the name of Jake. Apparently, he was a difficult prisoner and eventually found himself in solitary confinement in the "sounding room," a walled-off area at the terminus of one of the cavern's passageways. It received its name from the fact that the high copper content of the room's walls causes human voices to assume an eerie metallic timbre, an experience that many contemporary visitors still find quite disturbing. Its effect on the

Four-story cellblock with observation deck and ramp entrance. Photo circa 1890. (Historic Preservation & Museum Division of the Connecticut Commission on Culture & Tourism)

ears is similar to the sensation one feels when a vibrating tuning fork is placed against the skull.

Jake, finding himself bored, decided to see how far up his legs he could force the iron shackles welded around each of his ankles. With little effort, he was able to get them up from this original position to a point above his calves. Unfortunately, the swelling that quickly ensued made it impossible for the shackles to be moved back down. Jake's pain kept increasing, but no one was around to hear his cries. Some hours later, a guard bringing him his ration of bread and water found Jake in agony and summoned the surgeon. There proved to be no way to remove the shackles, which were now well imbedded into the skin, and the surgeon found himself with no choice but to amputate both legs.

Anesthesia was unknown at the time of this incident. Horace Wells, a Hartford dentist, would not discover this effect of nitrous oxide for another quarter-century. The only relief available to Jake to get him through the ordeal was an abundant supply of rum from Viets' tavern.

Despite his age, Jake survived the operation, and a sympathetic state legislature commuted the balance of his sentence. Phelps reports that Jake was able to support himself, despite his condition, for many years afterwards.

In 1815, about four years after Prince had entered Newgate, the state greatly expanded the facilities at the prison. Two buildings were added along

Looking west through entrance arch toward guardhouse and end of cell block. Photo circa 1890. (Historic Preservation & Museum Division of the Connecticut Commission on Culture & Tourism)

the southern perimeter. The first contained a cooper shop, an infirmary, a shoemaker shop, and a kitchen. The second building, built directly into the southeast corner of the prison wall, contained prison cells on the first level and a chapel on the second. At the opposite end of the prison yard, in the northeast corner, the prisoners would busy themselves in a newly constructed wagon shop.

The state's motivation in adding these new work facilities was hardly benevolent; rather, it was founded on pure economics. The market for hand-wrought nails was drying up, and it was becoming increasingly difficult for the prison to find buyers for its inventory. Consequently, the decision was made to abandon nail making and to diversify into other trades, the major ones being barrel making and shoemaking.

By 1822, the diversification of the work force was well implemented. The overseers' report for that year lists the following occupations: 16 shoemakers; 10 coopers; 12 nailers; 5 wagon, sleigh and plow makers; 1 turner; 4 blacksmiths; 1 filer; 1 basket maker; 1 washer; 1 cook; 2 sawyers; 1 "taylor"; 2 coal and water carriers; and "one old and infirm, unable to labor."

With the construction of the new cells, the expectation was that the cavern would cease to be used for housing the general prison population. That did prove to be the case for some years, although even with the new construction, concerns persisted about possible overcrowding. The 1822 report reaffirms that concern, where the overseers state, "at present all convicts are accommodated with lodging in rooms above ground—if # increases may have to resort to lodging in caverns."

It did not take very long for that concern to become reality. The following year's report states that half of the 109 convicts imprisoned by year's end were housed in the caverns. Many of the prisoners clearly preferred being relegated to their underground home for the night. The guards kept their distance, and the inmates were relatively free to engage in activities that would have never been permitted on the surface. In his autobiography, William Stuart describes the desirability of the caves over the newer cells:

> We chose these lower huts in the summer for sleeping because they were cool, and because, moreover, we could digest our plans unmolested. The loudest cry could not be heard upon the ground, as the upper surface of the shaft was closed by a trap door fastened from above. We would pick up tallow in the daytime and carry it down to give us light in the pitchy darkness that overspread the vast cavern. Some nights were spent gambling, others in fiddling and dancing, others in arranging schemes to obtain our liberty, and others in devising plans to punish that world by whose arbitrament we were excluded from the enjoyment of life.[6]

At ground level, life in the new cells was at best a mixed blessing. Prince and the other prisoners were now being spared the darkness and dampness of the cavern, as well as the effort of negotiating the long ladder up and down the shaft. But these miseries were replaced with others that many prisoners considered even more onerous.

The cavern, despite its dampness, did offer the prisoners the relative comfort of a constant temperature of about 50° to 52° Fahrenheit, regardless of whether the outdoor temperature was 0° or 90° Fahrenheit. The new cells were much more susceptible to outside temperatures, especially in the summer. Stoves enabled the cells to remain somewhat comfortable in the winter, but the prisoners were completely at the mercy of the summer's heat and humidity. Some years later, Louis Dwight, whose interest in Newgate will later be discussed in considerable detail, wrote about the conditions in these cells in 1826:

> We found the prisoners more filthy than any which I have ever seen, except those of the Jail in Washington city. The night rooms were in the same state, nearly, as in the heat of summer, when one hundred and nine convicts were lodged in five small rooms. The largest room was about 21 feet by 10, and 6 feet high, with very little ventilation, and in this room were lodged thirty-two men. It would have been said by most persons, that this number of men could not live in that room a single night. The narrow space, the loathsome bedding, the vermin would take life.[7]

These conditions were considerably aggravated by the fact that these were congregate cells. The influx of the prison population meant that several prisoners were frequently crammed into a cell, with one inmate's head lying next to the feet of his neighbors on either side. Add to this situation the facts that the honey pots were well used in the course of the night and that many of these prisoners routinely neglected to make use of the limited opportunities for washing either themselves or their clothing, and the extent of the misery found in these new cells on a hot summer's night begins to be appreciated.

In short order, these new cells became extremely dirty, with food brought in from the prisoners' daily rations and inevitably spilled buckets of urine and feces. The vermin soon followed. Further, the constant infusion of new inmates, most of whom were already infected before they arrived, constantly frustrated the keepers' efforts at maintaining a modicum of sanitation. William Stuart, never at a loss for colorful and pertinent detail, describes his accommodations with similar disgust:

> It was night when we got to the prison, and I was introduced to my five years' residence. The rooms were only lighted with a small heavily grated window pane, overstocked with lice, fleas and bed bugs, and the floor five inches deep of slippery stinking filth. I exclaimed in the language of Milton, "Hail horrors! and thou infernal hell, receive thy new possessor."[8]

Depictions such as this, as graphic as they may be, cannot do justice to the depths of the squalor and misery to which Newgate's prisoners were subjected. Stuart certainly recognized this, as he continued his commentary:

> There are facts in the world too terrible to be believed, and infinitely exceeding the most extravagant fiction; and these facts are so gross and so abhorrent to the human mind, that they can obtain little credence from community. The poverty of language is such, that no description, however faithfully wrought, can ever approach the truth, and the reader is left to conjecture the revolting character of such a state of things. One view only staggers our faculties, and we step backwards in amazement and horror. Loathsomeness and putridity, united with billions of entomological living specimens, shock the senses of a man uninured to filth, and he instantly feels that in such cases nothing but fire can act successfully as a purifier and health preserver.

There were no murderers at Newgate prison, at least no convicted ones. By 1815, murder was one of the few remaining capital offenses in Connecticut, and persons convicted of that crime were quickly dispatched to the gallows. That did not mean, however, that the criminal population of Newgate was any less venomous or violent. Of the fifty or so inmates in the prison at the time of Prince's arrival, nine were serving life terms for attempted murder or rape, five were serving lengthy terms for arson, and most of the others were burglars and horse thieves. The most innocuous crime represented in the prison was forgery. Clearly, these were not men disposed to be particularly charitable or considerate of the needs of others. They were not the types who would have been inclined to be accommodating towards an elderly former slave by making extra room for him in the cell, and so Prince most likely was subjected to the same crowded and suffocating conditions as were the other prisoners. The old prisoner may well have had occasion to recall another similar situation, nearly nine decades earlier, when he had found himself crammed into the hold of a dark and filthy slave ship.

Newgate may well have been a place of consummate misery, but it did not attempt to keeps its horrors from the public eye. Quite to the contrary, throughout the first quarter of the nineteenth century, the prison's notoriety caused it to become one of the state's most popular tourist attractions. The official overseers' report states that some 5,400 visitors came to Newgate in 1810. The keepers and guards recognized an opportunity when they saw it, and they derived a nice incidental income by providing these tourists with impromptu tours of the prison grounds and, for the more adventurous, portions of the caverns. For many people, Newgate presented a sideshow form of diversion, as they took in the appalling sights and nauseating smells of the place, with the relief of a perfumed handkerchief always at the ready. As the volume of visitors confirms, the general population derived some macabre pleasure from interacting with these filthy dregs of society, who were without doubt the worst congregation of miscreants any of them would probably ever have occasion to encounter in a single place.

Once the caverns were no longer being used exclusively for housing, the prisoners began to be allowed some diversions after their day's labor. After they had finished their work quotas, usually by late afternoon, the prisoners were free to engage in other handiwork that suited them; more than a few of them were able to make pocket change by selling woven baskets to the tourists, which profits were usually spent at the tavern, through the courtesy of Prince's good offices, or those of a cooperative guard, as courier.

The religious needs of the prisoners were not overlooked, although there was a presumption that all the prisoners were protestant Christian, or ought to be. In the earlier years, services were held on the bare ground of the nail shop. In about 1815, however, the second floor of the southeast cellblock was converted to a chapel large enough to hold 250 worshipers, and the public was regularly invited to participate in Sunday services. This event must have provided these visitors as much with entertainment as it did an opportunity for worship, as they would first hear the clamor of the chained prisoners making their way up the stairs and then watch them file into the front pews of the small chapel. The service proceeded with visitors and prisoners alike surrounded by guards incongruously holding a bayoneted musket in one hand and a hymnal in the other.

These were the conditions under which Prince subsisted, and somehow managed to survive, during his incarceration at Newgate. The prison, grossly dirty and overrun by vermin, by the early 1820s was universally decried as a den of abject misery and suffering. For an aging, sickly former slave, however, this wretched place had long since become home.

• 11 •

Freedom Delayed

$\mathcal{P}$rince had been old and sickly on his arrival at Newgate and now, a decade or so later, his condition certainly had deteriorated, although he was still ambulatory. Even though the prison was properly regarded as a hellhole, and the keepers and guards understandably were not the kindest of men, nonetheless they took to heart their legal obligation to safeguard those entrusted to their care. Consequently, Prince's advanced age, aggravated by his yaws, presented the Newgate administration with a unique problem they recognized themselves poorly equipped to handle.

Perhaps only secondarily out of concern for Prince, the guards made several attempts over the years to convince him to leave the prison, but he consistently refused their offer. Perhaps Prince was simply applying the old adage that the devil you know is better than the devil you don't know; in his situation, however, the first half of that maxim was less metaphorical than is usually the case. His fear of the unknown, of what life as a free man would hold for him outside the prison gate, was so great that he had steadfastly chosen to remain in Newgate, amongst thieves, rapists, and worse, subsisting in the ubiquitous filth and sharing his sleeping quarters with vermin large and small.

The guards must have been persistent, because on one occasion Prince decided to take them up on their offer. What a curious mixture of emotions must have overtaken him as he stood outside the wall, taking a last look back into the prison yard as the guard slowly closed the gate to shut him out. Years earlier, he had stood in this same spot, fearing the unknown as the gate had opened to let him in to the prison; now, the same fear overcame him as he left behind his home for the past several years. But Prince's apprehension had to be tempered by the joy of knowing that, for the first time in more than nine decades, he was a free man. This was the dream that had sustained him throughout his life, the dream so bitterly frustrated by George Starr's challenge of Philip Mortimer's will, and the dream seemingly lost forever when that frustration set in motion the chain of events that had sent him to Newgate.

After an obligatory visit to Viets' tavern, Prince was on his way. The journey back to Middletown covered about twenty-eight miles, and the condition of the roads probably had not improved appreciably in the years since his trip in the other direction. Even in good weather, it was a hard day's journey, assuming Prince was fortunate enough to obtain a ride for the entire distance. Otherwise, he would have had to beg a series of rides, which easily would have extended the trip's duration to two or more days.

Upon his arrival in Middletown, Prince found a community that was still in its downward spiral after the collapse of the maritime economy. Only fifteen or so years had passed since the embargo, but already the town had lost nearly all of the shipbuilding industry and associated trades that had been its sustenance for nearly a century and a half.

Although the fact of Prince's return to Middletown is well documented, the precise date remains unknown, and it might be significant in one respect: Because George Starr died in 1820, knowing whether Prince returned to Middletown before or after that event might shed some light on the decision he soon would be making.[1] Certainly, if Prince returned prior to Starr's death, it is easy to envision a less-than-hearty reception for the old slave. Not only Starr, but friends of his as well, would not be disposed to facilitate Prince's transition back into society, and they were in positions of power to control Prince's access to the limited opportunities for assistance then available to the town's poor. Even in the first quarter of the nineteenth century, a social safety net did exist for providing minimal sustenance to those in need. One commentator notes that "[b]y 1800, poor relief was the single largest item in the town budget."[2]

Obviously, Prince was far too old and sick to be able to provide for himself. The extent of social services available in the town, however, suggests that the community would have been able to provide him with basic food and shelter and perhaps even medical care.

But Prince had returned to a community whose population was quite different from the one he had left behind. Few familiar faces, both friendly and otherwise, were to be seen. None of Prince's contemporaries were still around. Many of the buildings may have been familiar, but the people busying themselves in the Main Street shops and along the docks were all strangers to him.

It did not take Prince very long to come to the realization that his dreams of freedom, the driving force that had sustained him through decade after decade of degrading servitude and painful illness, would not be realized in Middletown. For him, freedom delayed had indeed become freedom denied; there was but one home for Prince now, and it was a home surrounded by twelve-foot stone walls.

What thoughts occupied Prince's mind as he made his way back to Newgate? Was he filled with anger and resentment, that dreams held so dear for so long had dissipated beyond hope? Was he perhaps consumed by despair, believing that Middletown could not provide him a home in which to live out his remaining years? Or was he perhaps more concerned with a much more immediate and practical fear—that he would not even be permitted to return to prison?

Phelps reports that Prince had to beg the guards to readmit him into Newgate. They must have been both surprised and amazed to see this near-centenarian back at their door; surprised, not only that Prince was there at all, but that this sickly old man had even been able to tolerate the return trip; and amazed that anyone would want to return willingly to the confines of Newgate, a place so terrible that men had risked their own lives, and taken those of others, in their efforts to escape the confines of these dreaded walls.

Once again, Newgate had become Prince's home, this time as a matter of choice rather than at the direction of a judge's sentence. Perhaps this is the particular aspect of Prince's life that Phelps was alluding to when he wrote that "his life was a tale of misfortunes, and his fate won the commiseration of all who knew him."

· *12* ·

The Counterfeiter

*P*rince had been a prisoner at Newgate for nearly nine years when William Stuart arrived in 1820 to serve his five-year sentence for counterfeiting. As a literate man, and one who had earned his Newgate sentence through criminal cunning rather than criminal violence, Stuart was in a select minority. Most of Newgate's prisoners had never had the benefit of even a rudimentary education; had they been so fortunate, quite possibly many of them would have forsaken their lives of crime in favor of more honorable activity.

Stuart was quite the opposite. Although he came from a family of moderate means, he obtained only four years of formal schooling. It is obvious from his writing, however, that Stuart was subsequently inspired to teach himself the rudiments of a classical education. Despite the benefit of this acquired knowledge, he nonetheless saw fit to apply his intellect to less-than-honorable endeavors. Neither was he motivated by poverty, since at the age of ten he inherited three thousand dollars, a sizeable sum at that time, when his father died. Although Stuart easily could have succeeded at any career he might have chosen, he derived considerably more satisfaction from a swindled dollar than from an honest one.

From a historical perspective, it is fortunate that William Stuart embarked on his life of criminal adventure. Had he not done so, he would have never spent nearly six long years at Newgate, and history would have been deprived of the single most important first-person insight into the misery that was inflicted on this place's occupants on a daily basis. Stuart's autobiography, of course, deals with much more than his years in prison, but his descriptions of those years are rich with information and perspectives that simply cannot be found anywhere else.[1] It is certainly appropriate to accept many of his experiences as typical of what all of the other Newgate inmates, including

Prince, had to endure. For instance, Stuart's impressions of his first hours at Newgate no doubt were consistent with the reactions of every first-time visitor to the prison, and certainly Prince's; it is difficult to imagine that any of them, however deprived their former lives, ever had to contend with this degree of squalor, even in the slums of the country's largest cities.[2]

Even within the limitations of prison life in Newgate, it did not take long for Stuart to find ways to ply his skills to his advantage, beginning with counterfeiting. Working as a cooper, or barrel maker, Stuart found he had access to all the materials he needed. This is how he describes the process:

> I cut out molds in two fragments of pine boards, filled them with finely levigated chalk, and then inserted a 25 cent piece in the chalk and squeezed my mold together; then I took them apart, bought pewter buttons from the prisoners, melted them down, and run the metal in my molds. Thus I coined money and bought my small stores of Beach, the merchant. Before he was aware of the fraud, I had passed ten dollars upon him, all in my prison coined 25 cent pieces.[3]

His mischief was soon discovered, but even in defeat the new prisoner was hardly inclined to be submissive to authority. He defended his activity to Captain Tuller, the prison keeper, with characteristic impudence. "I was sent here for counterfeiting," he told Tuller, "and I shall lose my skill unless I do a little at the business."

Stuart did not hold his fellow inmates in very high esteem. "I was disappointed in the character of my associates," he writes, "for I had been led to expect that they were shrewd, sagacious and cunning. Instead of that character I have never met in my intercourse with mankind, such a number congregated together so void of the natural powers, capabilities, and instincts peculiar to our race."[4]

Disdain for his cohorts did not deter Stuart from gaining their confidence to aid in his own misadventure. Many of these inmates were serving sentences far in excess of Stuart's five-year term. Although escape was a common nighttime topic in the caverns among these men, Stuart's relatively short sentence might suggest that he would have no interest in any escape attempt, particularly in the company of associates he regarded as so intellectually wanting. But that would quickly prove not to be the case.

Stuart's first escape plan was fairly simple. Since the caverns were dug into a hillside, there were a few horizontal shafts that made their way towards the sloping westerly surface. Some were actually open to the outside; these were not suitable escape routes, however, since long ago they had been filled with large timbers bolted together. Other shafts stopped short of the surface, and Stuart deduced that a modicum of additional digging would provide him and his associates with an easy escape route. They dug for ten nights, hiding the dirt by scurrying it to other caverns. Unfortunately, one of the prisoners had divulged the plan to the keeper; when Stuart finally broke through, he was unpleasantly greeted by a guard's discharge of a blank cartridge into the hole.

One stool-pigeon inmate had been released shortly before this incident, and so he avoided the wrath of his former companions. Another potential informant, however, was not so fortunate. Stuart tells of his plan to punish this man by separating him from a good part of his tongue, or, as the would-be surgeon puts it, "operating according to the Russian fashion." The man's last-minute pleas for mercy, coupled with his promise never again to divulge information learned within the caverns, persuaded the good doctor to spare this patient his painful punishment.

From Stuart's activities to this point, an observer could well conclude that this prisoner stood apart from the bulk of the prison population, relying on intellect, wit, and persuasion, rather than crude violence, to achieve his objectives. Soon enough, however, Stuart would show himself to be no better than the worst of his fellow inmates, whom he scornfully dismissed as possessing "no more thinking powers than a calf in a clover field."

The failed escape attempt did not deter Stuart from contriving a different plan, this time involving a general insurrection of the entire prison population. This attempt definitely would not be as stealthy, or as benign, as the last one; instead, Stuart was planning a direct attack on the guards. The plan was refined over a period of several weeks, and Stuart received assurances from all of the inmates that they were solidly behind him.

One of the guards, Corporal Rowe, had apparently taken a dislike to Stuart and "made himself restless and unhappy in his desire to annoy me." It was no coincidence, then, that Rowe was on duty in the nail shop at about 7:30 on the morning of May 23, 1823, when Stuart gave the signal for the attack. He struck Rowe on the head from behind with an iron bar, sending him falling to the floor. Another inmate promptly disarmed Rowe of his sword and one of his pistols.

Believing Rowe to be incapacitated, Stuart quickly made his way up the stairs to overtake Bacon, the other guard on duty in the nail shop. A fight ensued for control of Bacon's pistol, but before that contest could be freely decided, the prison blacksmith struck Stuart above his left eye with a red-hot iron bar.

Despite this wound, Stuart was able to maintain his hold on Bacon, standing behind him and firmly grasping Bacon's crossed arms at the wrists. By this time, Rowe had recovered sufficiently to make his way up the stairs, along with Sergeant Griswold, in pursuit of Stuart. They found him soon enough, but Stuart was using Bacon as a shield, preventing either guard from taking a clean shot at their target. Realizing that he could not maintain this standoff indefinitely, Stuart began edging his way over to Griswold. When he was close enough, he let go of Bacon and tried to grab Griswold's pistol.

Stuart failed in the attempt, succeeding only in deflecting the pistol downward, so that when it discharged, it struck him squarely in the groin and leg. The wound was severe, but not enough to stop the determined instigator. He managed to make his way down to the lower end of the nail shop, where most of the prisoners were gathered, hoping to spur them to action. They must have sensed the futility of the effort, however, since none was willing to rise to the cause. Stuart's autobiography recounts his dismay and disgust with this turn of events. "I could not rally them," he writes. "They were in perfect confusion, a panic had seized them, and in the cooper's shop they were all huddled up like a flock of sheep when attacked by the dogs."[5]

Already twice wounded, Stuart was soon to learn that the extent of his suffering was not over. By now, Captain Tuller had returned to the prison and had made his way to where Stuart was making his unsuccessful plea for help. Tuller's sword struck Stuart squarely on the back, causing him to fall to the floor. Writhing in the dirt of the nail shop floor and bleeding from his three wounds, he finally gave up the fight. Two guards quickly subdued him, and the uprising was over.

The accuracy of a career criminal's autobiography is understandably suspect, since there is a strong likelihood that the author has engaged in exaggeration, and perhaps even prevarication, in an effort to bolster his status in the story or to deflect responsibility for his acts. This suspicion is especially justified in Stuart's case, since deception was the linchpin of his criminal life. Fortunately, Stuart's story is corroborated by none other than Captain Tuller, who saw fit to submit a report of the incident to the *Connecticut Courant*, Hartford's weekly newspaper.[6] The article is brief enough that it can be reprinted in this account, and readers can judge for themselves the accuracy of Stuart's own description.

INSURRECTION AT NEWGATE

At about half past 7 o'clock A.M., the officer who was on duty in the nailor's shop, was requested by a prisoner, in a by part of the shop, to examine his work—He stepped to him for a moment, and was in the act of turning to leave him, when he received a blow with a fire-shovel on the side of the head, which knocked him down, and for a short time rendered him insensible to what was passing.

Having effected this object, which seems to have been a preconcerted signal for further proceedings, three of the desperadoes, one having secured the officer's cutlass, another armed with the fire-shovel, with which the officer was knocked down, and the third with some other weapon, calling on their comrades to follow, and exclaiming "the day is ours" rushed to the walk where the centinel [*sic*] was posted: Two of them immediately seized his gun, while the others made several cuts at him with the cutlass but without much effect; when in a lucky moment the sentinel wrested the cutlass from him and threw it to a distance. The officer of the shop, having by this time recovered a little from the shock, occasioned by the blow he had received, made his way to the walk and discharged his pistol. The ball passed through the arm of one of the prisoners, engaged with the sentinel, and grazed his side.

A sentinel who was in the yard at the time, after giving the alarm in the guard room, proceeded directly to the shop, and was met at the door by an axe thrown at him, by one of the insurgents. He instantly leveled his piece and was upon the point of firing at the fellow, when an axe from another quarter struck him in the breast; the motion of his body occasioned by the blow, directed the muzzle of his gun from its object, and consequently the charge did not take effect. About this time the serjeant [*sic*] of the guard entered the shop, and seeing the struggle on the walk, sprang to the spot and ordered them to desist; not being obeyed, he discharged his pistol at one of them, who received the ball in his groin. At the same instant a corporal and three sentinels arrived, and were in the act of firing, when the insurgents cried for quarters, and gave up the contest.

A shower of hammers, axes, bars of iron, sledges, &c. filled the air at the onset, but fortunately none of the guard were much injured by them.—these missiles appeared to be directed mostly at the blacksmith, who is one of the mechanics employed at the prison, and was at work in the shop. The son of Vulcan acquitted himself manfully, by laying some of them lustily over the head with a red hot bar of iron.

It is evident from every circumstance, and from all the information which has been collected, that a great proportion of the convicts were engaged in the plot, and had the assailants proved successful in the quarter where the attack was made, numbers would have rallied to their assistance from the other shops.

The plan, it is understood was, to kill such of the guard as made any resistance, secure the remainder under the hatches, set fire to the prison, and make off.

The convicts who were most active were, William Steward, Josiah King, Benjamin Beach, Shadrach Burr, Zebulon Stafford, John Bassett, Elisha Fenner, and William Mingo.—Steward and King were wounded, the other six are well secured with heavy irons.

The subscriber was within a few rods of the prison when the disturbance commenced, on his return from Hartford, and arrived at the shop just as the affray had ended.

Much credit is due to the officers and guard particularly to those who were engaged in the contest, for the courage and presence of mind which characterized their conduct during the whole affair which lasted about five minutes.

The officer who was first attacked received a severe though not dangerous wound, and the centinel [*sic*] on the walk was slightly wounded. No other of the guard were injured.

E. TULLER, Prison Keeper

New-Gate Prison, May 27, 1823

Although there are discrepancies in some of the particulars of the two accounts, Stuart appears to have been accurately reporting his central involvement in the affair, as well as the extent of his injuries. Certainly, Prince's advanced age, now approaching 100, suggests that it is highly unlikely he was among the "great proportion of the convicts" involved in the plot, although he may well have become aware of it during the planning stages. More important, however, is the fact that Newgate was Prince's voluntary home, and he would have no reason to participate in Stuart's scheme.

Stuart and Prince may not have shared much in terms of their prior lives, their education, or their mores, but nonetheless they did share one very meaningful common experience: the many miserable and degrading aspects of Newgate prison. Both of them subsisted on the same wretched food, slept in the same bug-infested beds surrounded by the same ubiquitous grime and dirt, and chased away the same rats.

Stuart was obviously an intelligent man, yet he was willing to risk his life in an ill-conceived escape attempt, with less than two years remaining on his sentence. This degree of desperation certainly confirms the extent of suffering that permeated prison life at Newgate. Perhaps inappropriately, Stuart likened the prisoners' situation to that of the oppressed American colonists. "Such I felt to be our condition in this prison," he wrote. "By virtue of law we were here confined, and our oppressor was entrusted with the lives and welfare of men, for which he was held irresponsible."

Stuart was constantly engaged in a battle of wits with Tuller, and the results of that conflict were the more likely direct motivation for the uprising. Stuart had steadfastly refused to reveal to Tuller the identity of the guard who was supplying him with rum from the tavern across the road; an exasperated Tuller ultimately placed Stuart in solitary confinement in the dungeon. It was after Stuart emerged from nearly two weeks in the absolute darkness of that sepulcher that he began to devise his plot.

After the insurrection, Stuart's wounds did not deter him from continuing his battle with Tuller. A number of doctors examined the injured prisoner, and they uniformly concluded that he would not survive. Despite this prognosis and the patient's emaciated condition, Tuller kept Stuart in irons for six months as he languished in bed. Finally convinced that Stuart was indeed on his deathbed, the captain then had an apparent change of heart. He went to Stuart and told him that he could have anything to eat that he desired. Although truthful in that offer, Tuller had an ulterior motive for making it. Having been struck from behind, Rowe could not identify his attacker. Although other prisoners had identified Stuart as the culprit, their credibility was so poor that their testimony would never have been adequate to support charges against him. With his act of kindness, Tuller was trying to extract a deathbed confession from Stuart so that he could finally close the book on the incident.

Stuart would have none of it. Despite his condition, he was hardly ready to concede either his imminent demise or his culpability. He summoned enough strength to curse Tuller for his belated gesture of kindness. Recalling the conversation, Stuart claims to have exclaimed, "You say you will send to Hartford to get me any thing I want. This is nice. Here I have been for more than six months starving and slowly perishing for want of proper food. What have I had? A burnt crust of sour bread soaked in old sour and musty cider, and now that I am going to die, you offer to give me food and take off my irons. No, let them be on, and I will go to hell with them jingling to let them know that I am coming."[7]

Eventually, Stuart did begin to recover, although his wounds continued to drain profusely on a regular basis. Realizing that he was still under threat of indictment, however, Stuart resolved not to let his wounds heal too quickly. When he was alone, he would immerse his foot for an hour in a pail of cold water, "and the result was, I took cold in the sore, and it would be full of pain, then break and run again for many days." Stuart believed that he could convince Tuller that he was still in danger of dying and consequently there was no point in bringing him to trial. Additionally, he wanted Tuller to see that his inability to work make him an unprofitable charge to the state and, more important, to Tuller himself, who consistently deflected the prisoners' labor to his own financial gain. If Tuller saw Stuart as more of a burden than a benefit, he might well be inclined to discharge him from prison.

The months continued to pass, with Stuart's condition showing little improvement. Eventually, the one-year statute of limitations came and went, and consequently Stuart was never charged for his involvement in the failed insurrection. Even after he was immune from prosecution, however, he refused to acknowledge culpability for the attack on Rowe.

As Stuart was nearing the end of his five-year sentence, his condition had improved to the degree that he was able to get around on crutches and work at basket weaving. Of course, reaching the end of his sentence in no way meant that Stuart would then be released; as was the case for all prisoners, there was then the matter of expenses. Not only did a prisoner have to endure the hardship of his incarceration, but he was also required to pay for the dubious privilege by working it off in prison at the rate of five dollars per month.

In Stuart's case, his expenses amounted to $375. At the stated rate, it would take him over six years to work off his debt, thus more than doubling his original sentence. The keeper had the prerogative, however, of waiving part or all of this obligation, and Stuart was determined to have Tuller release him. Already four months beyond his sentence, Stuart persisted in feigning continued injury with his secret cold-water treatments. "At other times," he writes, "when walking over the yard, if Tuller or the officers of the guard were in sight, I would stub my toes and tumble upon the ground, and groan as if I had hurt me in a shocking manner."[8]

After much persistence, Stuart finally convinced Tuller to let him go for a payment of $20. Hobbling across the prison yard on crutches, Stuart made his way to the nail shop and managed to borrow that sum from some of the inmates, promising to repay them after his release. Returning to Tuller, Stuart gave him the money, expecting to gain his freedom then and there. Tuller, of course, had other plans.

"Stuart, you shall not go now," he told his prisoner. "You contrived with Smith to cheat me."

"Well, give me back the money," Stuart replied.

"No, I will not, I will keep the money and you too."

"Ah, Captain, this is hard and cruel, and I have been punished enough to satisfy any reasonable man. Have pity on me, and my poor family."[9]

This last plea apparently had its intended effect on Tuller, who finally agreed to release Stuart if he paid two dollars more. Stuart borrowed the additional money, and Tuller, this time true to his word, issued the discharge. "The gate was opened," Stuart writes, "and I cursed the place and left it."

Relief was hardly the sole emotion that filled Stuart's heart and mind at this moment. Apparently, he also felt great sense of satisfaction, as can be discerned from the next sentence of his account: "I threw away my crutches and went to Buck's tavern and got some rum, and lounged about all day."

It did not take long for Tuller to learn that he had been had. The next day, the angry captain marched across the road to the tavern to confront his former charge. Brandishing his sword, Tuller tried to chase Stuart from the tavern, and the general environs of the prison as well. "Had I known that you could move about so easily," Tuller exclaimed, "I would have kept you here as long as grass grows and water runs."

Knowing that Tuller was completely powerless over him, Stuart took such delight at the degree to which his continued presence upset the captain that he stayed around for three more weeks before making his way home. When he did commence his journey, however, it was with a new resolution that his life of crime was over. Additionally, he left Newgate with strong views about the prison's deficiencies and the effect that horrendous place had on everyone who had the misfortune of serving time behind its stone walls.

"Newgate was a high school for rogues," Stuart would later write, "and few prisoners ever left it as tyros in the science of iniquity. Crowded in small apartments, away from the surveillance of its officers, every crime was concocted with all the nice manipulations of a chemical professor, and if any man left the place unimproved in the arts of deviltry, it was owing to the obtuseness of his mental powers."[10]

Even though Stuart most likely was on the teaching side of that equation, for the remainder of his years he remained resolute in his decision to avoid a life of crime. Still a young man of thirty-seven at the time of his release in 1826, he turned his back on his prior professions of counterfeiting and horse thievery, instead devoting himself to the quiet life of a family man and farmer.

It was not just the fear of returning to prison, however, that kept him on the road of respectability. "I abandoned crime as profitless," he later revealed, "as the sure precursor of hopeless ruin. It lost all its charms, and entailed on me miseries incalculable."[11]

Neither was Stuart ever apologetic for initiating the failed uprising. "This encounter I did not dignify with the name of crime," he wrote. Quite to the contrary, he viewed those five minutes as a pivotal point in the history of Newgate prison. "An important consequence to the welfare of prisoners flowed from it," he continued. "It opened the eyes of legislators to see the glaring evils consequent upon prison life and morals, and the causes of perpetuity in crime."[12]

It is tempting to discount Stuart's self-congratulatory commentary as nothing more than an attempt to render justifiable and even meritorious an event that easily could have had disastrous results. The reality, however, is that Stuart was quite accurate in his descriptions of Newgate's failures, and the legislature would soon be taking action to remedy the state's notorious reputation for continuing to maintain this unenlightened facility.

The reformed ex-convict flattered himself, however, in asserting that his five minutes of glory were the impetus for what was to come. Ironically, this call for change would not come from a prisoner, either former or present, nor from the judiciary. Instead, Connecticut's prison system was about to be shaken by a man armed with nothing more than a bible.

· *13* ·

The Bible Peddler

*L*ouis Dwight harbored no illusions about what lay beyond the stone walls coming into view. Although he was amply familiar with Newgate's notoriety, his experiences over the last year made him believe himself fully prepared for what he was about to see.

Dwight's journey was as unique as the man who had undertaken it. Having set out from Boston in late October 1824, he was intent on riding horseback to visit every state prison and several county and local jails scattered throughout the country. Ostensibly, Dwight's primary mission involved delivering miniature bibles to the prisoners, but there was a much more personal element behind this journey that would see him riding alone over thousands of miles of sometimes rugged terrain and through the worst weather conditions that each season had to offer.

But such conditions were precisely what he wanted, and even believed he needed. The arduous nature of his trip, he was convinced, offered him a necessary opportunity to challenge himself physically and to rebuild the sickly body that was cheating him from fulfilling his goals in life. And these were not merely his own objectives; they were goals he knew, with all his soul, that God Himself had ordained him to accomplish.[1]

From his earliest years, Louis Dwight had exhibited a piety and a devotion to his Christian faith that was not merely exemplary—it was all-consuming. The last of three sons, Louis was born in 1793 to a family that could trace its Massachusetts lineage back to 1635. He was raised in Stockbridge, nestled in the Bershire mountains of the westernmost part of the state. His father, Henry, was the county clerk, and his mother, Abigail, was of the Hartford Wells family.

Abigail was left a widow in 1804, and within the year young Louis was sent to Bethlehem, Connecticut, a small town in the Litchfield hills, to live with and study under the Reverend Dr. Backus. Upon his return home some months later, both Louis and his mother were delighted to come to the realization that this young man was indeed destined for a life doing God's work. In the following years, Louis never varied from that ambition, and in due course he found himself at Yale, eagerly preparing for his career at the pulpit.

However much Louis may have believed himself destined for this life, even destiny has a way of succumbing to unforeseen events. For Louis, such an event occurred in 1813 in a chemistry lab at Yale; Louis accidentally inhaled an excessive amount of "exhilarating gas," now commonly referred to as "laughing gas." The effect on Louis was both severe and permanent. Not only was his voice forever ruined, but his entire constitution was also rendered weak and chronically ill.[2]

More devastating to Louis than his deteriorated state of health, however, was the realization that his dream of preaching was never to become a reality. Forced to abandon his studies, Louis returned home both physically emaciated and emotionally demoralized. Believing that a milder climate might hasten at least his physical recovery, Dwight set out on a southern tour and did indeed return generally much improved, although his voice still remained impaired by the accident.

The record is silent as to Dwight's activities over the next several years; he probably remained in Stockbridge, assisting his mother in maintaining the household. In about 1818, however, Louis decided to make another attempt at seminary studies, and he entered the theological seminary at Andover, Massachusetts, just north of Boston. Although he graduated and was ordained in 1822, Dwight must have come again to realize that his ruined voice would forever place severe limitations on his access to the pulpit. In what would prove to be a pivotal decision in his life, Dwight elected not to seek a pastoral appointment and instead accepted a position in the fledgling American Tract Society.[3]

William Jenks, Dwight's biographer, does not provide any information regarding Dwight's physical characteristics, but he does give the reader a comprehensive description of his subject's complex personality and temperament:

> Affectionate and kind, he was yet resolute and firm. Of a pleasing address, he yet would sacrifice no conspicuous convention. Faithful to his engagements, what he did he did with vigor and thoroughness. What he felt he was ever ready to declare, in a proper time and place, with frankness. His feelings were vivid and strong, and his friendships tender but permanent. His piety and attachment to the doctrine which distinguished the "Puritans," no one who knew him could doubt. The ardor of his zeal often, indeed, carried him beyond his physical strength, as, on many occasions, his family and friends perceived, and were not backward in expressing their fears.[4]

Louis did not work long at the Tract Society; within the year, he was lured away by a competing group, the American Education Society, which was primarily involved in missionary work and in subsidizing the training of preachers in various colleges around the nation. He apparently found this work satisfying enough to prompt him to settle in Boston, where he married in 1824. His new bride's father happened to be the publisher of a Boston religious newspaper, the *Boston Recorder*, and he immediately offered Louis a position as an editor.

The job proved to be quite demanding, and Louis' health began to deteriorate rapidly, to the point that there was concern about his likely survival.[5] Since Louis had had success with horseback riding, he bid his worried wife and friends farewell and headed off to Stockbridge "and the attentions of a devoted mother," a trip of about 150 miles.

The same friends who had thought him to be a "doomed man," as Jenks writes, must have been amazed to see Louis return, only slightly more than a month later, completely revitalized and in appreciably good health. But Louis realized that a return to the sedentary life of an editor would be suicidal, so he now was confronted with the dilemma of how to direct his newly recovered energies.

Dwight saw the challenge as one of combining his need for physical activity with his still strong desire to participate in a meaningful religious ministry. He had already visited the Southern states shortly after the Yale incident, and the results had been very beneficial to his health. Why not repeat that trip, but add to it a work dimension? But what should that be?

Jenks does not give credit for the idea, but eventually it was decided that Louis Dwight would embark on a horseback trip of considerable duration and distance, visiting in the process all of the state prisons and a number of county jails to distribute bibles to the prisoners.

On October 28, 1824, Louis set out from Boston, his horse laden with saddlebags full of miniature bibles provided him by the American Bible Society. Revitalized by both his physical activity and his newly discovered sense of purpose, he wrote home that he was convinced that he had finally found "*the work* which my Lord would have me perform."

If Dwight was correct in concluding that he had finally found his life's work in ministering to prisoners, he was quite mistaken in believing that his activities would be limited to addressing their spiritual needs. Dwight had yet to set foot in a prison cell, to speak with a prisoner, or, frequently even worse, to deal with prison administration. In many of the institutions Dwight was to visit, neither cleanliness nor godliness was present to any discernible degree; Louis would soon come to realize that his real calling was to minister, not to the souls of these miscreants, but rather to the foul-smelling and abused bodies in which those souls subsisted.

This realization did not visit itself upon Louis spontaneously as an instance of divine revelation. His letters clearly demonstrate that Dwight saw his early prison visits as mainly pastoral in nature. In New Haven, for instance, he reports that he spent an hour in conversation and prayer with a woman under sentence of death.[6]

It did not take long, however, for Dwight to realize the urgency of a more immediate, if not higher, calling than preaching. His letter regarding his visit to Baltimore Penitentiary gives the first inkling of what Louis was beginning to see as his real vocation: to let the world know what evils were occurring behind America's prison walls and to do what he could to alleviate the deplorable conditions he was witnessing.

Such terrible conditions existed, Dwight believed, primarily because they remained largely unknown to the general population. Now, more than ever, he realized the necessity of improving his health so that he could carry on this task. "You will probably know, at some future day," he wrote about Baltimore, "if my health is spared, what I this day witnessed. There is but one sufficient excuse for Christians, in suffering such evils to exist in prisons, in this country, as do exist; and that is, that they are not acquainted with the real state of things. In one or two years, I hope it will be more apparent than it is now, that I am not spending my strength for naught."

Although Jenks writes generally about the deplorable conditions of the prisons Dwight visited throughout the country, he describes only one specific incident. Three women and four children were being kept in a single cell in a District of Columbia jail. The children, ranging in age from four to twelve years, were orphans and were being kept in jail to save them from being sold as slaves, since they were children of a black woman and a white man. The deceased father's will had granted his children their freedom, but the will's executor was intent on selling them as slaves in order to settle debts of the estate. Although the marshal was saving the children from bondage by placing them in this environment, it appears he did nothing to alleviate the inherently difficult conditions they had to endure in the jail cell. There was not a single bed, not even a blanket, to be had for the cell's seven occupants, and the youngest child, who was ill, had nowhere to lie but upon the stone floor.

Dwight was both indignant about this situation and frustrated over his complete inability to do anything about it. His frustration, however, served to fuel Dwight's resolve to make the public aware of the atrocious conditions existing behind America's prison walls. American patriarchs may well have eagerly imported the ideas of Cesare Beccaria from Europe after the revolution, but four decades later few if any modern notions of penology had been implemented.[7] It is quite possible that at this point Louis Dwight was not even aware of Beccaria or his work, but they were of one mind regarding the need for prison reform. Dwight ends his letter with a statement that leaves no doubt about his having found the cause he had been searching out for so many years:

> I am constrained to go on my way with an assurance, when I shall bring before the Church of Christ a statement of what my eyes have seen, there will be a united and powerful effort in the United States to alleviate the miseries of prisons. This expectation is my support.

Eventually, Louis Dwight would come to recognize that he would need more than just ecclesiastical support to accomplish his goals, but certainly faith was a strong influence in fueling his early enthusiasm. So devoted was Dwight to his newly acquired cause that he chose to continue his tour of the Southern states rather than return home when he received word in Richmond that his daughter had been born.

In May 1825, Louis returned to Boston, both physically and psychologically regenerated, despite the hardships he had endured and the misery he had seen. His journey had taken him over three thousand miles, and he had visited most of the state prisons in the country, as well as numerous county and local jails. But his return did not mark the end of his work; rather, it merely afforded Dwight an opportunity to gather his thoughts and to act upon an idea that had been developing in his mind throughout his trek. Within a month, Louis had set up meetings with a number of prominent politicians, businessmen, and clergymen, all of whom had previously been interested in either a reform of the penal code in general or in the plight of prisoners at the local jail. Despite his broken voice, Dwight's eloquence in describing the conditions he witnessed rang loudly with this receptive group, and on June 30, 1825, the Boston Prison Discipline Society was founded.

Although Louis's journey had provided the newly formed Society with a great deal of information from which to begin the process of focusing and directing its future efforts, there remained one conspicuous hole in its data: Newgate Prison. Since there was no convenient way for Dwight to reach the Southern states other than to travel the Post Road through Connecticut, and since he did so not once, but twice, it is difficult to conclude that Dwight's failure to visit Connecticut's state prison was inadvertent. To turn the phrase, the strong suggestion is that Dwight was saving the worst for last.

That visit took place in early November. Dwight may well have believed himself sufficiently hardened by his earlier experiences to be fully prepared for what awaited him beyond Newgate's twelve-foot stone walls. Returning to Hartford after a visit of several days at the prison, however, Dwight wrote back to his fledgling Society:

I returned, last evening, from Newgate. After spending nearly a week in its filth, investigating subjects more loathsome than its polluted air, I found myself at night entirely prostrate, desiring only to be at rest. This morning I was refreshed, but it has required the whole day to restore me to my wonted strength. Our minds have been so entirely engrossed, night and day, during my absence from Hartford, that I required two or three days and nights for repose. I do not know that I was ever so completely exhausted. I feel the need of your prayers that I may be supported, guided and blessed in this arduous work. I need a double portion of wisdom and grace. There are many miseries to be relieved; many dark places, which are full of cruelty, to be exposed; many minds to be made acquainted with the facts, before the most miserable portion of the human family will be relieved.

Counted among the "subjects more loathsome than its polluted air," of course, was Prince Mortimer. At the time of Dwight's visit, Prince was about 101, and the sight he presented, as well as the conditions under which he was subsisting, must have played no small part in forming Dwight's opinion of Newgate prison. But Prince was by no means the only "loathsome" subject to capture Dwight's interest. William Stuart, who would have eagerly provided Dwight with reams of information about the miseries of the prison, had been released only a few months before Dwight's arrival. But there was certainly a respectable assemblage of characters who would easily qualify under Dwight's definition.[8]

Dwight's Christian orientation probably would have prompted him to provide some degree of comfort to these wretched men even if he had encountered them in open society. As wretched as they were before their imprisonment, however, their confinement in Newgate only served to make them even more pathetic, or "loathsome."[9]

Once Dwight's Prison Discipline Society became fully operational, it began publishing annual reports, beginning in 1826, describing in great detail the conditions in all of the state and county prisons and what was occurring in each jurisdiction to improve those conditions. The Second Report, for 1827, gives a succinct but telling description of the horrors of Newgate:

> In the Old Prison in Connecticut, if the prisoners themselves had been permitted to build a Prison, where they could have the greatest facilities for concealment, with the least possibility of detection; where they could serve their master with none to molest them, it is difficult to conceive how the end could have been more effectually attained. In a Prison constructed as that is, it must require nearly as many keepers as prisoners to prevent communication between the latter. This remark is applicable to the shops, and other buildings, scattered throughout the yard. In the dungeons, seventy feet under ground, formerly used as night rooms, some of the prisoners

volunteered to return to them, as places of confinement at night, and assigned as the reason, that they could there curse, and swear, and fight, and do other unutterable abominations, without having it known to anyone. There probably has never been on earth a stronger emblem of the pit than the sleeping rooms of that Prison, so filthy, so crowded, so inclined to evil, so unrestrained.[10]

Louis Dwight was not alone in his condemnation of the abominable conditions at Newgate; the prison's notoriety was national in scope and was an ever-present embarrassment to the state. Calls for reform were increasing, and the state legislature had finally begun to pay attention. In May 1825, several months before Dwight's visit, the legislature had appointed a committee to investigate the conditions at the prison and make recommendations for either improving Newgate or removing it somewhere else.

That committee consisted of three men, John Russ, Martin Welles, and John Peters. Welles, a prominent attorney in the Hartford area, quickly became the committee's spokesman and authored all of its reports.[11] The report submitted in 1826 is even more damning of Newgate's conditions than was Dwight. Where Dwight was content to simply make reference to "unutterable abominations" committed in the caverns, Welles minced no words in describing what was being alluded to:

[t]he crime of sodomy has been perpetrated in numerous instances with entire shamelessness and notoriety. If that unnatural crime is ever perpetrated, we should look for its commission among men shut up from all the enjoyments of society; among hoary heady convicts, condemned to long imprisonment, and whose passions and principles have been corrupted and degraded to the lowest point of debasement, and who are at night in numbers of from four to thirty-two persons locked together in cells which are not subjected to official inspection.[12]

The crimes to which Welles was making reference were, for the most part, crimes in the truest sense of the word. The 1825 prisoner list confirms that a substantial percentage of Newgate's inmates arrived there while in their teens, some as young as 13.[13] There can be little doubt that a substantial number of instances of "unutterable abominations" were involuntary, committed against boys forced to submit to the will and strength of more seasoned veterans of inmate life.

As much as Dwight was upset about the atrocious conditions under which the Newgate inmates had to work, eat, and sleep, he was equally enraged, as a man of the cloth, at the freedom these inmates enjoyed, to be able to engage in such criminal activity with impunity. The dark recesses of the caverns, and the nooks and crannies of the hodge-podge collection of buildings, offered numerous opportunities for "abominations," both voluntary and otherwise. Dwight's call for reform were doubtless motivated as much by a desire to put an end to "unutterable abominations" as well as to do away with abominable living conditions.

Welles's criticisms went beyond those expressed by Dwight, however, in denouncing the fact that Newgate was serving as a school for criminals. Seasoned veterans passed on to the newcomers not only their trade secrets but also their contempt for the society that had placed them behind the walls of Newgate. "No efforts are spared," Welles wrote, "to render the young convict unprincipled and profligate; he is taught to believe that society has cast him off, and shut him out from all the enjoyments of life, and this wrongfully—that this is accomplished by the wealthy and powerful, who have always waged war against the rights of the poor; and he is made to feel that society, having injured him, he has a natural right to revenge upon it."

This constant freedom of interaction between the prisoners, then, quickly was seen by the legislature as the root of all of the problems inherent in Connecticut's state prison. As Welles put it, the buildings at Newgate were "every thing that they should not be, and nothing that they should be." Far from providing an opportunity for rehabilitation, Newgate served only to turn wayward boys bad, and bad men worse, so that they returned to society more bitter than ever and more desirous of continuing their lives of crime.[14]

One of the charges given Welles's committee was to consider adding a building to the Newgate facility, perhaps to provide cells for solitary confinement for recalcitrant inmates. The committee quickly came to realize that this was not a viable solution; the buildings at Newgate were simply unfit for ensuring prison discipline and effective supervision.[15]

Not everyone shared this opinion on the desirability of closing Newgate. Welles acknowledged the initial appeal of the argument in favor of keeping the facility open: "It is this, 'That New Gate as a Prison, has, both abroad and at home, such a dreadful notoriety among criminals; such a wide spread reputation as a place of severe and terrible punishment, that it furnishes over every other prison a strong and peculiar inducement to abstain from crime.'"

The facts, however, did not support this argument. Out of the 117 prisoners in Newgate in 1825, 26 were repeat offenders. Comparable figures for the state prison in Massachusetts showed recidivism at only half that rate. Further, the ratio of convicts to the general population was much higher in Connecticut than in other states. New Hampshire, with a population of 244,000, had only 70 inmates in its prison, while Connecticut, with its population of 275,000, harbored 117. Such statistics, Welles argued, confirmed as a myth the notion that Newgate's horrors operated as a meaningful deterrent to crime in Connecticut.

Of course, finances were a ubiquitous aspect of any change in Newgate's structure, or any replacement of the facility, and Welles was highly critical of the fact that Newgate was a constant drain on the state's financial resources. The various trades to which the prisoners were put, such as nail making, blacksmithing, and coopering, never generated nearly enough income to cover expenses.[16] With no small degree of envy, Welles surveyed the activities of other state prisons in New Hampshire, Massachusetts, and New York. In each of these states, the prison was located near a quarry, and the state was able to derive substantial income from the labor of the convicts in cutting and hammering stone.

Welles's committee was making its investigation at the same time that Louis Dwight was forming the Prison Discipline Society and visiting Newgate. It could hardly be expected that these two inquiries would remain independent for very long. At some point, the men began collaborating and sharing both information and ideas. Welles must have seen Dwight as a tremendous source of information as to prison conditions and administrative techniques in other states; Dwight, for his part, would have quickly seen in Welles, and his committee, an opportunity for his fledgling Society to have a direct influence on the construction of a new prison.

There was nothing surreptitious in the way that Dwight went about trying to influence Welles, and Welles in turn made no secret of the extent of his reliance on Dwight's assistance. His report gives express recognition to "the experience and suggestions of Mr. Louis Dwight, of Boston, who has for the last year devoted himself to the subject of prisons and their condition." Dwight's assistance, however, was not limited to describing the conditions that then existed in Newgate and elsewhere; more important, Dwight sought to influence how Connecticut would resolve its prison problem. He did so by furnishing Welles with copies of "the plans and systems of various prisons" and by educating Welles on what he perceived as the most appropriate plan for constructing a new prison.

Although the American prison reform movement was still in its infancy at this time, nonetheless there were two well-established competing schools of thought regarding which path prison reform should follow. Known as the Auburn and the Pennsylvania systems, both plans certainly agreed on what evils should be addressed, but their advocates had sharply diverging views on how to resolve the problems of America's prisons. The particulars of these plans will be discussed in detail in the next chapter, but for now it is sufficient to know that Louis Dwight was a passionate advocate of the Auburn plan. Welles's report leaves no doubt but that Dwight heavily influenced Welles's committee to come out in favor of the Auburn plan, and to adopt that plan in any new construction.

No small part of that influence can be traced back to a letter Dwight wrote to Welles, to which he attached an engraving of Auburn prison in New York, along with a narrative description of its features.[17] The letter goes on to report Dwight's encouragement with the fact that the Massachusetts legislature was seriously considering building a new prison in Charlestown under the Auburn plan, and it ends with Dwight's offer to render "any service to you in regard to New Gate." The Welles report, written some four months later, attests to the fact that Welles did indeed avail himself of that offer.

A later letter of Dwight's to the Welles committee confirms the extent of the persuasive powers of the secretary of the Boston Prison Discipline Society; apparently, Dwight was able to procure a contribution of fifty dollars from the Connecticut legislature in support of the Society's work.[18] Dwight goes on to praise the legislature for its vote to abandon Newgate, which he states to be "on the whole the worst prison, except one, which I have found in traveling about four thousand miles."

Dwight did not limit his advocacy to Welles and his committee. He was the consummate lobbyist, tirelessly espousing his views to anyone who would listen, including the governor. Only a couple of months after his visit to Newgate, Dwight had caught the ear of Governor Oliver Wolcott and engaged in correspondence with him about prison reform in general and the conditions at Newgate in particular. In one such letter, written at a time when Dwight was actively working with Welles, Dwight relates to the governor in considerable detail the progress of prison reform legislation in Massachusetts, particularly in connection with anticipated construction costs for the new prison proposed for Charlestown.[19]

The influence of Louis Dwight in securing the passage of legislation that would forever close the doors of Newgate prison cannot be underestimated. His loud and constant accusations of the abuses being committed within those walls, his advocacy of a reform system that promised to rid Connecticut forever of such abuses, his securing allies within both the legislature and the executive branch—on all of these fronts, Dwight was both a guiding light and a moving force.

Dwight's visits, as well as those of Martin Welles and his committee, certainly had made Prince and the other Newgate inmates aware that things were about to happen. Certain of the more hardened members of the prison population were probably quite content with the situation as it was, with all of the opportunities for mischief, and worse, that Newgate's haphazard assemblage of structures and caverns offered them. The majority, however, most likely welcomed the possibility that they would soon be redeemed from this hellhole that the state called a prison. It is doubtful that they had any idea of what was being proposed to replace Newgate, but they certainly could not believe that anything else could possibly be worse.

Little did these men know how much of an impact this diminutive man with the hoarse voice would have on their lives. And little did they know, nor did anyone else at that time know, that their torment was far from over; it was simply about to assume a different form.

· *14* ·

Three and a Half Feet

$\mathscr{D}$wight's ardent lobbying for a new prison to replace Newgate, coupled with the Welles committee's conclusions that the old prison could no longer be justified on either moral or economic grounds, easily carried the day. On May 3, 1826, the Connecticut General Assembly adopted a resolution appointing Martin Welles and his two committeemen as prison commissioners and directing them "to purchase, in behalf of this State, the lot of land situated in Wethersfield, offered to the State by the heirs of Justus Riley, late of said town, on the terms and at the price proposed by the proprietors, together with any land near to, or adjoining the same, not exceeding in value the sum of Five Hundred Dollars, for the site of New Gate prison."[1]

The resolution was also specific as to how the prison was to be built. The commissioners were directed "to cause to be erected on said lot suitable buildings for a State Prison, upon the principles of the plan submitted to this Legislature." Those plans, of course, were the very ones that Louis Dwight had so eagerly presented to Welles and the governor only a few months earlier. They were plans of Auburn prison, a recently completed facility in New York.

The Auburn plan, as it would soon come to be called, was not merely a design for a physical structure. The plan went far beyond merely prescribing the construction particulars of the building; it also included elements relating to prison administration and finance. Its most compelling feature was the Auburn plan's strict measures for enforcing prison discipline. Little did Prince and his fellow inmates realize that on May 3, 1826, a force had been set in motion that would fundamentally alter every facet of their lives as prisoners: how they ate, how they slept, how they worked, and even how they could think.

Before examining the particulars of the Auburn plan and how it was implemented in the new state prison (which ultimately was named Wethersfield State Prison, not New Gate), it is worthwhile to discuss some of the characteristics of the site chosen for this new facility. Welles's committee had expended considerable time and effort studying possible alternative sites for the new prison. Having seen the success of other states in employing prisoners as marble quarry workers, the committee's first thought was that a similar opportunity might be available somewhere in Connecticut. Unfortunately, good marble simply did not exist in the state; the only alternative worthy of consideration was a brownstone quarry, in east Middletown. Although this stone was highly desirable for a variety of uses, its soft texture required care and skill in handling, and these were not qualities to be expected from a prison work force.

Other locations were also considered around the state, but they were not centrally located or easily accessed for transporting raw materials or finished goods. Ultimately, the committee settled on a site along the Connecticut River in Wethersfield. This community is situated immediately south of Hartford, easily accessible by boat. Additionally, the proposed site was located on a cove with a deep channel and whose banks offered an ample supply of fine sand and clay from which bricks could be manufactured.[2]

An added advantage to brick making, Welles was quick to point out, was the fact that no special skills were required for many of the tasks, and thus all of the prisoners could be made productive participants in the industry:

> We have also reason to believe from these statements that this is a business in some part of the details of which, all may be employed, as well those who have no faculty to learn, as the old, the imbecile, and the intractable—and that daily tasks may be set and ascertained. It is a fact, that at our prison there are about thirty prisoners who are called *loose hands*, who have no capacity to learn, and who are unqualified for any labor now performed at the prison. These men are placed at no regular employment, and are a heavy burthen on the institution. Men of this class, it has been supposed, might with a few others of better faculties, be beneficially placed at the business of brick making.

Clearly, the economic aspects of a new prison were of paramount concern to Welles; more than half of his twenty-five-page report is devoted to prison finances, both actual at Newgate and anticipated at Wethersfield, while only three pages discuss the moral and social reasons for remedying the shameful conditions at Newgate.

The plans for Wethersfield were based on a new prison system advocated by Louis Dwight and founded on a strict disciplinary regimen for prisoners. Although first implemented in New York, this new system could trace its origins to Philadelphia and the time of the Revolution.[3] In 1786, Pennsylvania had been the first state to adopt significant penal law reform, eliminating the death penalty for all crimes except murder.[4] But this was only the tip of the reform iceberg. Except for murder, all other crimes for which the death penalty had been imposed would now be punished by "continuous hard labor, publicly and disgracefully imposed."

The expected deterrent effect of this new rule never materialized; in fact, it backfired. The increased public awareness of the misery imposed upon prisoners at Philadelphia's Walnut Street Jail resulted in heightened demands that the deplorable conditions of the jail be remedied.

It was from these circumstances that the Philadelphia Society for Alleviating the Miseries of Public Prisons was born in May 1787. In addition to the goal expressly set out in its name, the Philadelphia Society also advocated the adoption in Pennsylvania of a new system of prison discipline, based on the idea of solitary confinement. This was not to be merely a temporary method of punishment for recalcitrant prisoners, such as William Stuart experienced at Newgate;[5] what was being proposed was quite different in character and was to be undertaken for quite a different reason.

Pennsylvania was not alone in recognizing that not only was congregate housing at the root of most of the problems existing in its jails, but it also perpetuated recidivism, as young inmates were hardened and corrupted by close-quarter association with their elders. Pennsylvania was alone, however, in resolving to address the issue at this early time. Furthermore, its problems were aggravated by the fact that the change in the state's penal laws, doing away with corporal punishment in favor of incarceration, resulted in a significant increase in the number of convicts. In 1790, the state took the first step toward resolving this situation by constructing a number of solitary cells at the Walnut Street Jail, which was then also converted into a state prison. The intent, according to the enabling act of 1790, was to isolate the "more hardened and atrocious offenders." Unfortunately, there quickly proved to be more qualifying prisoners than there were cells to accommodate them; in short order, these cells had to be converted into congregate units, and the entire experiment quickly deteriorated into a dismal failure.

Although the failure of the Walnut Street facility was recognized within a few years of construction of the new cells, another quarter century would pass before Pennsylvania would make a second attempt at resolution. In 1818, the Pennsylvania legislature passed enabling legislation directing the construction of two new prisons, the Western and Eastern state penitentiaries. Although there was a consensus that these prisons would be built on the solitary confinement plan, the Philadelphia Society became so entangled in bickering over details that the final authorization did not occur, and the first stones were not laid, until 1829.

A large part of the problem lay in the fact that the prisons would be so costly to build. The structure built at Cherry Hill, ultimately to be known as Eastern State Penitentiary of Pennsylvania, was so massive that its footprint covered nearly twelve acres and it took six years to complete. Prisoners began to be accepted, however, after the first section was finished in late 1829. Blake McKelvey gives the best description of the facility:

> Branching out from a central rotunda, like the spokes of a huge wheel, the seven massive stone corridors of the prison provided easy access to the rows of cells that flanked them. Each of the four hundred large solitary cells, 8 by 15 and 12 feet high in the center of their vaulted roofs, could be entered only from these corridors, but each was provided with an individual exercise yard, likewise securely walled about to prevent any communication between the convicts.[6]

Several debates had delayed construction. There was a contentious argument over the selection of an architect, as well as debate over what types of work the inmates would do in their cells. The enabling legislation directed that the prisoners be placed in solitary confinement at hard labor. But what kind of hard labor could they undertake within the confines of their individual cells? The answer to this question was heavily influenced by a concern over the types of tools that might be used and whether they could be diverted for criminal purposes. Ultimately, the decision was made that the inmates' activities would be limited to such things as spinning, weaving, dying, and shoemaking.[7]

Even though Pennsylvania was dragging its heels throughout the 1820s in implementing its solitary confinement system, the plan was well known and was being carefully studied in other states, particularly New York. This northern neighbor had been dabbling in its own series of experiments with solitary confinement. The original Auburn prison, erected in 1816–1817, had been built on a plan of congregate housing that could accommodate as many as a dozen prisoners in a single cell. An additional wing constructed in 1821, however, contained solitary cells in which the most difficult prisoners were to be placed. Although fully aware of the design elements of Pennsylvania's system, New York chose not to follow it when these new cells were erected. Instead, this "north wing" of Auburn prison was built on a new plan, never before implemented in any prison in the world. This cellblock, a precursor to the "Auburn plan," as it would come to be known, made no provision for exercise yards, nor did the cells include enough room for in-cell manual labor. The cellblock constituting this north wing was essentially a building sitting within a building, so that the cells themselves had no windows nor views to the outside. The prisoners would be afforded no work opportunities, either in their cells or anywhere else.

The north wing of Auburn was, very consciously and explicitly, an experiment in human behavior. The eighty unlucky prisoners chosen for this experiment were divided into two groups. The members of the first group were simply placed in these very small solitary cells and left there, with absolutely nothing to do. Their only other human contact came when the guards brought them their meals. The second group fared only slightly better: they were placed in solitary cells three days per week and kept in the congregate areas the rest of the time. A third study group, not part of the eighty and consisting of younger prisoners, worked in the prison shops six days per week.

After two years, the results of these varying forms of incarceration were evaluated. Not surprisingly, those convicts kept in solitary confinement were considerably more ill than the other two groups, and a number of them had become insane. This was certainly not the expected or desired outcome; New York was simply trying to come up with a plan for imposing greater discipline on difficult prisoners, not to punish them by rendering them insane or severely and chronically ill.

New York's first experiment with solitary confinement was such a dismal failure that the legislature outlawed the practice in the state's prisons, and the governor pardoned those convicts who had participated in the experiment. But the prison administration at Auburn was not to be denied. Since neither extreme of incarceration—congregate housing or solitary confinement—was successful, was there perhaps a middle ground that could get the job done?

That middle ground turned out to be the Auburn plan. It was the system that, in short order, Louis Dwight would come to know and love, and the virtues of which he enthusiastically broadcast to other states, particularly Connecticut and Massachusetts. The plan involved placing the prisoners in solitary confinement at night, but having them work in a congregate area during the day. In this way, the daily human contact offered by the work environment would avert the instances of insanity and illness frequently seen in prisoners subjected to unbroken solitary confinement.

The plan, although not as psychologically demanding as its Pennsylvania rival, was no picnic. Superimposed upon the entire scheme was an extremely demanding disciplinary structure: first and foremost, the inmates were required to observe constant silence, both at work and in their cells. They were not permitted to make eye contact, either with their superiors or between themselves. The marches back and forth from the cells to the work area were made in lock step; each prisoner would march with his right arm extended and his hand resting on the shoulder of the man in front of him. This was hardly a march in the military tradition, with soldiers holding their heads high, proudly showing their might and their willingness to use it in defense of their country. No, the lockstep march of Auburn's prisoners was similar in name only; their gait was directed to be slow, even halting, their heads down and their eyes downcast. The entire process was intentionally designed to fill the prisoners with a sense of shame, both for their present status and for the crimes they had committed.

None of this, of course, was intended merely to be punishment for its own sake. Each aspect of the Auburn system had its own specific goal: the labor, to enable the convicts to defray the cost of their incarceration, and the solitary confinement, to eliminate corruption of younger prisoners and to provide time for quiet contemplation of the dubious fruits to be harvested from a life of crime.

As the Auburn system's chief apostle, Louis Dwight brought to his job a devotion that possibly surpassed even his devotion to his faith. Dwight may not have been the natural father of the Auburn plan, but he certainly quickly became its favorite uncle. This is how he described his beloved prison:

> At Auburn we have a more beautiful example still of what may be done by proper discipline, in a prison well constructed. It is not possible to describe the pleasure which we feel in contemplating this noble institution, after wading through the fraud, and the material and moral filth of many prisons. We regard it as a model worthy of the world's imitation.[8]

Dwight continues his praise of Auburn with words that could easily be mistaken as a description of the contemplative life of a monastery:

> The whole establishment, from the gate to the sewer, is a specimen of neatness. The unremitted industry, the entire subordination and subdued feeling of the convicts, has probably no parallel among an equal number of criminals. In their solitary cells they spend the night, with no other book but the Bible, and at sunrise they proceed, in military order, under the eye of the turnkeys, in solid columns, with the lock march, to their workshops; thence, in the same order, at the hour of breakfast, to the common hall, where they partake of their wholesome and frugal meal in silence. Not even a whisper is heard; though the silence is such that a whisper might be heard through the whole apartment. The convicts are seated, in single file, at narrow tables, with their backs towards the center, so that there can be no interchange of signs. If one has more food than he wants, he raises his left hand: and if another has less, he raises his right hand, and the waiter changes it. When they have done eating, at the ringing of a little bell, of the softest sound, they rise from the table, form the solid columns, and return, under the eye of the turnkeys, to the workshops. From one end of the shops to the other, it is the testimony of many witnesses, that they have passed more than three hundred convicts, without seeing one leave his work, or turn his head to gaze at them. There is the most perfect attention

to business from morning till night, interrupted only by the time necessary to dine, and never by the fact that the whole body of prisoners have done their tasks, and the time is now their own, and they can do as they please. At the close of the day, a little before sunset, the work is all laid aside at once, and the convicts return, in military order, to the solitary cells, where they partake of the frugal meal, which they were permitted to take from the kitchen, where it was furnished for them as they returned from the shops. After supper, they can, if they choose, read Scripture undisturbed and then reflect in silence on the errors of their lives. They must not disturb their fellow prisoners by even a whisper.[9]

If this was the picture Dwight was painting to his Connecticut friends, he certainly had to be aware that he was being less than forthright about conditions at Auburn. The inmates' cells, where they would retire to "read Scripture" and "reflect in silence," were nothing like the large ones proposed under the Pennsylvania plan. Rather, each cell was only three and a half feet wide, seven feet deep, and seven feet in height. Assuming a cot covered an area at least two and a half feet by six feet, precious little room was left for standing, let alone any kind of exercise. Also, Dwight's suggestion that the inmates could read in their cells overlooked the fact that they had no independent light source; the only dim lighting came through the 18-by-14-inch barred opening in the cell's door. Similarly, there was no plumbing of any sort; they took no water to drink or wash with, and a bucket served each inmate as his toilet from dinner until the following morning.

Despite these conditions, Dwight was quick to extol their superiority over earlier prisons. There can be no doubt that he had Newgate in the front of his mind when he continued with this passage:

> It is hardly necessary to add, that at Auburn there is an exclusion of all the positive evils of the old system which arise from crowded night rooms, evil communication, instruction in all the arts of pickpockets, thieves, incendiaries, and counterfeiters, and, above all, from the existence of a crime which is not fit to be named among Christians.[10]

Dwight interrupted his glowing description of Auburn to make only passing criticism to the reality that the Auburn prison administration had a chronic problem with enforcing the rules, since many prisoners were not automatically submissive to this intense degree of discipline.[11] In 1821, the legislature had expressly permitted flogging as a means of enforcement, and the warden was quick to make frequent and intense use of this tool. Captain Elam Lynds, Auburn's warden at the time and for several years thereafter, was adamant in his defense of the whip. When questioned about its need by

Tocqueville, who visited the prison around 1831 as part of his famous tour, Lynds reportedly answered:

> I am convinced to the contrary. I consider the chastisement by the whip, the most efficient, and, at the same time, the most humane which exists; it never injures health, and obliges the prisoners to lead a life essentially healthy.... I consider it impossible to govern a large prison without a whip. Those who know human nature from books only, may say the contrary.[12]

Louis Dwight, his Auburn allies, and their Pennsylvania rivals could debate the relative merits of their competing systems ad infinitum (and Dwight did just that, until the last day of his life), but for the Connecticut legislature, finances were the order of the day. On this issue, there was no contest: the per-unit cost of a cell in Pennsylvania was $1,650, while a cell at Auburn could be built for about $91. Ultimately, the final cost of the Cherry Hill facility had skyrocketed to a staggering $772,000 by the time it was completed in 1836. In comparison, the Welles commission's report to the Connecticut legislature claimed that the entire prison could be constructed at a total cost of slightly more than $25,000.[13] With such assurances of reasonable initial cost, buttressed by the promise that prison industry would make the operation more than self-sustaining, the project was approved in early May 1826.

The committee immediately purchased the parcels needed for the prison, and within two months construction was underway. Despite poor weather, progress continued unabated, and within fourteen months the new prison, although not entirely complete, was secure enough to enable the first prisoners to be moved.

The 1827 prison commissioners' report, penned primarily by Martin Welles, presents a clear description of what the state had been able to erect in only a little more than a year:

> The principal building is 177 feet long, by 48 in width.—The external walls are 3 feet thick at bottom, gradually diminishing to 2 feet 2 inches at top. The average height of the walls from the commencement of the foundation is 36 feet. The whole laid in lime mortar. The windows adjacent to the night rooms and prison yard are all substantially grated. There are copper gutters around the whole roof, and tin conductors to carry off the water—an expense not estimated in the last report.
>
>   At the east end of the main building, are a Guard room, Warden's Office,—hospital and medicine room—an apartment for confining female convicts, and sundry other rooms for the use of the establishment, in the whole 17—exclusive of closets, with a cellar under the whole, 50 feet by

"Connecticut State Prison" circa 1830–1842. D. W. Kellogg & Co., Hartford, Conn., lithograph. (The Connecticut Historical Society Museum)

48—At the west end, a building is erected for confining the convicts on the plan of the celebrated prison at Auburn, containing 138 night rooms,—the length of which is 79 feet, width 19, and height 30 feet, from the floor of the lower tier of cells, with a deep stone foundation. The external and center walls thereof are 1 foot 8 inches thick, and the partition walls one foot thick. Each night room is 7 feet long—3½ wide and 7 feet high in the clear,—and is ventilated through a flue in the center wall, which is carried the whole height of the building and discharged through the roof, thereby securing a free circulation of air.—The doors of the night rooms, are oak plank, 3 inches thick, with four Iron bolts passing horizontally through each door, the whole width thereof.—Every door has a grated space, 18 inches by 14, for the admission of air and light, to each door will be attached a strong lock, made by the Convicts at New Gate, from a pattern furnished the Commissioners, by the politeness of Mr. Lyndes, Agent and keeper of the prison at Sing Sing.[14]

On June 27, 1827, less than a year after construction had begun, Wethersfield accepted the first twenty transferees from Newgate. Twenty more followed suit on August 14, and on September 29 the remainder of the prison population made the trek. In all, Wethersfield greeted 121 inmates as its doors formally opened for business on October 1, 1827.

That is not to say, however, that 121 cells were now occupied; seven women had been among the transferred prisoners, and they were not to be housed in solitary cells.[15] Instead, a single congregate cell had been constructed to meet the housing needs of the female inmates.

Among the men transferees, Prince Mortimer was the most senior, not only in age but also in terms of time spent incarcerated, having endured sixteen years at Newgate before the move. Curiously, only sixteen of the inmates had been imprisoned for more than five years, and only nine were lifers. At the other end of the spectrum, thirty-two were serving sentences of two years or less. Based on this latter number, and the rapid turnover of inmate population it suggested, it is easy to see why the legislature considered the 138 cells more than adequate to meet the state's needs for some years to come.

On the eve of the move, one convict, apparently surmising that escape from Wethersfield would be next to impossible, decided to give it a final try at Newgate. Abel Starkey, a counterfeiter only three years into his twenty-year sentence, prevailed on the guards to let him spend the last night in the caverns. In the dead of night, Starkey attempted to climb a rope up the well shaft, but the following morning he was found dead at the bottom of the shaft. Indications are that one of the guards had also been bribed to lower the rope down to Starkey. As the unsuspecting prisoner was attempting his climb, the guard cut the rope, and Starkey fell to his death. The incident was formally classified

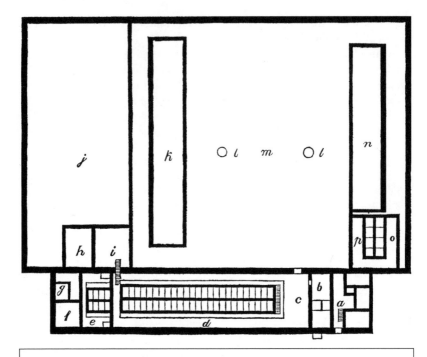

South Front. *a*, entry; *b*, guard-room; *c*, open space, used for morning and evening prayers; *d*, area, 11½ feet wide, open from the ground to the roof, around 200 men's cells, 7 feet long, 7 feet high, and 3½ feet wide, arranged back to back in 4 stories; *e*, area around 32 women's cells; *f*, women's work-room; *g*, women's hospital; *h*, store-room; *i*, kitchen; *j*, women's yard; *k*, workshops and chapel above; *l*, *l*, wells; *m*, men's yard; *n*, workshops; *o*, area in front of cells for punishment; *p*, area in front of cells for lunatics.

Plan of Wethersfield from Boston Prison Discipline Society.

as an accident, but sabotage becomes a more credible interpretation in light of the additional fact that in the morning the hatch cover at the top of the well was found unlocked, and Starkey's pockets were empty of most of the money he was known to keep on his person. Whatever the case, accident or not, on September 29 one less prisoner would be making the trip to Wethersfield State Prison.

Since the state did not have sufficient wagons and men to transport and guard all these men, the services of local townsmen were solicited. Road conditions had not much improved since the day Prince had made the trip in the other direction, so the seventy-one prisoners sat shackled to the beams of four wagons for the four-to-five hour trip to Wethersfield.[16]

One reporter, however, appears to have gotten carried away in describing

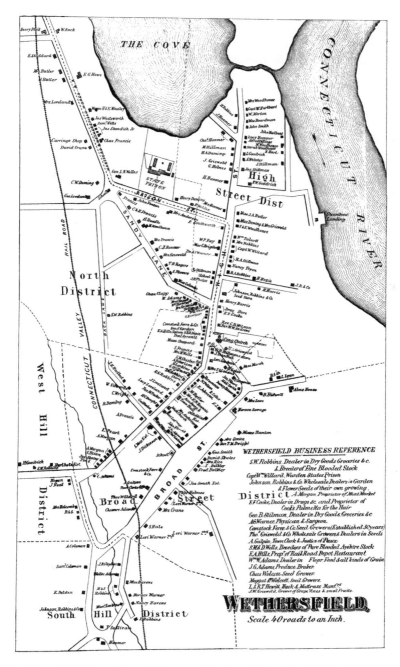

Detail from 1869 Baker & Tilden Map of Wethersfield, showing location of State Prison in relation to Cove and Connecticut River. (From Atlas of Hartford City & County, Conn.)

the event, claiming that the entire prison population was made to walk the twenty miles while fettered in wrist and ankle chains.[17] As unlikely as that depiction might be, nonetheless the group must have been both tired and hungry when they arrived at Wethersfield. Those feelings probably faded quickly, however, as they beheld for the first time their new homes, and began to ponder their future lives within the forever silent confines of a three-and-a-half-foot cell.

· 15 ·

Moses and Amos

$\mathcal{H}$aving resolved to close forever the gates of Newgate prison on the filth, vice, and corruption that had festered within its walls, the legislature was not about to subject its new prison to the same administration that had piloted the old one to its degenerate condition. Even before the first stone had been set at Wethersfield, the search was on for a new warden. Since Wethersfield was to be America's shining star in the world of prison reform, whoever was chosen would have to be a man with proven ability to maintain discipline. That ability, however, also had to be coupled with a record of achievement that would confer immediate credibility upon the new institution, even before its doors were open for business. Finally, the new warden needed to have a demonstrated commitment to humane treatment and to providing his inmates with religious instruction.

Only a few men in America at that time could boast a resume that satisfied all those requirements. Of course, the Auburn plan was already in effect at the prison bearing its name, but there was one factor that disinclined the prison commissioners from approaching Auburn's warden or any of his subordinates: Auburn's frequent resort to the whip to enforce discipline. On this matter, Louis Dwight's influence was very heavily felt; he had seen the beatings at Auburn, and as much as he was a fervent advocate of the plan, he strongly objected to the ubiquitous presence of the whip as the favored disciplinary tool.

At the urging of Dwight, the prison commissioners undertook discussions with Moses Pilsbury, who was then warden of the New Hampshire state prison. By promising Pilsbury complete discretion in the choice of his subordinates, they were soon able to induce Moses, who was forty-nine at the time, to move to Connecticut to oversee the final construction at Wethersfield and to set up the prison administration.

Pilsbury had only one real concern in steadfastly insisting on hiring rights: he wanted his son, Amos, to serve as assistant warden, just as he was doing in New Hampshire.

It took no time at all for the prison directors to recognize the perceived wisdom of their choice. They were charged by law to make annual reports to the legislature in the spring of each year, and the first report, given April 10, 1828, was glowing in its praise of Moses Pilsbury. "We consulted gentlemen from different parts of the State," wrote Welles, "who with entire unanimity, concurred with us, in the opinion, that we should be most fortunate, if we were able to obtain to the state, the services of Mr. Pilsbury. The result so far has not disappointed our expectations."[1]

The directors were indeed pleased to see the Auburn plan running so smoothly, and they were particularly encouraged that the plan's promised rehabilitative benefits were already appearing to bear fruit. "We believe that the means of mutual corruption are effectually cut off," Welles wrote to his fellow legislators, "and that the most practiced and hardened offender, will be obliged to lock up in his own breast, his schemes, his secrets, and his arts; and that the young offender, who perhaps has been detected in his first offence, may be again received into society, without the fear that he has been made worse by his imprisonment."[2]

Of course, Pilsbury had the benefit of a set of regulations with very specific rules for everyone involved in prison life, beginning with the warden himself, then down through the deputy warden, the overseers, the watchmen, the prison physician, and finally, of course, the prisoners themselves. Although he was required to visit each cell on a daily basis, the warden's primary duties were to keep the prison books and to negotiate contracts. The day-to-day supervision of prison operations was left to the deputy warden; he had complete charge of lesser prison officers and employees, and he was also directed to "see that the convicts are diligent and industrious."

The rules for the inmates were brief in number, but all-inclusive in scope:

1. Every convict shall be industrious, submissive and obedient, and shall labour diligently and in silence.
2. No convict shall secrete, hide, or carry about his person, any instrument or thing with intent to make his escape.
3. No convict shall write or receive a letter to or from any person whatsoever, nor have intercourse with persons without the prison, except by leave of the warden.
4. No convict shall burn, waste, injure or destroy any raw materials or article of public property, nor deface or injure the prison building.

5. Convicts shall always conduct themselves toward the officers with deference and respect; and cleanliness in their persons, dress, and bedding, is required. When they go to their meals or labour, they shall proceed in regular order and in silence, marching in the lock step.
6. No convict shall converse with another prisoner, or leave his work without permission of an officer. He shall not speak to or look at visitors, nor leave the hospital when ordered there, nor shall he make any unnecessary noise in his labour, or do anything either in the shops or cells which is subversive of the good order of the institution.

In less than two hundred words, these regulations laid out the entire philosophy and structure of the Auburn plan and left little room for error or misunderstanding on the prisoners' part as to what was expected of them.

An inmate violating any of these rules could be quite certain of punishment, but one of the distinguishing features of Wethersfield's version of the Auburn plan was the warden's disdain for the use of the whip. Although Pilsbury had the express authority to punish transgressions with as many as ten stripes, the directors were "happy to say, that since the Warden has taken charge of the Institution, corporal punishment has not been inflicted in any case."

Pilsbury was also true to his obligation to provide the convicts with religious instruction.[3] The inmates' work days began and ended with a service, usually a reading from the bible; on Sundays, a local clergyman would visit the prison and provide a more formal service. As gratifying as all this may have been, it appears that Welles was at least a bit skeptical about its ultimate effect on the inmates. "What effect these efforts to instruct, to reclaim and reform these men, shall have upon their future characters, or how permanent will be the impressions which they have received," he wrote, "it is not for us to say."

A second feature that distinguished Wethersfield from Auburn, much to the delight of everyone, was the fact that it became a profitable enterprise from the very beginning. Although Welles's designs for a brick-making factory would never materialize, the prison was able to let out the inmates' labor to a number of private concerns, who would bring raw materials to Wethersfield to be fashioned into finished goods within the confines of the prison yard. Ironically, these were the same types of activity that had been running a deficit at Newgate for years: a shoe shop, a cooper's shop, a carpenter's shop, a smith shop, and even the original nail shop, which was successfully using up the raw materials that had been wasting away in Granby. After only six months in operation, Pilsbury was able to inform the legislature, rather proudly, that the prison showed a profit of $1,017.19, after all expenses of administration. That figure may appear rather small in today's economy, but in 1828 it represented over one-thirtieth the cost of construction of the entire prison.

Unfortunately, all of the early records of individual prisoners have been lost, so particular information about Prince's life in Wethersfield, to the extent such information may have ever existed, is gone forever. At the time of Welles's first report, Prince Mortimer was about 104, and one would suspect that he was probably bedridden, or nearly so, merely by virtue of his advanced age. Apparently, however, that was not the case. The directors' report, in addressing the prison's ability to meet the medical needs of the inmates, points out that "not a case of severe sickness has occurred, nor has it been found necessary to order a single prisoner to the Hospital."[4] This fact is confirmed in the prison physician's report, filed at the same time, in which he states, "Among the male convicts not one individual was confined to the hospital, or so much indisposed as to require confinement to the bed, or any thing like a regular course of medication."[5]

If Prince was not confined to the hospital, indeed, apparently had never even been in the hospital, then where else could he be within the limits of the prison grounds? Only two options present themselves: either he was part of the general prison population, working and living as they did, or he was languishing in his cell. The latter possibility is rather unlikely, however, considering the fundamental precepts of the Auburn plan. Here was a system premised on the notion that the activities of each and every prisoner were controlled during every minute of every day; the last thing the administration would tolerate would be a situation where an inmate was permitted to remain idle, as had occurred on a regular basis in Newgate. Here, every prisoner was expected to be productive and to help defray the cost of his incarceration. If Prince was not so debilitated as to require hospitalization, or even confinement to his cot, as the physician's report would suggest, he was probably required to perform some form of labor, however light it may have been. Such a situation, as inhumane as it might seem to twenty-first-century observers, certainly would have been in accord with Martin Welles's report to the legislature in 1826, where he had advocated brick making as an appropriate activity because the work could be performed by the entire prison population, including "the old, the imbecile, and the intractable." There is no small amount of irony in such a circumstance, with Prince still being productive some thirty years after he was described in the inventory of Philip Mortimer's estate as "sick with yaws — £0."

Wethersfield and Auburn prisons were built long before the development of special facilities for juveniles or the criminally insane, so members of such groups would periodically be found in the general prison population. One look at the plan of Wethersfield, however, confirms that no thought whatsoever was given to accommodating the special needs of such a population, even on a limited basis. The same holds true for the elderly. Although Welles's comment confirms his recognition that the elderly would be part of the prison population (since a certain percentage of prisoners always would be "lifers"), no provision for their needs was made beyond the general infirmary.

Just as Martin Welles was extolling the successes of Wethersfield to the state legislature, so also was Louis Dwight singing its praises to a much larger audience, by means of the third annual report of his Prison Discipline Society. Dwight took pride in comparing the old and the new from a number of perspectives. "The stillness of the night is preserved by a watchman," he wrote, "walking silently in front of the cells, and a striking contrast is here found to the oaths and blasphemies, which issued from the old night rooms at Newgate."[6]

Dwight had played no small role in encouraging Welles's committee to consider Pilsbury as the new warden, and his Third Report showed little restraint in praising the decision to hire him:

> In Connecticut, Moses C. Pilsbury, the warden of the new Prison at Wethersfield, in addition to the provision, which he makes on the Sabbath for public worship, regularly reads the scriptures to the assembled convicts, every morning and evening, and, in their behalf, offers prayers to the Father of mercies. He is, besides, faithful in counsel, affectionate in sickness, and lovely in his Christian sympathies towards those committed to his care, without losing any thing in his prompt and successful attention to business and discipline. He mingles the principles of obedience and affection in his government and instructions, so that the principles of obedience and affection flow spontaneously towards him from the hearts of convicts.[7]

Dwight's choice of adjectives in describing Pilsbury is certainly unexpected; Moses is perhaps the only warden in history ever to be described as "affectionate" and "lovely." The irony of Dwight's words, however, will become more meaningful in light of subsequent developments at Wethersfield Prison.

The remainder of 1828 and the first half of 1829 saw Wethersfield continue to exceed expectations in terms of both income and successful prison discipline. The directors' report of May 1829 is so comfortable with the situation that, rather than give a detailed report of the year's events, it simply repeats verbatim the observations of the prior year regarding the benefits of solitary night cells, the advantages of abandoning the whip in favor of more effective but less abusive disciplinary tools, and Pilsbury's commitment to religious instruction.

Having dispensed with such observations, Welles then goes on to discuss at some length what he perceives as the main reason behind the significant increase in the prison population over the prior year: inconsistent sentencing by the judges throughout the state. Prince's sentence of life imprisonment could well have been on Welles's mind as he made this observation:

Perhaps however there are no instances in which so striking an inequality is presented, as in the respective punishments for manslaughter and an assault with intent to kill, by our statute the first is punished by an imprisonment for three years, and the second, by imprisonment for life or a shorter period, at the discretion of the court. It is believed, that in many instances of a conviction of an assault with intent to kill, the proof has shown that there existed such an excitement of the passions, such a sudden heat, or such an affray, as would have induced a Jury in case death had ensued the assault, to have found the prisoner guilty of manslaughter, and not of murder. If this opinion is correct then this singular case is presented. A man in a quarrel or under some sudden excitement assaults and kills another, is found guilty of manslaughter and imprisoned for three years — another person under the influence of a similar excitement, makes a similar assault and wounds his antagonist, but does not kill him, and he is imprisoned for life.

Certainly, Welles's observation is supported by the list of prisoners who transferred from Newgate. Prince was one of eleven lifers who had made the trek to Wethersfield. Of these, two others besides Prince had been convicted of attempted murder; three were serving their sentences for attempted rape, and one for rape. Only one was a convicted murderer; the remaining lifers were in for assault, bestiality, and burglary.[8] On the other hand, ten other inmates had been convicted of attempted rape and had received sentences ranging from a maximum of twenty years to as little as three years. Prince's sentence, for attempted poisoning where there was no actual harm inflicted, stands in sharp contrast to those received by three of his fellow transferees. Already, Prince had been imprisoned for eighteen years, while others convicted of attempted murder were serving sentences of three, six, and twelve years.

Financially, the new prison was continuing to be an unexpected source of income for the state. The warden's report for the fiscal year ending March 31, 1829, showed a profit of $3,220.41. In only a year and a half, the prisoners' labor had managed to defray over a tenth of the cost of construction of the prison. One cannot help but wonder whether Pilsbury's reluctance to enforce discipline with the whip was not in part motivated by a desire to keep every prisoner, even recalcitrant ones, and even ancient ones, as productive as possible; Pilsbury knew full well that an inmate subjected to ten lashes would certainly require a recuperative period of at least a day or two, during which time he was not in the shops adding to the warden's bottom line.

Suffering from poor health, Moses retired in 1830, even though he was only fifty-two at the time.[9] He may well have realized when he accepted the position of warden that he would only be at the helm for a short time, and that was why he was so insistent on appointing his son, Amos, as assistant warden. Born in 1805, Amos was only twenty-five years of age when he succeeded his father as warden. Despite his youth, Amos Pilsbury was no stranger to prison administration. His father had introduced him to this field of endeavor in New Hampshire; at the age of nineteen, Amos began working as a watchman and guard at the state prison at Concord. Ironically, this employment came about quite by accident: Although still in his teens, Amos had become skilled as a tanner, but at that particular time the demand for leather goods was unusually low and he was unable to earn a satisfactory living at that trade. He returned home to Concord to live with his parents and began his prison employment with the expectation that it would only be a temporary position, to be abandoned when the demand for leather goods revived.[10]

Now, only six years later, Amos was being appointed warden of what was generally considered the best prison in America, if not the world. Despite Amos' youth, nothing but praise could be heard for the success of his first year as his father's successor. The opening years of Wethersfield's operation had been such a resounding success, however, that even Louis Dwight was sounding complacent in his Society's 1830 report. In that survey of the nation's prisons, encompassing well over a hundred pages of text, Dwight saw fit to limit his discussion of Wethersfield to this solitary paragraph:

> The New Prison at Wethersfield, Conn., continues to sustain the high character given to it, the last year, in the official communications of the State authorities, which were published in our last Report. As an example of neatness, order, quiet industry, mild and wholesome discipline, faithful instruction, economy, and productive labor, it stands, at least, on a level with the Prison at Auburn. In one respect, it was without a parallel, so far as our knowledge extends, in the history of Prisons. The proceeds of labor, of an average number of about 150 prisoners, exceeded the whole expense of their support, including the salary of the officers, by the sum of $5068.94.

Although Dwight would never abandon his fervent advocacy of the Auburn system over the competing Pennsylvania plan, for the moment he was focusing his efforts on his new crusade, debtors' prison. Things appeared to be going quite well in Wethersfield, particularly with respect to the prison's finances, which was probably the greatest appeal that the Auburn plan presented to anybody in any of the other states with an interest in prison reform and the power to implement it. So, with Wethersfield's success under Amos's guidance a fait accompli, Dwight felt free to expand the scope of the Society's interests and pursue the very real problems of America's debtors' prisons.[11]

Even foreign visitors were impressed with the administrative capabilities of the young warden. William Crawford, an English prison administrator who toured American prisons in 1832, was unabashed in noting that "much of the success of the penitentiary is owing to the peculiar enlightenment of the warden, Mr. Pilsbury."[12] Crawford's final comment on Wethersfield is no less glowing. After noting that the absence of whipping as a disciplinary instrument showed in the faces of the inmates, who would even dare to take surreptitious opportunities for forbidden communication in the work shops, Crawford concludes:

> On the other hand, the evil arising from this comparative relaxation of discipline is in a great degree compensated by arrangements of a highly valuable character, which render this penitentiary more deserving of attention than perhaps any other (conducted on the principle of association) in the United States. The enlightened feeling which induces, and the vigilance which enables, the warden to dispense with degrading punishments, reflect great credit on his management; while the persevering and judicious labours of the excellent chaplain (who resides in the prison) cannot fail to be most beneficial to the objects of his care. It is impossible to doubt that much good has been effected at this penitentiary in the way of reformation.

Visitors from the other side of the English Channel were similarly impressed. Touring the country at about the same time as Crawford, Alexis de Tocqueville and Gustave de Beaumont were particularly interested in prison reform and were intent on visiting Wethersfield, as well as Auburn and Sing Sing. George Wilson Pierson, in his classic *Tocqueville in America*, saw fit to report the following except from the *Hartford Mirror*'s article the day after the Frenchmen's departure:

> They have been through many prisons in the Union, but express an opinion that for regularity of discipline, for the good order that prevails throughout the institution, for the neatness and precision with which its concerns are managed, as well as for the profits made to accrue from the labor of the convicts, that the Wethersfield prison is not inferior to any which has come under their inspection.[13]

Amos Pilsbury was not the only person, however, who was instrumental in shaping Tocqueville and Beaumont's opinions about Wethersfield prison. Martin Welles was no less inclined to make the acquaintance of these notable foreign visitors and in fact invited them to dine at his home, only a short half-mile walk from the prison grounds.[14]

Pierson reports that it was a pleasant dinner, with Welles spontaneously drawing up plans and hypothetical balance sheets for his French guests for a 500-man prison built on the Auburn plan.[15] They left Wethersfield completely unaware that they, along with Louis Dwight and the other singers of the praises of Connecticut's prison, had all been duped.

· 16 ·

Old Soldiers

$\mathcal{W}$hen Tocqueville and Beaumont departed Hartford opining that Wethersfield was among the best prisons they had ever visited, they did so in complete ignorance of a dispute that had been fomenting for nearly two years. The meticulously clean cells and workshops furnished no hint of the fact that Martin Welles and Amos Pilsbury were in the midst of an acrimonious battle that went to the heart of the prison's management, and in which the prisoners, Prince included, had become the unfortunate pawns.

Even though his early directors' reports were laudatory of the Pilsburys' results, Welles had never made a secret of his dislike of both of them, particularly Amos; he considered the young warden ill suited for his post, both by temperament and by character. After Moses's retirement in April 1830, the three directors were faced with the task of appointing his successor. Moses, of course, wanted to see his son in that position, and to that end both father and son lobbied John Russ and Samuel Huntington, the other two directors. Welles had doubts about Amos, however, and expressed them without reservation to anyone who would listen, much to the dismay of the Pilsburys. But by the time of the vote, Welles had been unable to win over his fellow directors, and Amos was appointed by a vote of two to one. Russ and Huntington, although acknowledging their concern over Pilsbury's youth, nonetheless decided that they would "make the trial of Mr. Pilsbury," as they stated in their directors' report of 1830.[1]

Two issues in particular were troubling to Welles. First was the information that Amos frequently had been seen inebriated in Concord when he was the assistant warden of the New Hampshire prison. In addition, Amos had been discharged by the warden (his father's predecessor at Concord) for forcing his way into the warden's desk by making a false key.

Neither had Amos's time as assistant warden at Wethersfield been free of controversy, even though the 1829 directors' report was replete with praise for the financial success of the prison and the disciplinary capabilities of its officers, particularly Moses and Amos. "The results of the experiment are now before the public," they concluded. "We can say truly, they have exceeded our highest anticipations, both as it respects their moral and pecuniary character; and we are not aware of the existence of any cause which shall produce results less gratifying in the future."[2] The ink was hardly dry on that report when events began to occur that severely tested the accuracy of that prediction.

Moses was absent from Wethersfield for the entire month of June 1829, leaving Amos in complete charge of the prison. Although even before Moses's departure the prisoners had been complaining of insufficient food, the situation came to head under Amos's watch. During the months of July and August, the first of a series of incidents took place that together would set the stage for the bitter conflict that was to follow.

The several workshops in the prison were run by private contractors, who paid the state for the services of the prisoners. Since prison profits were directly related to the number of hours that the warden could charge to these contractors, the warden was loath to relieve inmates from their work because they were sick. The Pilsburys were fond of discounting claims of illness, dismissing such complaints as prisoners "playing the old soldier," meaning that they were feigning illness to avoid work. Many genuinely sick prisoners were so fearful of the treatment they would receive from the Pilsburys that they preferred working while sick to attempting to be relieved from work by making their condition known. The problem was aggravated by the fact that the prisoners were not permitted to speak to anyone other than the warden or his deputies, especially not the prison physician, Dr. Woodward, nor any of the directors.

In June 1829, a young prisoner by the name of Botsford complained to his overseer in the shoe shop that he was ill. Amos, being advised of the situation, dismissed Botsford's complaint as another instance of a prisoner "playing the old soldier," refusing to allow him to see the physician and directing that he remain on the job. After about four weeks, Botsford's condition had deteriorated to the point that Amos could no longer deny the truth of the situation and allowed him to be seen by Dr. Woodward.

Some months later, for reasons that will be discussed later, Woodward set forth in a certificate the particulars of his observations:

> Botsford was now permitted to consult me. I found him extremely ill with all the symptoms of general dropsy, not only of the limbs, but the cavities, his feet were swelling, his abdomen greatly distended with water, his breathing was laborious and distressed, his pulse was one hundred and twenty or twenty-five in a minute, greatly irritated and palpitating; tongue much

furred, appetite gone, flesh wasted, he had had for weeks a severe and wasting diarrhoea [*sic*] which still continued, he complained of great weakness,
said he was quite unable to labor, that he could not ascend the stairs to his
cell, without the occurrence of great distress in breathing, and palpitation
of the heart, which seemed to threaten immediate death. Upon examining
his symptoms, I at once saw the danger of his case, and prescribed such
remedies as I thought most likely to relieve him.[3]

A few days later, Woodward was astounded to be informed that Botsford
was feeling much better and that Amos Pilsbury had ordered him back to work.
Within another few days, Botsford was back in Woodward's care and had the
distinction of being the first patient to be received in the prison hospital, some
two years after the prison's opening. This was not because Wethersfield had
gone all that time with no significant illness; rather, it was due to the fact that
the Pilsburys had deemed the space better suited for use as a paint shop.

Four days after he had been taken off the job, Botsford was dead. That
same day, another prisoner, by the name of Fagan, was admitted to the hospital
with similar symptoms. The overseer of the chair shop, where Fagan worked,
informed the physician that he had reported Fagan's condition "repeatedly" to
the Pilsburys, but they dismissed the case as another prisoner "playing the old
soldier."

Fagan was dead within two weeks, and in short order three more prisoners died, all of the same symptoms, and all because, Woodward asserted,
their treatment had been delayed until it was too late. The day after Botsford's
death, Woodward had informed Welles of the situation, and in short order
the directors adopted a by-law giving the prison physician the ultimate power
to decide whether an inmate was too sick to work and forbidding the warden
from denying any prisoner access to the physician.

The Pilsburys were incensed over this new regulation, seeing it as a direct
affront to their authority, and they blamed Welles and Woodward for instigat-
ing the attack. Ironically, the Pilsburys still retained substantial control over
the affairs of the hospital, thanks to the financial arrangements that had been
made at the time that Moses signed on. The agreement was that sick inmates
would not be fed from the same reserves used for the other prisoners; rather,
Moses's family would be responsible for their meals and would be reimbursed
for these provisions at the rate of one dollar per inmate per day. Consequently,
the Pilsburys were in the position of being able to routinely ignore Woodward's
dietary directives, and they fed the hospital patients as they saw fit.

These were the circumstances that prevailed at the time of Moses's retirement, and they easily explain Welles's opposition to the appointment of Amos
as warden. Such issues were quickly overshadowed, however, by a series of
other problems that arose soon after Amos took charge.

In addition to being extolled as a stellar example of the Auburn plan, Wethersfield and its administration were being praised for their fiscal success, turning a handsome profit to the state by letting out the prisoners' work to private enterprise. Of course, income was only half of the equation; the other half consisted of the prison's expenses. To the extent that the Pilsburys were able to keep those expenses to a minimum, their figures were that much ahead.

In 1830, Welles became aware of the extent to which Amos Pilsbury was willing to cut corners on expenses. Pilsbury's report for that year showed that he had expended $3,190.60 on prison provisions, meaning that the cost of a prisoner's daily sustenance was 4.9 cents. The inmates' rations were not decided at the whim of the warden, nor anyone else; rather, they were specifically prescribed by prison rules. Each prisoner was to receive a daily allowance of one pound of beef, one-twentieth bushel of potatoes, one pound of bread, and supper of pea porridge, all of which was to be weighed on a per-ration basis. The cost of such a daily ration was 6 cents; thus, on the basis of the warden's own figures, he was spending nearly 20 percent less on the prisoners than he was obligated.[4]

This deficiency did not go unnoticed in the inmates' mess kits, nor by many who had opportunity to observe them. Welles would later write that "men have been seen to take the entrails of cattle slaughtered in the yard, and after cooking them in the lime which was slacking, have devoured them with great avidity. They have also been seen struggling with each other to get at the barrel where the wash of the cook room was placed, in order to get at such morsels of food as might be found there."[5]

Part of the reason for the shortfall in the prisoners' rations, Welles suggested, was that the Pilsburys were appropriating provisions for their own families' use. Such diversion initially might not seem very extensive, certainly not enough to account for a 20% deficiency in the provisions of an entire prison population. The Pilsbury families, however, were quite atypical in terms of size. Moses Pilsbury's family consisted of 22 persons, and Amos counted eighteen persons as members of his household. In addition, a number of the prison guards boarded with the Pilsburys, for which they each had two dollars per week deducted from their pay.[6] If all these persons were being fed from the provisions that were supposed to be going to the prisoners, the scope of the shortfall begins to make sense.

Welles's issues with Amos Pilsbury did not end with concerns about the prisoners' medical treatment and their starvation diet. The winter of 1831–1832 was particularly cold, and problems developed in connection with the prison's heating system. The cellblock had been designed with air vents leading into each cell, all fed from a central furnace, known as a Fowler's air heater, fueled by wood and drawing air from the outside. From the beginning, the system never worked well; it was poorly designed and the vents were of insufficient size to deliver adequate heat to the cells. Then, for reasons that are not at all clear, prior to the winter in question Pilsbury decided to move the Fowler's to a different location and to use the interior air for combustion.

The consequences of that decision were enormous. There was no plumbing in the cells; each evening, each prisoner would carry a bucket into his cell, and whatever use he made of it over the next twelve hours would remain there until the morning. With no outside air helping to dissipate the fumes, it took very little time before the stench became overwhelming. The only recourse available to the guards, who were suffering nearly as much as the prisoners, was to open the large windows of the outer hall to vent the building. Of course, this caused what little heat there was in the building to escape, so that at night the temperature in the cells would routinely drop into the low forties, sometimes lower.

As difficult as it was for the guards to endure this cold, it was even more uncomfortable for the prisoners. They were provided with no warm clothing; all they had were the satinette uniforms they worked in throughout the day. Their beds were bereft of sheets; even though the prison regulations required Pilsbury to provide them to the prisoners, he had never seen fit to make the expenditure. Likewise, their blankets were small and threadbare, offering little warmth.[7]

It was no surprise, then, that at one point during that winter forty-five prisoners were suffering from influenza. Since the hospital could not accommodate that many patients, they were left to remain in their cells, dependent on the limited good will of the guards to bring them food. Dr. Woodward later reported that some of the prisoners suffered from chilblains and frostbitten feet from exposure to cold while in their cells.[8]

When the time came for the directors to file their report in the spring of 1832, a dispute arose among them as to certain matters. Russ and Huntington wanted to include a statement censuring Dr. Woodward for submitting a certification to them regarding the illness and suffering of the prior winter because of the lack of heat in the cells.[9] The ostensible reason for the censure was that Woodward had not informed them of these conditions when they were occurring. The real reason was that they disputed Woodward's claims; Huntington had even written in the directors' book, a notebook kept in the warden's office for the exclusive use of the directors to communicate between meetings, that he thought the cells to be too warm.

Welles refused to sign the report if the censure was to remain. Huntington refused to budge, and even added the following statement, praising the work of Amos Pilsbury:

> Before closing this Report, the undersigned deem it a duty they owe the public, as well as an act of justice to the Warden, to express our opinion with regard to the general management of the Prison concerns for the last year.

We have endeavored throughout the year to keep a vigilant oversight on the conduct of those who have had charge of the government and discipline of the Prison; and we are happy in being able to state, that nothing has fallen under our observation to impair our confidence in their fidelity to the State, or in their judicious and reasonable government of the convicts—while the public interest has been faithfully consulted, as is clearly indicated by the pecuniary results of the year, we are persuaded that the feeling of humanity have not been disregarded, in the discipline and general treatment of the prisoners.[10]

Welles, of course, continued to refuse to sign the report, which was submitted with only the signatures of Russ and Huntington. Five days later, Martin Welles, who was also the Speaker of the House at that time, submitted a counterreport, challenging the findings of the other directors and setting out in considerable detail his reasons for withholding his signature from the majority. Pilsbury, apparently recognizing that the best defense is a good offense, immediately submitted a petition to the legislature seeking an investigation into Welles's allegations.

The lines were drawn for an inquiry that would consume several months and would extend its scope far beyond the issues of starvation and freezing. The investigation would also delve into Welles's claim that Pilsbury was systematically robbing the state by altering the prison books and appropriating goods and prisoners' services to his own use. Ultimately, though, this would prove to be a battle of personalities, and Martin Welles and Amos Pilsbury possessed perhaps the two strongest wills in state government at that time. The *Hartford Times*, a strong supporter of Pilsbury, was constant and unrestrained in its criticism of Welles. "Wherever he has been," the paper wrote, "he has caused a blight that has interrupted and destroyed social intercourse—he has estranged friends and produced discord in society."[11]

Welles, for his part, did not need a surrogate to make known his contempt for Pilsbury. After laying out in his counterreport instance after instance of "gross and abusive treatment," Welles concluded by stating that he could not commend Pilsbury to the legislature "as a safe depository of so tremenduous [*sic*] a power as is given to the Warden of that Prison, over the comfort, health and lives of the unfortunate, although criminal men, who are committed defenseless to his care."[12]

In response to Pilsbury's petition, the legislature appointed a committee of three of its members to undertake an investigation and conduct a hearing into Welles's allegations. The particular charges being asserted against Pilsbury were:

1. That the accounts were not kept according to law.
2. That the Prisoners suffered from want of food.

3. That they were for several weeks furnished with bad water.
4. That they suffered from cold and bad air.
5. That the sick prisoners were treated with great cruelty.
6. That the Bye-laws [*sic*] were disregarded.
7. That depredations were committed on the public property.
8. That the prisoners were illegally punished for misconduct.
9. That the Prisoners were permitted to leave the Prison and go at large.

Over the next several months, the committee took dozens of depositions from nearly everyone who had business with the prison during the period at issue. They heard from directors, guards, overseers, physicians, Pilsbury family members, and workmen on the addition to the prison built in 1830.[13] Ironically, they refused to take testimony from the inmates, the group most directly affected by the prison conditions, accepting Pilsbury's argument that "no Warden would be safe if prisoners might be examined against him."[14]

Ultimately, the committee issued its report, which is remarkably brief, considering the extent of the testimony and the number of depositions available to it. To the utter amazement of everyone familiar with the testimony, the Committee exonerated Amos Pilsbury on each and every allegation. The only "official" record is the committee's report. None of the many depositions and extensive testimony has survived as any part of that "official" record. Fortunately for historians, however, an unofficial record was compiled, some two years after the hearings, by a group of citizens who were incensed over the committee's decision and were determined to provide the public with a more complete basis for evaluating that decision.

The material is compiled under the official-sounding title, "Minutes of the Testimony Taken Before John Q. Wilson, Joseph Eaton, & Morris Woodruff, Committee from the General Assembly, to Inquire into the Conditions of Connecticut State Prison, together with Their Report and Remarks Upon the Same." The "Minutes" include much more than a record of the actual committee proceedings; they also reprint significant excerpts from many depositions, some of which were accepted into the record and were presumably considered by the committee, others of which the committee flatly disallowed. In addition, a great deal of the actual witness testimony is presented, as well as arguments of counsel for the state and for Amos Pilsbury.

The most intriguing aspect of this compendium, however, is the portion falling under the heading "Remarks Upon the Same." In this section, each aspect of the committee's ruling is minutely examined and mercilessly criticized under a discipline that skillfully blends legal principles with simple logic and an abundance of common sense. But even more remarkable than the drafting skill displayed in the "Remarks" is the fact that their author is anonymous. Readers will look in vain for any express indication of whose hand penned this clear and convincing counterpoint to the contrived reasoning of the committee.

In truth, there can be little doubt as to the author. Only one man was so engrossed in this struggle, and so versed in its facts, as to be able to write with such precision and such passion: Martin Welles. His authorship becomes even more likely when the origins of the "Minutes" are disclosed in the first paragraph: "At a large meeting of the inhabitants of the Town of Wethersfield, held for the purpose of considering the expediency of publishing the evidence taken before the Committee appointed by the Legislature to examine the condition of Connecticut State Prison."

Anyone reading the "Minutes" is likely to conclude, as did Martin Welles, that the committee could have reached its conclusions only if it engaged in a constant and systematic disregard of the evidence. Nonetheless, they decided as they did, and history, at least officially, has exonerated Amos Pilsbury.

Even those inclined to accept the committee's conclusion, however, cannot deny the facts on which they were premised. During the two years in question, prisoners suffered. They were systematically deprived of each of the three essentials for human life: adequate food, shelter, and clothing. More important to this study, however, is the fact that Prince Mortimer, then approaching the end of his eleventh decade, was undeniably subjected to such conditions. There are a few references in Dr. Woodward's testimony to certain prisoners, including "Guinea," Prince's birth-country nickname, being in the hospital at the time that Botsford and Fagan died. It is comforting to believe that, at least in some respects, Prince was spared these difficult conditions, that perhaps some guards took pity on him and provided him with extra rations, clothing, or blankets. Unfortunately, absolutely nothing in the testimony of dozens of witnesses supports such speculation. Certainly, if Pilsbury had engaged in such acts of benevolence, he would have been sure to present them as part of his defense. But even if such acts did occur, they likely were not sufficient to elevate Prince's circumstances to anything that most persons would consider appropriate for a man of his extreme age and its inevitable infirmities.

The committee's report plodded systematically through the list of accusations, in some instances simply refusing to believe the evidence and in others explaining it away. The "Remarks" author (since Welles's identity cannot be conclusively established, he will subsequently be referred to as the "commentator") was not about to let these instances of willful disregard of the truth go unchallenged. The commentator began by asserting that the committee members could not even acknowledge who were the real parties in interest in the dispute. The committee's preamble made reference to the parties being the state of Connecticut and Amos Pilsbury. "The real parties," the commentator noted, "are the suffering and complaining prisoners, on the one hand, and Amos Pilsbury and his accomplices on the other."[15]

The essence of the committee's finding on the first accusation, that Pilsbury failed to keep the prison's books according to law, was that "he is not a *perfectly* correct book keeper [emphasis in original]" and that "He has committed mistakes to which all book keepers are more or less liable." In response, the commentator noted that at least three witnesses had testified that the books for the period in question were more than $1,000 out of balance, a significant amount at that time. More damning, however, was the testimony of an auditor that he detected evidence of originally correct entries being erased and falsified. The accusation had now gone well beyond issues of Pilsbury's lack of bookkeeping competency; there was evidence of intentional fraud. The committee, to the commentator's obvious frustration, did not even mention such evidence; instead, it simply found the charge not proven and suggested that the warden could benefit from someone to assist in keeping the books, since he was so obviously busy with countless other duties.

The elements of the second accusation, the lack of adequate food, have already been discussed. The entire text of the committee's findings on this issue comprises less than 400 words. They did not address any of the particulars of the accusations, contenting themselves with merely stating their conclusion that the charge was not proved. They also saw fit to comment that "the Wethersfield prison is remarkable for the healthfulness of the convicts," since the death rate was considerably lower than many of the other northern state prisons. They also noted that any problems with the quality and adequacy of the prisoners' food had been resolved by hiring a matron to do the cooking and ensure compliance with the by-law requirement that each portion be measured.

This finding was perhaps the most infuriating one for the commentator, ignoring as it did so much credible testimony from so many reliable sources. He begins on a purely logical point, asking how a problem can be resolved if there was no problem in the first place. Additionally, the evidence clearly showed that Pilsbury could not account for nearly one-third of the required rations. "Can the Committee be serious," the commentator asks, "when with such documents before them they can say that the prisoners have not suffered from hunger?"

Witness after witness had testified to their observations regarding the paucity of the prisoners' rations. Even worse, there was corroborating evidence that "the prisoners were seen scuffling to get at the morsels of food in the swill barrel; they were seen struggling too for potatoe [*sic*] skins and eating them with a ravenous appetite, devouring cattle's feet from which the oil had been extracted, and which were thrown out in their uncleansed state, roasting potatoes and the entrails of cattle in lime and devouring them."[16]

Then follows what is perhaps the commentator's most scathing indictment of the committee's findings:

> Against this mass of evidence, not a syllable, not even the slightest particle of testimony has been produced except the *opinion* of two or three individuals who were occasionally at the Prison, and who thought the rations were sufficient, such as Deacon Stillman. There is not the slightest attempt to prove that before 1830 the rations had been given to the prisoners, and for all this period the Messrs. Pilsburys stand wholly undefended. Condemned by their own books, condemned by the testimony of every officer who has spoken on the subject, and finally condemned by the proof of the disgusting and brutal acts of the prisoners driven to desperation by the extremity of their suffering. If this charge is not proved there is no faith or efficacy in human testimony. There is a degree of wanton cruelty and barbarity in the conduct of the Warden as disclosed in this testimony, which must excite the indignation of every humane man who examines the subject.

Other deprivations were also alleged, and proven, but not to the satisfaction of the committee. For instance, for some six or seven weeks during the summer of 1830 problems arose with the well used to provide water to the prisoners. Apparently, refuse from the kitchen was being emptied into a drain that contaminated the well. One witness testified that it smelled and tasted like putrid clams; another, like stagnant bilge water. Despite his awareness of the problem, and despite the fact that a good well was available only a few feet from the prison entrance, Pilsbury refused to allow the prisoners access to that water. He moved to correct the problem only when pressed by the directors. The commentator, his level of indignation rising to nearly the same level as it had earlier, condemns Pilsbury of being "guilty of an outrage which few men except this Committee will defend or excuse."[17]

The facts relating to the freezing temperatures in the cells have already been discussed. Here is the committee's finding in exonerating Pilsbury on this accusation:

> The Committee are aware that there is a great difficulty in using artificial heat and at the same time preserving a pure atmosphere where so much is consumed, by the perpetual breathing of so many men! But from all the testimony which the Committee have heard on this part of the case, they are persuaded the convict, when once in his cell, enjoys as much of warmth and purity as are to be found in the filled tenements of a crowded city, and at no time does he suffer more hardships than an ordinary seaman on a voyage.[18]

In fairness to Amos Pilsbury, this particular issue was really a dispute between two directors, Welles and Huntington, the newly appointed director and, not insignificantly, a political foe of Welles. The commentator suggests that Huntington's sole intent in prison matters was marked by a spirit of opposition to Mr. Welles. The commentator continues:

> Mr. Welles in December 1831, thinks the prisoners suffers from *cold*. Mr. Huntington the next week with the thermometer at zero, thinks they suffer from heat. Mr. W. think the air offensive; Mr. H. thinks it sufficiently pure. Mr. W. prefers a ventilation by heated air through the ventilation furnace. Mr. H. prefers a ventilation by cold air through the windows and doors, in December and January; Mr. Huntington appears to have been influenced by this contentious spirit throughout, and who can "set down or sum up" the amount of suffering it has occasioned the unhappy convicts.

Another accusation, certainly not nearly as odious as the others, dealt with Pilsbury's alleged disregard for the prison regulations. He was accused of allowing inmates to leave the prison grounds on personal errands, including walking his children to school. He was also accused of appropriating the services of male and female prisoners in his kitchen, the total value of which was about $3,000.00.

Again chastising the committee for its complete disregard of overwhelming testimony, the commentator states, "But there is another light in which the practice may be considered as still more glaring. We mean the promiscuous intermingling in the Warden's kitchen of these abandoned women with the male convicts. The bare statement of the fact is enough to raise the question, how any Committee sensible to the decencies and moralities of life could have given even it implied sanction to such a practice."

The final charge was nearly as egregious as the ones relating to starvation and freezing. Pilsbury was accused of illegally punishing inmates "for breaches of the Prison discipline." One of the features of Wethersfield that Louis Dwight was particularly proud to emphasize was its disavowal of the whip as a disciplinary tool. Obviously, if the Pilsburys were disinclined to use the whip, they had to come up with some alternate punishment that would encourage compliance with prison rules. Their solution, which was specifically permitted in the by-laws, but only under limited circumstances, was to confine prisoners to their cells while also removing their bedding and boarding up the small door opening to leave them in complete darkness.

The commentator is quick to note, however, that the by-laws only permitted the removal of bedding in cases where the prisoner "injures the furniture of his cell." The evidence, however, was replete with instances where Pilsbury had used this punishment indiscriminately, as a means of punishing even the most minor violations. Although obviously not as physically painful as a whipping, Pilsbury's favored punishment certainly presented its own brand of suffering.

In the winter, especially, the inmate found himself in a pitch-black cell for as much as a week at a time, with no bedding and little clothing for protection from the bitter cold that permeated the entire cellblock. Dr. Woodward had testified that one such prisoner, Whitman, had actually suffered frostbite while in his cell.

The summer was probably not much better, as the prisoner was confined to his small space, with no air circulation to offer even the slightest relief from the heat and humidity, to say nothing of the stench emanating from his bucket.

The psychological elements of this punishment were probably as intense as the physical ones. The committee attempted to dismiss its severity, however, by stating that the duration of this punishment was within the complete control of the prisoner. "In taking the bed of the prisoner," the committee reported, "he is left to his choice, the moment he submits, a rap on his cell door, (which can be heard in every part of the Hall) will bring a watchman to the spot, he can have his bed again, and lay himself down, and go to sleep."[19]

The commentator is quick to point out that the committee was in error in concluding that the inmate was in such control of his fate. He comments:

> It is rather difficult to suppose that the writer of this statement believed in its truth. In a few sentences above he states that this was practiced as a *punishment*, and had nearly "superceded" all others, for prison offenses. And does he *now* mean to state that a prisoner guilty of an offence or which he is about to be *punished*, can escape by simply rapping upon his cell door and submitting? It must follow as a matter of course, from such an *ingenious device*, that a prisoner may infringe any rule or disobey any order, and *escape punishment*, unless indeed *it is his pleasure to suffer*. [Emphasis in original]

On each and every charge, then, the committee found in favor of Amos Pilsbury. In light of such strong evidence proving culpability, however, it is certainly difficult to conclude that the committee acted with anything close to the impartiality that is expected of such inquiries. History has seen fit simply to accept the fact of Pilsbury's exoneration and has not troubled itself with examining the correctness of that conclusion. Certainly that has been the case with the more prominent scholarly texts on prison history. Stuart Holbrook, in *Dreamers of the American Dream*, summarizes the entire episode in three sentences:

> The temporary retirement of Amos Pilsbury was occasioned by political appointees to the state board of prisons who preferred a warden more amenable to suggestions. There was not much "give" to the granite Pilsbury. He resigned at once, then demanded an investigation by a legislative com-

mittee. His stand was wholly exonerated, and he returned as warden within a few months.[20]

Orlando Lewis, in his classic *The Development of American Prisons and Prison Customs, 1776–1845*, gives the incident slightly more attention, but not much:

> The charges against the administration of Mr. Pilsbury were investigated by a Legislative Committee in 1832, and were typical of similar allegations against prison executives rising from time to time in other States. Briefly, it was claimed that the account were not kept according to law; that the prisoners were not getting enough food; that for several weeks they were furnished with bad water; that they suffered from cold and bad air; that the sick were treated with great cruelty; that the by-laws were disregarded; that there were depredations upon public property; that the prisoners were illegally punished, and that prisoners were permitted to leave the prison.
>
> In general, the charges were either "not proved" or "explained."[21]

Blake McKelvey's *American Prisons: A Study in American Social History Prior to 1915* ignores the hearings altogether.[22] His only comment about these years at Wethersfield is: "Connecticut had the good judgment to call the able warden, Moses Pilsbury, from New Hampshire to manage its prison; and for twenty years this self-made administrator, and his son Amos who succeeded him, maintained the best penal institution in the country."

History, then, has pretty much forgotten the events that took place in Wethersfield, Connecticut, in 1830–1831, and Amos Pilsbury went on to achieve prominence as a pioneer in American penal reform.[23] The discussion presented in this chapter may well call into question the appropriateness of history's judgment, but that has not been its primary, or even its incidental, purpose. The facts brought out at the hearing were, in large part, undisputed. The only question was whether they were sufficient to hold Pilsbury accountable for the suffering and privations that occurred under his watch. The fact that the committee exonerated Pilsbury does not alter the fact that such suffering took place.

More to the point in connection with the story of Prince Mortimer is the fact that many of the events did not deal with specific inmates; they affected the entire prison and each and every prisoner, including Prince. In the last years of his life, he endured not only the expected ravages of his extreme age but also the poor diet and bitter cold to which all of the prisoners were subjected.

On March 11, 1834, the heart that for eleven decades had been faithfully giving life to Prince Mortimer decided that it had had enough. More than a century and an ocean removed from where he had commenced his incredibly long and arduous journey, Prince died. The prison kept an area near the banks of the cove where it buried inmates whose remains were not claimed by family. Prince's body was lowered into its unmarked grave, and no doubt the prison chaplain said a prayer in the presence of only the few inmates charged with the task of being pallbearers.

Some eighteen years earlier in Cummington, Massachusetts, a young William Cullen Bryant had just penned *Thanatopsis*, almost immediately acknowledged to be the most significant work of poetry produced to date in America. In writing so perceptively about the role of death as part of the human condition, the seventeen-year-old certainly did not have in mind an old slave who was then languishing in the caverns of Newgate prison, only fifty miles to the south. In his final hours however, Prince might well have taken some comfort from Bryant's closing verse:

> Thou go not, like the quarry slave at night,
> Scourged to his dungeon, but, sustained and soothed
> By an unfaltering trust, approach thy grave
> Like one who wraps the drapery of his couch
> About him, and lies down to pleasant dreams.

· *17* ·

Acidum Arseniosum

The information under which Prince Mortimer was convicted accused him of being "a person of wicked mind and disposition, maliciously intending to poison and murder" George Starr. There can be no doubt that Prince's actions put Starr at great risk. There is also a rational basis for attributing criminal intent to Prince, since Starr's successful probate appeal sixteen years earlier had denied Prince his freedom. But might there not be an alternative, but equally reasonable, basis for explaining Prince's actions?

There is only one piece of evidence relevant to the question, and it is disappointingly inconclusive. One of the Newgate prisoner lists, compiled in 1825 at the behest of Martin Welles and his committee investigating the prison, sets forth the prisoners' names, along with each's date of conviction, crime, and age. Under the last column next to Prince's name, the warden inscribed, "He says old enough to know better."

Assuming Prince actually said those words, they constitute the only reported statement directly attributable to him throughout his entire life. Unfortunately, it is so ambiguous as to shed no light at all on what, if anything, might have been motivating Prince on August 5, 1811.

Arsenic is certainly a dangerous poison, and in Prince's time was used extensively, both on land and at sea, to control vermin. Despite its inherent danger, however, arsenic was also well established as a component in several medications used to treat a variety of ailments. Nor was such treatment relegated to the outer fringes of medical practice; a number of treatises, authored by prominent physicians in the early nineteenth century, cautiously advocated the medicinal use of arsenic. Although antibiotics have generally replaced arsenic in modern medicine, it does continue to be administered in some skin disorders and blood dyscrasias.[1]

Acidum arseniosum is a by-product of the process of smelting cobalt. The acid is initially gaseous, but then condenses into a loose gray powder. The early nineteenth-century manufacturing process then involved mixing that powder with potash and heating it again, after which the arsenic assumed its ultimate form as white lumps, which were then crushed into a powder.

On occasion, arsenic was mistaken for sugar, and obvious dreadful consequences would ensue. Could this have been the case with Prince? In stating he was old enough to know better, might the old slave simply have been chastising himself for not being attentive enough to avoid making a stupid—yet potentially fatal—mistake when dissolving what he thought was sugar in his master's chocolate drink?

Alternatively, of course, Prince's statement can just as easily be viewed as a complete admission of guilt, indicating that he should have been wise enough to avoid becoming involved in an ill-conceived scheme to murder George Starr.

A third possibility, however, hovering somewhere between those two interpretations, also suggests itself. Rather than trying to do in his master, could Prince have been attempting to engage in some amateur doctoring, providing some surreptitious assistance to a perhaps stubborn old man who was refusing to seek treatment for some undisclosed malady?

The suggestion is not as outlandish as it might initially appear. By this time, arsenic's medicinal uses were solidly established. In 1810, Dr. John Redman Coxe, a physician and professor of chemistry at the University of Pennsylvania, published the second edition of *The American Dispensatory*.[2] His list of ailments appropriately treated with an arsenic compound included cancer,[3] intermittent fever (malaria),[4] cutaneous diseases,[5] and rheumatism. As this short list confirms, in 1810 the medical community saw arsenic as beneficially used in treating illnesses as varied as cancer and warts.

By no means did Coxe minimize arsenic's potentially dangerous nature. "No other escharotic possesses equal powers in cancerous affections," he wrote, "but unfortunately its good effects often do not go beyond a certain length, and if in some cases if effects a cure, in others it must be allowed it does harm."[6]

Coxe was hardly alone in espousing such views. Dr. John Bard, writing in Crane's *The American Medical and Philosophical Register* (1811), saw arsenic as useful in the treatment of scrophula, a form of tuberculosis resulting in the inflammation of lymph nodes in the neck that would ultimately evolve into abscesses and ulcers.[7] In Prince's time, scrophula was commonly seen in children, since it was often acquired from drinking unpasteurized milk. Bard relates his success in treating a patient, and completely curing him, by administering "the arsenical solution" at the rate of twelve drops three times a day.[8]

Certainly, Prince would not have had any particular knowledge of the specialized medicinal uses of arsenic. The treatises discussed above do demonstrate, however, that arsenic was in common use as a treatment for a wide variety of illnesses, and so it would not be unexpected for Prince to be at least generally aware of its medicinal properties. That likelihood becomes even greater when considered in the light of Prince's own affliction with yaws. A comprehensive and nearly contemporaneous discussion of the illness is given in Robert Thomas, *Modern Domestic Medicine* (1829).[9] Dr. Thomas had spent time in the West Indies and had practical experience with this primarily tropical disease. One of his recommended treatments for the early stages of yaws was to administer internally a mixture of sublimed sulphur and antimonial powder. He then suggested "washing them down with a decoction of the woods, such as sarsaparilla, &c."[10]

One of the tonics set out in Thomas's text describes the ingredients for making decoction of bark; the formula includes, not surprisingly, a "solution of arsenic, four drops to eight."[11]

If such treatment was being made available to yaws patients in such a remote area as the West Indies, it is even more likely that Prince's masters, situated in a well-populated and prosperous town like Middletown, Connecticut, would have made at least equivalent treatment available to him. Prince himself, then, may well have had personal experience with arsenical solutions at some point or points in his long life. If so, obviously a much stronger case can be made for the likelihood of his familiarity, even as a slave, with arsenic's medicinal uses. Even if that was not the case, it certainly appears that, along with the general population, he would have had at least a passing acquaintance with such use, much to the same degree that most of us, not schooled in medicine, have a passing acquaintance with antibiotics. We certainly are not familiar with the particulars of their various formulations, but we do know what they are and what they are capable of treating.

Of course, the mystery of whether Prince acted criminally, innocently, or naively can never be solved. If he was justly convicted, his life still remains an unusual example of perseverance in the face of extraordinarily prolonged injustices. If, in addition to all that he endured, he was unjustly convicted, his life becomes all the more tragic.

Postscript

$\mathscr{P}$rince Mortimer probably still would recognize many aspects of the Middletown of the twenty-first century, even though nearly all the buildings of his time have long since given way to more modern replacements. Main Street, which in Prince's day was wide enough to house the town courthouse and schoolhouse in its center, has yielded none of that width to progress. The Connecticut River is still there, of course, but an eight-lane highway denies convenient access to its banks.

The harbor itself is not even a shadow of its former self; the shoreline offers no evidence of the area's former maritime glory. A restaurant and a small park now occupy the space where tall ships once docked to unload their precious cargo from foreign ports, and the slavers theirs. The view, however, remains essentially the same; the combination of the river's change in direction, coupled with the treed slopes gently rising from each shore, is still as inviting and pleasing to the eye as it was when Philip Mortimer sat on his porch and took it in with young Philip at his side.

Mortimer's home, his "mansion," as he described it in his will, was lost to the railroad in the 1870s. By that time, the ropewalk had long since suffered a similar fate. One component of Middletown's geography, however, remains as readily identifiable as ever: Mortimer Cemetery. Completely enclosed by high stone walls and iron fences, it counts a somewhat larger population than it had in 1794, when Philip Mortimer was laid to rest beneath his modest gravestone.

George Starr is Philip's immediate neighbor, only a few yards distant. His sepulcher, set into a small hillside, is imposing when compared with Mortimer's humble flat stone and looks down directly at him. One cannot help but wonder whether this was Starr's final retort to the man who, through his last will and testament, would have denied Starr his progeny.

Newgate Prison still stands, although many of the buildings are in ruins following a fire in 1904, as well as the expected destructive effect of more than two hundred winters on their fragile stone walls. Thanks to the efforts of the former Connecticut Historical Commission, the perimeter wall is still intact, as is the guardhouse. Designated a National Historic Landmark in 1973, Newgate is regularly open to the public under the supervision of the Connecticut Commission on Culture and Tourism. Hours are posted on the commission's web site, www.cultureandtourism.org/history/museums.html. In the late 1960s, the caverns became more accessible with the construction of a new accessway built into the western slope. As is the case with Middletown's harbor, the years have done nothing to diminish the beauty of the prison's western view.

Wethersfield Prison did not fare as well. Over the years, the size of the prison had grown considerably. New construction was practically a chronic feature of the prison's landscape, with additions in 1830, 1835, 1846, 1888, 1889, 1895, 1897, 1899, and 1917. In 1963, however, all prison activity came to a halt when a new state prison opened in Somers, three towns away from Granby, Newgate's host community. Just as Prince and his fellow inmates had made the trek south in 1827, now their successors were returning to the rolling hills of northern Connecticut.

Within four years of Wethersfield's abandonment, the prison was demolished, and a new home for the state's motor vehicle department was erected on the site. The only physical evidence that a prison once stood there is a small memorial stone, lying inconspicuously flat at ground level and not far from the banks of Wethersfield Cove, commemorating the unmarked graves of Prince Mortimer and those other prisoners who died during the early decades of the prison's 136 years of operation.

Martin Welles was hit hard by the committee's decision to exonerate Amos Pilsbury. In short order, he resigned as a prison director and withdrew from active involvement in any prison affairs, closing the door on nearly a decade of intense involvement in Connecticut's prison system. He also turned his back on all his years of public service as both a state senator and a representative, where he had served for a time as speaker of the house. Additionally, for some years Welles had been working under an appointment from the legislature to revise the state's criminal laws. He abandoned all involvement in government life, contenting himself for the next three decades with practicing law and overseeing, through his sons, his land investments in Ohio and Illinois. Welles died in Wethersfield in 1863.

After his dismissal and subsequent rehiring, Amos Pilsbury went on to serve as warden at Wethersfield Prison until 1845. If conditions similar to those prevailing in the prison's early years continued after Pilsbury's return to office in 1833, it is difficult to imagine that they would have gone unnoticed or ignored for such a long period. Perhaps Pilsbury, despite his exoneration, was nonetheless chastened by the Welles-inspired investigation and amended his ways and attitudes towards the prisoners whose well-being he controlled. Whatever the cause, those several succeeding years under Amos's administration passed without any renewed criticism of his disciplinary regime.

In 1845, the political community seized upon the warden's position as a worthwhile object of patronage, and Amos Pilsbury was discharged. Even before then, however, Amos had been receiving solicitations from Albany to supervise the construction of a new county prison that would house 600 inmates, more than twice the number at Wethersfield. Now unemployed, Pilsbury finally accepted the offer and ended up spending the next decade as warden at Albany.

Being a county prison, Albany did not hold the same stature as Wethersfield or any other state prison. That did not make the prison any less of a challenge, however, since its population consisted primarily of short-term convicts, and Pilsbury's charge was to keep the prison shops profitable in the face of an ever-changing work force. But he did succeed, managing to turn a profit for the county coffers, just as he had in Wethersfield.

In 1855, at the urging of New York's governor, Pilsbury left Albany to assume a new position as administrator of Ward's Island in New York harbor. Originally intended as a refuge for sick or needy immigrants, the facility had also become a home for a significant population of the city's homeless. During the four years of his tenure, Pilsbury managed to reduce by nearly 80 percent the cost of maintaining the facility, while at the same time significantly improving the condition of its hospital.

Pilsbury's success at Ward's Island caught the attention of the New York City Police Commissioners, who at the time were intent on finding a new superintendent. Knowing that the position had suffered from a lack of authority in the past—the mayor was the real seat of power in the police department—Pilsbury initially rejected their solicitations. Ultimately, he accepted, but only after exacting a written "understanding that all power and authority (consistent with Law) necessary to enable me to fill the office with credit to the public, the Commissioners, and myself, shall be conferred upon me as Chief Executive Officer of the Police Department."

City politics being what they were, it was not long before the commissioners' assurances began to be tested. The election of 1859 saw Fernando Wood returned to office as mayor, and within months he was pressuring Pilsbury to detail a dozen officers to City Hall, thereby removing them from Amos' control. Seeing this request as merely an opening salvo, Pilsbury refused to comply. The mayor took his grievance to the Police Board, which upheld the mayor and effectively withdrew from Pilsbury the very authority he had demanded as a condition of taking the position.

Less than fourteen months after assuming his new position, Amos Pilsbury was proffering his resignation.

Once again, Pilsbury was out of a job, but once again his period of unemployment would be short lived. He was promptly rehired as warden at Albany, where he remained until his death in 1873. In true Pilsbury fashion, Amos's son, Lewis Dwight Pilsbury, made a career of prison administration, eventually becoming the first superintendent of the entire prison system of New York State.

The investigation at Wethersfield Prison did little to dampen the influence of Louis Dwight in the world of prison reform. Even as Pilsbury's version of the Auburn system was under attack, Dwight was successfully convincing a number of other states to adopt the plan in favor of competing efforts by proponents of the Pennsylvania alternative. By 1833, eleven states had joined New York and Connecticut in approving Auburn-inspired prison systems. In contrast, only Pennsylvania, New Jersey, and Maryland had implemented a system of complete solitary confinement.[1]

In succeeding years, however, Dwight's influence began to wane, in large part because of damage he was inflicting on his own credibility by making frequently untrue or outlandish accusations regarding the defects in the Pennsylvania plan of complete prisoner isolation. Nor was his credibility helped when he began revealing his visions for the ultimate implementation of his beloved Auburn plan. Dwight's first hint of this expanded vision occurred in the Prison Discipline Society's Fourth Report, in which he suggested that the Auburn plan presented society at large with "a principle of very extensive application to families, schools, academies, colleges, factories, mechanics' shops."[2]

This suggestion was not an isolated instance of irrational exuberance, to use the modern idiom. In his Eighth Report, Dwight wrote again of his vision regarding the potential application of the Auburn system beyond prison walls. He saw useful application in a variety of public institutions and even in families. Auburn and Wethersfield prisons acted as social observatories, Dwight believed, and he suggested that nocturnal isolation "would be useful, in all establishments, where large numbers of youth of both sexes are assembled and exposed to youthful lusts." Isolation, he also maintained, "would greatly promote order, seriousness, and purity in large families, male and female boarding schools, and colleges."[3]

Such ideas were no more acceptable to the public at large in the 1830s than they would be today. Dwight's influence began to wane, however, primarily because of his intense and intolerant attacks on the Pennsylvania system and its advocates. Dwight was not only a fervent advocate of the Auburn plan; he was still, as he had always been, a religious zealot. For him, the Auburn plan was not merely a proper means of prison administration; it was also a means of assisting troubled souls in finding salvation. In his mind, then, anyone opposed to Auburn was also an enemy of God.

The relationship between Amos Pilsbury and Louis Dwight went back to the days at Concord, when Dwight had been instrumental in convincing Moses to accept the Wethersfield warden position. Throughout the 1830s, their friendship had been constant; Amos even named one of his sons after Dwight. It must have been particularly painful, then, for Dwight to receive a letter from Amos in June 1839, informing him that Amos had gone over to the other side. Dwight had sent out an inquiry letter, probably to a number of wardens, asking for brief responses to a number of questions, among which was: "Are you an advocate for solitary confinement day and night, with solitary labor?"

Of course, the question was describing Dwight's nemesis, the Pennsylvania plan. Page after page of the Prison Discipline Society's annual reports was devoted to criticizing every aspect of that competing system. Imagine Dwight's dismay to read Pilsbury's response:[4]

> I have, since 1833, been in favor of the Pennsylvania system of solitary confinement day and night, with labor. I have believed that it was the carrying out of our system. I believe that there are many difficulties that may happen under our system, that cannot happen under the Pennsylvania system. . . . I have believed that when the public are willing to go to the expense of building a Prison such as they have in Philadelphia and Trenton, (the only two on this principle that I have ever visited,) that it would be an improvement over ours. The cells or rooms are well ventilated, and, if kept clean, must be a very comfortable place for labor, sleep, &c. . . .

If even Amos Pilsbury, the warden of Louis Dwight's pride and joy, the prison he held out as the shining example of his beloved Auburn plan, was wavering, Dwight must have realized that he was in trouble. Indeed, the days of the Auburn plan, and those of the competing Pennsylvania plan as well, were numbered, but Dwight was not destined to see that happen.[5] Louis Dwight died July 12, 1854, after delivering a sermon to the inmates of the South Boston Asylum for the Insane Poor. Lacking the focus and inspiration of its founder, the Boston Prison Discipline Society became a rudderless ship and in short order ceased its activities. During its twenty-nine-year history, however, Dwight and his Society had shamed most states into taking note of the conditions under which they housed their prison population and in the process profoundly affected the development of American prisons and the lives of most of their inmates. The Society left as its legacy twenty-nine annual reports that constitute the most comprehensive study of early American prisons in existence.

Notes

Chapter 1: The Trial (pp. 1–8)

1. The ritual dialogue for the clerk's activities in a criminal trial, from the arraignment and reading of the information at the commencement of trial to the taking of the verdict, has changed little since Prince's time. In each clerk's desk was found a daybook, in which the clerk recorded essential information, such as the case being tried, the names of witnesses, and the disposition of the case. On the last page or two of the book were inscribed instructions on how to read the information to the jury and how to solicit the jury's verdict. These instructions do not appear to have been established under authority of any statute or rules of court; rather they have been passed down from generation to generation of court clerks, on the inside back covers of courtroom daybooks throughout the state. The passages set out in the text were taken from the very daybook containing the record of Prince's trial. See Connecticut State Library, State Archives Record Group No. 3, Middlesex County, Judgments and Defaults, 1798–1904.

2. Much of the information regarding yaws is extracted from Hackett, C. J., *An International Nomenclature of Yaws Lesions*, 1957, published by the World Health Organization. A warning to those who might have an inclination to pursue this subject in greater detail: the photographic case studies are explicit and may well be very disturbing to many readers.

3. Ironically, in 1638 Connecticut was the first colony to adopt a "constitution"; for 180 years, its Fundamental Orders would operate as the essential document regulating all aspects of the colony's legal system. In 1818, however, the state would be the last of the original states to adopt a constitution based on the federal concept of separation of powers. The story of the state's prolonged debate over its constitutional destiny is an interesting one, best described in Wesley Horton's *The Connecticut Constitution: A Reference Guide*, Greenwood Press, 1993. Those seeking a more abbreviated account of this subject should consult two articles appearing in the same issue of the *Connecticut*

Bar Journal: Henry S. Cohn, "Connecticut Constitutional History—1636–1776" and Wesley W. Horton, "Connecticut Constitutional History—1776–1988," both published in the *Connecticut Bar Journal*, Volume 64, No. 5, October 1990. Lay readers should not be deterred by the fact that these histories are published in a legal journal; both articles are eminently readable and highly informative accounts of the developing legal system under which Connecticut's colonial population lived, worked, and died.

4. There were other defendants, however, who were similarly prosecuted of common law crimes in disregard of statutory requirements, and who sought redress in the courts. One such person was Steven Danforth. In 1818, Danforth was imprisoned in the county jail in New Haven. In an escape attempt, he attacked the jailer with a heavy piece of oak taken from the top of a hogshead, striking him on the head five times, clearly with an intent to kill. Danforth was charged with a common law crime, by means of an information rather than the statutory crime, which would have required an indictment by a grand jury. In this account of Prince's trial, the supposed arguments of the parties are taken from the state Supreme Court's decision in *State v. Danforth*, which sets out at considerable length the legal arguments surrounding the issues being raised. Interestingly, in upholding Danforth's common law conviction, the court relies to some degree on precedent, mentioning the fact that, in the course of the preceding seventeen years, there had been five similar convictions of persons under common law prosecutions in disregard of the statutes. One of those five was Prince Mortimer.

Chapter 2: The Early Years (pp. 9–19)

1. Although Whittier was only a boy of four at the time, the severity of this storm and its aftereffects left an impression on him that was to last a lifetime; it would be fifty-five years before the Massachusetts Quaker would reach back into his earliest memories to relate his recollections of this storm of the century. The blizzard's intensity would not be matched until the famous blizzard of 1888.

Whittier's experience with the blizzard of 1811 in his childhood home of Haverhill, near the shoreline north of Boston, was not unique to that part of the northeast. Middletown, along with the rest of southern New England and Long Island, was also buried in gigantic drifts that trapped people in their homes for days.

2. The most authoritative source for information on weather in early America is David M. Ludlum, *The History of American Weather: Early American Winters, 1604–1820*, American Meteorological Society, Boston, 1966. Ludlum's account draws heavily from newspaper reports and a number of personal diaries to piece together a history of this era's weather that provides not only an accurate history of weather but also an interesting account of the men who were America's first weathermen. Weather observation at that time was always just an avocation, and its enthusiasts came from such divers professions as politics, farming, and the ministry.

3. Middletown's maritime history, although richest in the years before, during, and immediately after the Revolution, did continue to varying extents well beyond the town's declining reliance on the river in the early 1800s as its primary commercial

element. For a comprehensive discussion of the town's maritime history, see James L. McConaughty's essay, "Maritime Middletown," published as part of *A Pamphlet Containing Two Articles on Middletown and the Connecticut River*, James D. Young Company, Middletown, 1950.

4. The most complete source for information on the geography, geology, and history of the Connecticut River is Walter Hard, *The Connecticut*, Rinehart, New York, 1947. Hard devotes an entire chapter to Middletown, in which he traces the town's connection to the river from its earliest beginnings in the mid-1600s through the following two centuries. Hard sees Middletown's experience as a microcosm of the American experience, not only during that period but also considerably before. Consider the last paragraph of the chapter: "So here at the great bend in the river one may see the march of American civilization since the day when Adriaen Block first discovered the village of Sequins, the smoke from whose signal hill had been spreading tidings for red generations. And across the river to this day the tracks of the dinosaur are visible in the sandstone quarries, carrying the story back to the days before man came to the valley."

5. In view of the fact that Prince remained active for such a long period, there is a good possibility that he was spared the worst symptoms that yaws had to offer and that the disease simply arrested at a stage that still permitted Prince to work. Even if this did occur, however, Prince definitely continued to suffer from the disease well into his seventies, if not later. The inventory of Philip Mortimer's estate, filed with the Probate Court in 1796 when Prince was about seventy-two, describes him as "sick with yaws."

6. A good account of the type of treatment that would have been available to Prince is given in Robert Thomas, M.D., *Modern Domestic Medicine: Being a Treatise Divested of Professional Terms on the Nature, Causes, Symptoms, and Treatment of the Diseases of Men, Women, and Children in Both Warm and Cold Climates*, 1829. Dr. Thomas had spent time in the tropics and was personally familiar with yaws and its symptoms. In yaws' early stages, Thomas recommended assistance in bringing out the eruptions with a mixture of sublimed sulphur either given by itself or mixed with "two grains of antimonial powder, and ten of that of gum of guaiacum, washing them down with a decoction of the woods, such as sarsaparilla, &c." Once the eruptions became dry, Thomas suggested administering a mild preparation of mercury. He did give this caution, however: "But should the salivary glands and mouth shew [sic] the mercurial influence, by a discharge of spittle or great tenderness in the gums, the further use of mercury should be suspended for a time, and then be recommenced in smaller doses."

7. In comparison to the extensive material detailing the development of southern plantation slavery, northern slavery has not generated a significant body of research. The single most informative study of slavery in Connecticut is Ralph Foster Weld's essay, "Slavery in Connecticut," commissioned in 1933 by the Tercentenary Commission of the State of Connecticut.

8. See Joel Lang, "The Plantation Next Door: How Salem Slaves, Wethersfield Onions and West Indies Sugar Made Connecticut Rich," *The Hartford Courant, Northeast Magazine*, September 29, 2002.

9. The ropewalk has all but disappeared from the American landscape. In the

heyday of sailing ships, these structures dotted the eastern coastline, with every ship-building community having at least one ropewalk in the vicinity. More massive than the ships they supplied, one by one these long slender buildings gave way to progress and development. The reasons for their demise varied: reduced demand was the principal culprit, of course, resulting from the advent of the steam engine. But another factor was the fact that each of these structures occupied a tremendous amount of land that was almost always in a commercial area near the water. As the area's commercial development intensified, the value of the land consumed by the ropewalk's vast size eventually exceeded the economic value of the facility, and so the ropewalk yielded its space to other activities.

Over fifty years ago, Samuel Eliot Morison, one of America's foremost twentieth-century historians, documented the story of one particularly resilient ropewalk in Plymouth, Massachusetts. His account, *The Ropemakers of Plymouth: A History of the Plymouth Cordage Company, 1824–1949*, Arno Press, 1976, c. 1950, was written only a year or so after the company had closed its doors on a century and a quarter of activity.

A portion of the Plymouth ropewalk was saved for posterity when a 250-foot section of the building was relocated to Connecticut's Mystic Seaport. Even at that length, the building is imposing; how much more impressive it must have been at its original size, more than four times the length of the preserved section.

Much like the ships it served, to the colonial mind the ropewalk evoked memories and feelings that went far beyond the building itself and the product it generated. Nowhere is this better exemplified than in Longfellow's poem, *The Ropewalk*, published in 1859. By that time, some degree of manufacturing had already been introduced into the process, but it is clear that Longfellow is reaching back to an earlier era, certainly one with which Prince would be completely at home.

THE ROPEWALK

In that building, long and low,
With its windows all a-row,
Like the port-holes of a hulk,
Human spiders spin and spin,
Backward down their threads so thin
Dropping, each a hempen bulk.

At the end, an open door;
Squares of sunshine on the floor
Light the long and dusky lane;
And the whirring of a wheel,
Dull and drowsy, makes me feel
All its spokes are in my brain.

As the spinners to the end
Downward go and reascend,
Gleam the long threads in the sun;

While within this brain of mine
Cobwebs brighter and more fine
By the busy wheel are spun.

Two fair maidens in a swing,
Like white doves upon the wing,
First before my vision pass;
Laughing, as their gentle hands
Closely clasp the twisted strands,
At their shadow on the grass.

Then a booth of mountebanks,
With its smell of tan and planks,
And a girl poised high in air
On a cord, in spangled dress,
With a faded loveliness,
And a weary look of care.

Then a homestead among farms,
And a woman with bare arms
Drawing water from a well;
As the bucket mounts apace,
With it mounts her own fair face,
As at some magician's spell.

Then an old man in a tower,
Ringing loud the noontide hour,
While the rope coils round and round
Like a serpent at his feet,
And again, in swift retreat,
Nearly lifts him from the ground.

Then within a prison-yard,
Faces fixed, and stern, and hard,
Laughter and indecent mirth;
Ah! it is the gallows-tree!
Breath of Christian charity,
Blow, and sweep it from the earth!

Then a school-boy, with his kite
Gleaming in a sky of light,
And an eager, upward look;
Steeds pursued through lane and field;
Fowlers with their snares concealed;
And an angler by a brook.

Ships rejoicing in the breeze,
Wrecks that float o'er unknown seas,

Anchors dragged through faithless sand;
Sea-fog drifting overhead,
And, with lessening line and lead,
Sailors feeling for the land.

All these scenes do I behold,
These, and many left untold,
In that building long and low;
While the wheel goes round and round,
With a drowsy, dreamy sound,
And the spinners backward go.

Chapter 3: *The Will to Be Free (pp. 20–30)*

1. Middletown's contribution to the war effort was certainly not limited to its shipbuilding. Even before the war, Philip Mortimer served as one of seventeen men in the town's Committee of Correspondence, set up to inspect the conduct of its citizenry and root out any British sympathizers. In the earliest days of the war, Captain Return Jonathan Meigs, along with fifty-six others from Middletown, promptly rushed to Boston after the first skirmishes at Lexington and Concord. Off the battlefield as well, Middletown contributed to the war effort in a variety of ways. Some of its men served as privateers, preying on British merchant vessels, and the town itself became one of the primary supply depots for the Continental Army's operations in New York.

The most complete discussion of Middletown's varied role in the war effort can be found in Albert E. Van Dusen's *Middletown and the American Revolution*, published in 1950 by the Middlesex County Historical Society as part of the city's tercentenary celebration, later reprinted by James D. Young Company, Middletown, 1976.

2. The law is very particular in describing different types of testamentary dispositions. A person making a will is said to "devise" real property and to "bequeath" personal property.

3. Only some three years earlier, the very courthouse in which Prince would later be tried and convicted had been erected at a cost of £850, by subscription pledges of the City's most prominent citizens. Thus, Mortimer's bequest was ample to cover the cost of construction of the granary and also was not an insubstantial percentage of his liquid assets.

Chapter 5: *Probate (pp. 36–41)*

1. John Warner Barber, *Connecticut Historical Collections, Containing a General Collection of Interesting Facts, Traditions, Biographical Sketches, Anecdotes, etc. Relating to the History and Antiquities of Every Town in Connecticut, with Geographical Descriptions, Illustrated by 190 Engravings*, Durrie & Peck and J.W. Barber, New Haven, 1849.

Without doubt, Barber (1798–1885) was the nineteenth century's most prolific writer of early state histories. In addition to the Connecticut edition, he wrote similar book-length histories of Massachusetts, New York, New Jersey and Pennsylvania, as well as substantial histories of individual communities, such as New Hartford and New Haven, Connecticut. He also wrote extensively on American history beyond these states; his titles, hardly humble in their self-aggrandizement, left no doubt in the reader's mind as to the scope of the text that lay beneath the cover page. His 1860 work, for instance, was entitled: *Thrilling Incidents in American History; Being a Selection of the Most Important and Interesting Events Which Have Transpired Since the Discovery of America to the Present Time.*

The following year, Barber brought in a co-author and expanded the text, as well as the title. *Our Whole Country; or, The Past and Present of the United States, Historical and Descriptive. In Two Volumes, Containing the General and Local Histories and Descriptions of Each of the States, Territories, Cities, and Towns of the Union; Also Biographical Sketches of Distinguished Persons. Illustrated by Six Hundred Engravings, Almost Wholly from Drawings Taken on the Spot by the Authors, the Entire Work Being on Their Part the Result of Over 16,000 Miles of Travel and Four Years of Labor.*

Barber's skills at communication were not limited to the written word. He was also an adept artist, and his histories are embellished with numerous drawing and sketches of the locales his text describes. Some, like the Middletown Main Street sketch, are fairly rudimentary, but others are quite detailed and provide a wealth of pictorial information on America before the advent of photography.

Chapter 7: *The Conviction Revisited (pp. 49–57)*

1. Apparently, selling a ropewalk was not a simple task; for much of the prior year, George Starr had run this same ad in the Middletown Gazette:

Ropewalk for sale
For sale, that well known Rope Walk, situated in the Main Street—for many years owned and occupied by the subscriber, with the Stock, Tools, etc. with or without the stock on hand. Said Walk for situation, length, and convenience, is not equaled in this State. The terms of payment will be made easy. Apply to George Starr or J. Lawrence Lewis.

Chapter 8: *To Newgate (pp. 58–69)*

1. This was the storm that Whittier would later immortalize in his epic "Snowbound." For an informative discussion of weather in America's early years, see Ludlum, *Early American Winters 1604–1820*, American Meteorological Society, Boston, 1966.

2. The most definitive discussion of Connecticut's early roads is Isabel S. Mitchell's *Roads and Road-Making in Colonial Connecticut*, an essay published in 1933 by the Tercentenary Commission of the State of Connecticut. Mitchell's account relates in great detail the particulars of Connecticut's long and difficult experience with road building.

Primarily, the problem lay in the way towns developed in the state, each around a town green, with property around the green being allocated to the residents for house lots, grazing lots, and farming. As the town grew, new inhabitants of the increasingly distant homesteads were confronted with the fact that their only way to town was by obtaining permission of other lot owners, many of whom were uncooperative, not wanting their grazing lots cut up by a road that would then have to be fenced.

The situation was even worse when it came to constructing roads between towns. In addition to the fact that the terrain was exceedingly difficult, there was no colonywide system for paying for these improvements. Each town was obligated to contribute both money and men to the effort, and most towns did so begrudgingly, if at all. Even as late as the time of the revolution, the general condition of the roads was extremely poor. Mitchell reports that in 1774, a surveyor inspecting the portion of the Lower Post Road from Stonington to New London wrote that the road was "past all conception bad," consisting of one continuous bed of rocks.

3. Many people mistakenly believe that there was only a single Post Road, beginning in New York and running through the Connecticut shoreline communities, along what is now U.S. Route 1. Although that route, known as the Lower Road, is certainly the most famous stretch of the Post Road, in fact there existed two other Post Roads. The Upper Post Road began in New Haven and headed north, slightly east of the modern Route 15, all the way to Hartford. There, the Road split again—the Upper Road continued north to Springfield, then turned east to Worcester and ultimately Boston. The Middle Post Road headed east from Hartford and veered northeast just before the Rhode Island line, joining the Lower Post Road in Dedham, about twenty miles south of Boston. For a complete history of the Boston Post Roads, see Stewart H. Holbrook, *The Old Post Road: The Story of the Boston Post Road*, McGraw-Hill, New York, 1962.

4. Even the title of Stuart's book tells much of the strong, self-assured personality of its author. *Sketches in the Life of William Stuart* was published by Stuart himself in 1856. Its subtitle continues, "The First and Most Celebrated Counterfeiter of Connecticut; Comprising Startling Details of Daring Feats Performed by Himself—Perils by Sea and Land—Frequent Arrests and Imprisonment—Blowing Out of Jail with Powder—Failure of Escape after He Had Led His Cowardly Associates Out of The Horrible Pit, in Simsbury, Into the Prison Yard, &c." It is obvious from Stuart's accounts that he survived his many ordeals through the liberal use of his wit and cunning. Except for one incident that will be discussed at length later on, he does not appear to have been a violent person, but instead confined his activity to crimes against property.

He certainly had little respect for authority, but it appears that he used his wit, rather than defiance, as his primary tool in showing that lack of respect. The following colloquy is representative of Stuart's manner of interacting with authority: "After the judge had sentenced me, I rose and asked his honor this question: "Suppose, sir," I said, "I die before my five years expire, shall I have to provide a substitute to serve out the remainder of my term? I hate to cheat the state; will you please to inform me in these matters, for I am ignorant of the law?" The judge smiled, and told me that in case of death these things would not be required of me. I felt better after the sentence of the court, convinced that justice would be subserved by my punishment."

5. For a discussion of the navy's long love affair with flogging, see Glenn, *Campaigns Against Corporal Punishment*, State University of New York Press, Albany, 1984.

Chapter 9: Early Newgate (pp. 70–77)

1. The Simsbury Copper Mines, as they were originally named, over the years have come within the limits of three different towns. In 1786, a portion of the Town of Simsbury, which included the mines, was set out as the new town of Granby. In 1858, Granby itself was subdivided, and the mines found themselves within the limits of the newly created town of East Granby.

2. Richard Phelps, in his classic *Newgate of Connecticut: Its Origin and Early History* (1844), suggests that Higley got carried away with his minting and soon started to issue his own copies of legal coinage. Phelps hesitates to call this activity counterfeiting; he notes that there is no record of a prosecution of Higley for that offense, but he also comments that Higley, upon being informed that he was infringing on the royal prerogative, was eventually persuaded to "suspend operations." In later years, counterfeiting became quite a popular crime; an 1810 list of Newgate prisoners notes that six of its forty-six prisoners were incarcerated for that offense. The punishment was quite severe, with prison terms varying from two years to as much as twelve years. Apparently, Higley, by managing to avoid prosecution altogether, did much better in this regard than his successors.

3. The popular belief is that Connecticut's Newgate was named after London's infamous prison bearing the same name, in the hope that the terror instilled by the English dungeon would rub off on Connecticut's neophyte copy. At least one scholar has disputed this notion. See Scanlon, "New Gate, New-Gate, or Newgate?" *Connecticut History*, Summer 1977, in which the professor asserts that the adoption of the name was not made at the time of the authorizing legislation, but was chosen entirely at random at a later time. In view of the fact that Connecticut's Newgate quickly acquired its own infamy as a place of misery, if not terror, the issue seems somewhat inconsequential.

4. Although Newgate's convict population harbored the worse criminals the colony, and then the state, had to offer, there were never any murderers confined there. The reason for that fact was obvious—murder was a capital offense, and those convicted of that crime promptly served their sentence at the end of the hangman's rope.

5. A modern visitor to Newgate will find a somewhat larger cavern. In 1830, two years after the prison's relocation to Wethersfield, the Phoenix Mining Company acquired the property from the state and attempted to resume mining. This effort continued for several years; as a consequence, the cavern was excavated to a total length of about 800 feet, and width of almost 300 feet. The height of the cavern also appears to have been enlarged from the five-foot height mentioned in the earliest reports.

6. See note 2 of chapter 8 for more information about this intriguing volume.

7. As meaningful as was the plight of the Tories in Newgate, the incident has not been the focus of much scholarly or even popular inquiry. There is but a single source for any appreciable amount of information about this period: *Newgate of Connecticut: Its Origin and Early History*, by Richard H. Phelps. First published in 1844, Phelps' book is replete with apparently long-lost references to primary and secondary source material about the Tories in Newgate.

8. The Tory problem was a major stumbling block in the peace negotiations that followed the war. England was pressing to have its supporters reinstated to all of the property they had owned before the war and even sought reparations for those cases where such restoration was not possible. The American sentiment was quite hostile to such notions, since there was not enough money in the new country's coffers to pay its loyal soldiers, let alone to expend any portion of its modest coffers on reparations to persons they still saw as traitors. In the end, a compromise was reached—Tory property would be returned to their former owners *as far as possible* (meaning that if the property had been destroyed during the war, there was no obligation to compensate for the loss), and the Tories would also be able to enforce pre-war debts. Also, the Tories were protected against prosecution for acts they had committed during the war. This final provision must have been particularly welcome to the Tories who, on three separate occasions, had expressed their frustrations by setting fire to Newgate prison.

Chapter 10: Mortimer, Prince (pp. 78–92)

1. Despite Newgate's prominent notoriety in the history of American penology, it has not commanded much attention on the part of commentators on that history. In the last two centuries only two writers have seen fit to relate Newgate's story with anything more than a superficial reference in a text on penology or in a newspaper or magazine article. The first, of course, is Richard Phelps's 1844 classic, *Newgate of Connecticut: Its Origin and Early History*, still available in reprint from Picton Press, Camden, Maine. Phelps gives a vivid description of the development of the copper mine in the colonial era, its subsequent conversion into a prison and then a holding place for Tories, and its eventual formal adoption by the State of Connecticut as its state prison. It is particularly rich in providing insights into the entire Tory experience in the state.

The major flaw in Phelps' presentation is his confusing indifference to chronology. Particularly in the chapters relating to Newgate's physical growth as a state prison, Phelps will relate events in the same paragraph that are years, even decades, apart. This defect can be remedied to a great degree, however, by cross-referencing the only other study of any consequence, William G. Domonell's *Newgate from Copper Mine to State Prison*, Richard Colby, Printer, Litchfield, CT (1998). Domonell's presentation is strictly chronological, tracing Newgate's history on nearly a year-by-year basis. Although perhaps not as colorfully presented as Phelps's, Domonell's study provides additional information not addressed by the earlier work, and his chronological presentation is indispensable for acquiring a full appreciation of Phelps's account. Domonell's inquiry goes even beyond Newgate's prison days, however, and discusses the subsequent reuse of the facility as a mine until 1857, its later use as a privately owned tourist attraction, and finally its development as a state-owned historic museum.

2. *A Revision of Swift's Digest of the Laws of Connecticut*, Volume II, 1853, p. 289.

3. William Stuart, *Sketches in the Life of William Stuart*, p. 193.

4. Charles S. Miller, *Peter Gilkey: A Connecticut Counterfeiter*, a Connecticut Heritage Booklet, 1989, Connecticut Heritage, Oxford, CT.

5. Phelps is quick to point out the gross inaccuracy of this portrayal; he footnotes the passage, stating that "Prince was never shackled, but was a harmless old Negro, and during all the last years of his life enjoyed the freedom of the prison." Unfortunately, Phelps' correction is itself somewhat inaccurate and misleading; although Prince appears to have been afforded some degree of freedom at Newgate, Phelps fails to note, as will be explored in subsequent chapters, that Prince went on to spend several years at Wethersfield prison, where conditions were quite different and the relative freedom of movement afforded at Newgate was but a receding memory.

6. William Stuart, *Sketches in the Life of William Stuart*, p. 173.

7. Prison Discipline Society, Third Report—1828, pp. 17–18.

8. William Stuart, *Sketches in the Life of William Stuart*, p. 165.

Chapter 11: Freedom Delayed (pp. 93–95)

1. Phelps writes, "Once he took his departure, and after rambling around in search of some one he formerly knew, like the aged prisoner released from the Bastille, he returned to the gates of the prison, and begged to be re-admitted to his dungeon home, and in prison ended his unhappy years."

2. Peter D. Hall, *Middletown: Streets, Commerce, and People, 1650–1981, A pamphlet written for the one hundred and fiftieth Anniversary of the Founding of Wesleyan University*, The Stinehour Press, Lunenburg, Vermont, 1981.

Chapter 12: The Counterfeiter (pp. 96–104)

1. See chapter 8, note 4.

2. See chapter 10, note 6, and associated text.

3. William Stuart, *Sketches in the Life of William Stuart*, p. 169.

4. William Stuart, *Sketches in the Life of William Stuart*, p. 173.

5. William Stuart, *Sketches in the Life of William Stuart*, p. 188.

6. This article appeared in the June 10, 1823, edition of the *Connecticut Courant*. The following parenthetical note appears above the headline: "[Omitted last week for want of room.]" Apparently, the editors did not deem an uprising at the state prison to be of greater interest to their readers than articles on farm produce or month-old reports from foreign journalists.

7. William Stuart, *Sketches in the Life of William Stuart*, p. 190.

8. William Stuart, *Sketches in the Life of William Stuart*, p. 204.

9. William Stuart, *Sketches in the Life of William Stuart*, p. 205.
10. William Stuart, *Sketches in the Life of William Stuart*, p. 209.
11. William Stuart, *Sketches in the Life of William Stuart*, p. 219.
12. William Stuart, *Sketches in the Life of William Stuart*, p. 209.

Chapter 13: The Bible Peddler (pp. 105–15)

1. There is only one source of information on the early life of Louis Dwight: *Memoir of Rev. Louis Dwight*, a short biography written shortly after Dwight's death in 1854 by William Jenks, a longtime friend of Dwight's, pursuant to a resolution of the Boston Prison Discipline Society.

2. Both terms are popular designations for nitrous oxide, which is produced by heating nitrate of ammonia to a red heat. Although the gas is still commonly used, particularly for dental procedures, much more is known about its proper administration than was the case in Dwight's time. It is safe to assume that Dwight's misfortune arose from an innocent accident in a chemistry lab, and not as a result of any extracurricular activities on the part of the college student.

3. This nondenominational Christian evangelical publisher had its roots in the New York (1812) and New England (1814) Tract Societies. Headquartered in Texas, and with a board of directors that includes the most prominent evangelists in the country, it continues its work to this day.

4. William Jenks, *Memoir of Rev. Louis Dwight*, p. 14.

5. Jenks writes that Dwight's confinement to a desk "brought on another attack of bleeding," accompanied by "severe pains in the chest."

6. Indications are, however, that this unnamed woman was never executed. In 1824, there were only two executions in Connecticut, both men. In fact, the last female executed in Connecticut was Ocuish Hannah, who was hanged for murder in 1786. Ocuish's execution was notable, not just for the fact that she was female, but also because at the time of her execution she was twelve years old. The incident is rendered even more poignant by the fact that it did not occur in the midst of some seventeenth-century witchcraft frenzy, but some six years after the end of the revolutionary war.

7. See the discussion in chapter 8 of Beccaria's work in the prisons of Europe.

8. A prisoner list compiled in May 1825, shows 117 inmates, and that number probably had increased somewhat by the time of Dwight's visit some six months later. The prison list confirms that these men had not been plucked from the higher levels of society when sentenced to Newgate. Only a relatively small number had been convicted of violent crimes: 10 for rape and 3 for assault or manslaughter. The vast majority were in prison for crimes against property: 57 for burglary, 8 counterfeiters, 9 for breaking in daytime, and 4 horse thieves.

9. The current meaning of "loathsome" connotes an element of detestability inherent in a person's character that is so repulsive as to make another want to turn away. Dwight was probably using the term in a less derogatory sense, referring more to the deplorable conditions under which the inmates were forced to live. It would be completely out of character for a man so imbued with a spirit of Christian charity to

suggest, by the use of such a term, that these men were so depraved as to make him unwilling to make any attempt at providing comfort.

10. Prison Discipline Society, Second Report—1827, p. 59.

11. Martin Welles's name is not consistently spelled the same by various persons or entities mentioned in this account. Legislative reports, etc., refer to Martin as "Welles," whereas Louis Dwight, in his correspondence and in reports of the Society, frequently refers to him as "Wells."

12. Report of the Committee Appointed by the Legislature of Connecticut, to Inspect the Condition of New Gate Prison. Submitted May Session, 1826. Printed by order of the Legislature. New Haven, Printed by J. Barber 1826.

13. James Bump was convicted of burglary on June 11, 1824, to a one-year term. He was thirteen years of age at the time.

14. Welles estimated that, in 1826, there were nearly 700 Newgate alumni walking the streets of Connecticut's cities and towns.

15. The caverns, of course, were by now completely out of the question as a continuing part of the prison. "We feel assured," Welles wrote, "that no Legislator—that no man—can, after visiting this *pit*, ascend from it and say, that this, either in a physical or moral point of view, is a fit and proper place for the confinement and lodging of his fellow man."

16. One element of Newgate's negative balance sheet, completely ignored in Welles' report, was the commonly recognized fact that prison administrators were routinely diverting income, raw materials, sundries, and prisoner labor for their own profit. William Stuart's autobiographical account, *Sketches in the Life of William Stuart*, cites just one example of this type of activity:

> Capt. Tuller was bound to give to each prisoner a suit of clothes at stated periods, and a blanket on which to sleep. The State paid him in cash, and he dealt out or kept the blankets and sold them as he liked. The State gave him five hundred dollars yearly as keeper of the prison. When he received the appointment, he was five hundred dollars in debt and a bankrupt; but after occupying the place for six years he paid off his debts and had remaining $12,000. This excess was obtained by cheating the prisoners out of their allowance, and charging it to the State, as if it had been used for the prisoners. Thus is iniquity punished, whilst other rascals are rewarded for fraud and theft.

One might question the reliability of Stuart's comments, since a mere prisoner could hardly be expected to have access to such information about the keeper's activities. William Stuart, however, was anything but a typical prisoner, either in intellect or cunning. In the several years he spent at Newgate, he certainly had ample opportunity to observe Tuller's methods and discern the keeper's dubious activities in cheating the state.

17. Louis Dwight, Letter to Martin Welles, January 26, 1826. Connecticut Historical Society Museum.

18. Louis Dwight, Letter to Martin Welles, et al., May 20, 1826. Connecticut Historical Society Museum. Dwight's fervor apparently more than compensated for his difficult writing style. His letter continues with this sentence: "If now, it shall appear wise for the legislature to abandon New Gate, which is in the language of the

Commissioners 'all that it ought not to be & nothing that it ought to be,' & to erect a new prison, on the plans proposed by them, which unites all the advantages, which appear to me important, I shall again feel, as I have felt in regard to the proceedings of the Massachusetts Legislature & of the House of Representatives of the United States, that there is no way of encouragement to proceed with new resolution in laying before the proper authorities of the different states the same facts, which were submitted to your own consideration."

19. Louis Dwight, letter to Governor Oliver Wolcott, January 23, 1826, Connecticut Historical Society.

Chapter 14: Three and a Half Feet (pp. 116–28)

1. Apparently, at this stage the intent was to continue using the old name for the new prison, perhaps as a reconciling gesture to those who had argued that the terror associated with the name still provided enough deterrent value to warrant keeping it.

2. It is difficult to do justice to the degree of detail contained in Welles's report without presenting verbatim a portion of it. Although Welles and Dwight were allies in championing the construction of a new prison, they certainly were approaching the project from different perspectives. For Dwight, of course, the social and moral aspects of incarceration were paramount, while Welles's support for a new prison was based more on the economic deficiencies of the existing facility. Here is a portion of Welles's cost-benefit analysis of a possible brick-making facility at the Wethersfield prison:

> We may assume the following statement as exhibiting the proper details of that business—viz.
>
> One man will in a season make of brick 100,000, which are worth at the river bank at least $4 per M.
>
> One cord of wood, which is worth from $3.50 to $4, will burn 4,000 brick.
>
> One yoke of oxen will be sufficient, if the materials are on the ground, to prepare, and with a proper machine fit the clay for ten men, supposing them to do nothing at carting brick.
>
> The result will then stand thus:—Fifty common men will make of brick, each 100,000 during the season—equal to 5,000,000, which at the river bank are worth $20,000. But from this estimate we will deduct one half on account of unforeseen expenses and the different character of the men. The statement, with this deduction, would then stand thus:
>
> Fifty prisoners will make 2,500,000 brick, which are worth, at $4 per M $10,000
>
> | | | |
> |---|---|---|
> | Deduct wood, at $1 per M | | $2,500 |
> | " loss on 5 yoke of oxen, at $10, | | 50 |
> | " keeping same 30 weeks at $1 | | 150 |
> | | | $2,700 |
> | Leaving as the income after all deductions, | | $7,300 |
>
> *Report of the Committee*
> *Appointed by the Legislature of Connecticut,*
> *to Inspect the Condition of New Gate Prison,*
> *Submitted, May Session, 1826, p. 17.*

3. The story of the development of prison systems in the United States has been told frequently, with varying degrees of detail. Two of the better accounts are Harry Elmer Barnes, *The Story of Punishment: A Record of Man's Inhumanity to Man*, Patterson Smith, 2nd ed. Rev. 1972, and Blake McKelvey, *American Prisons: A Study in American Social History Prior to 1915*, Patterson Smith, 1968 [c. 1936]. This chapter does not pretend to give the reader an exhaustive lesson on the subject; a basic understanding of the history of American prison systems, however, is critical to a full appreciation of the role that Louis Dwight and Wethersfield prison played in this story and of the forces that were controlling the conditions under which Prince Mortimer, aged about 103 when Newgate closed, was to live out his remaining years.

4. See the discussion in chapter 8.

5. See chapter 9 for Stuart's description of the Newgate dungeon.

6. Blake McKelvey, *American Prisons*, p. 11.

7. Perhaps the best description of day to day life at Cherry Hill is given in Miriam Allen DeFord's *Stone Walls: Prisons from Fetters to Furloughs*, Chilton Books, 1962. DeFord also provides a glimpse into the terror, or at least fear, that must have seized a new convict about to be inducted into the prison system:

> Cherry Hill was built and operated with just one idea in mind—to make it a model to the world. The building was circular, with all the cells opening outward, each into its small walled exercise yard. The prisoner in each cell worked, ate, and slept in it, and took his exercise alone in his own yard. He saw no other human being except prison officers and official visitors from outside, including clergymen; one or another of these visited him frequently and regularly, talked to him to find out his "state of mind" and to exhort him to better things, and left him reading matter. He was brought into the prison blindfolded, and throughout his term, which might mean the rest of his life, for there were many lifers—he never saw either the rest of the prison or any of his fellow inmates.

8. Prison Discipline Society, First Report—1826, pp. 36–37.

9. Advocates of the Pennsylvania system, for their part, were not any less fervent in their praise of the Eastern and Western state penitentiaries. Even as late as 1854, when the validity of both systems was beginning to be questioned, they were still expressing sentiments such as these:

> Pennsylvania, the precursor of all her sister states in the present system of prison discipline, has justified its wisdom before the world in the practical results of its successful administration in this institution. Anticipated evils, existing more in speculative humanity and morbid philanthropy than in substantive fact, have failed in their realization. Disease and mental imbecility so confidently predicted as necessarily incident to separate confinement, have resulted in health and intellectual improvement. Depraved tendencies, characteristic of the convict, have been restrained by the absence of vicious association, and in the mild teaching of Christianity, the unhappy criminal finds a solace for an involuntary exile from the comforts of social life. If hungry, he is fed; if naked, he is clothed; if destitute of the first rudiments of education, he is taught to read and write; and if he has never been blessed with a means of livelihood, he is schooled in a mechanical art, which in after life may be to him the source of profit and respectability. Employment is not toil nor labor, weariness. He embraces them with alacrity, as contributing to his moral and mental elevation. They help to fill the zodiac of this time, which would otherwise

be spent in unavailing complaint, and fruitless importunity for release. Shut out from a tumultuous world, and separated from those equally guilty with himself, he can indulge his remorse unseen, and find ample opportunity for reflection and reformation. His daily intercourse is with good men, who in administering to his necessities, animate his crushed hopes, and pour into his ear the oil of joy and consolation. He has abundance of light, air, and warmth; he has good and wholesome food; he has seasonable and comfortable clothing; he has the best of medical attendance; he has books to read, and ink and paper to communicate with his friends at stated periods; and weekly he enjoys the privilege of hearing God's holy word expounded by a faithful and zealous Christian minister.

Thus provided, and anxiously cared for by the officers of the prison, he is in a better condition than many beyond its walls guiltless of crime. He labors, but it is for his subsistence, like any other member of the community, and by his industry he relieves that community of the burden of his support.

Report of the Inspectors of the Western Penitentiary, 1854, Legislative documents, 1854, as quoted in Barnes, The Story of Punishment, p. 130.

10. Prison Discipline Society, First Report—1826, p. 37.

11. His somewhat indirect and rather mild criticism consisted of this single sentence: "We do not mean that there is nothing in this institution which admits of improvement; for there have been a few cases of unjustifiable severity in punishments."

12. Beaumont and Tocqueville, *On the Penitentiary System*, p. 201.

13. Ultimately, the cost of construction rose slightly, to about $30,000, because of a last-minute decision to expand the size of the prison yard. This additional cost was offset, however, by making limited use of some of the prisoners' labor during the final stages of construction.

14. Report of the Commissioners Appointed by the Legislature of Connecticut, at Their Last Session, To Build a New State Prison, 1827, pp. 8–9.

15. Of these seven, two were lifers, for murder and attempting to poison. The others were serving fairly short sentences: three for counterfeiting, one for adultery, and one for horse stealing. Thirza Mansfield, convicted of murder in 1825, spent twenty-six years in prison, dying at Wethersfield in 1851 at the age of seventy-one.

16. See chapter 8.

17. Benjamin, Howard W., "Scenes In and Around Granby," *The Connecticut Quarterly*, Volume I (1895).

Chapter 15: Moses and Amos (pp. 129–36)

1. Report of the Directors and Warden of the Connecticut State Prison: submitted to the legislature, May Session, 1828. Printed by Order of the Legislature. New Haven: Printed by Hezekiah Howe. 1828, p. 3.

2. Report of the Directors and Warden, p. 4.

3. Congregationalism may no longer have been the official religion of the rest of the state, but within the prison walls, it remained the order of the day. All prisoners, whether they were Protestant, Catholic, or heathen, or anywhere in between, were compelled to participate in Pilsbury's services.

4. Report of the Directors and Warden, p. 9.

5. Report of the Physician of the Connecticut State Prison, 1828, p. 18.

6. Prison Discipline Society, Third Report—1828, p. 9.

7. Prison Discipline Society, Third Report—1828, p. 13.

8. The burglary conviction is probably an instance of the court's enforcement of the habitual offender law, which is currently under attack in several jurisdictions throughout the country. The theory behind the law is quite simple: an accused who is convicted of a third felony offense has obviously failed at rehabilitation and is beyond hope. Society needs to be protected from such a career criminal and consequently that person is subject to life imprisonment. Prisoners challenging such laws assert that they are inherently unjust, since they do not take into consideration the nature of the prior convictions. It makes no difference whether the offenses were serious assaults or lower-level felonies, such as simple thefts or lesser nonviolent drug-related felonies; in either case, the prisoner's third conviction puts him behind bars for the rest of his life.

9. Apparently his illness, whatever its nature, was not life threatening. Moses retired to Derry, New Hampshire, and passed away in 1848, at the age of seventy.

10. There is but one source for biographical information on Amos Pilsbury: *Sketch of the Life and Public Service of Amos Pilsbury, Superintendent of the Albany Penitentiary, and Late General Superintendent of the Metropolitan Police*, published by Munsell & Rowland, Albany, 1860. The author is anonymous, described in the introductory notice only as "a distinguished gentlemen of New York City, who is familiar with the history of the family, has known the subject of the sketch from early manhood, and watched his successful career as a prison disciplinarian and reformer."

11. This would prove to be a much more formidable challenge than Dwight had encountered with Newgate. The practice of imprisoning persons simply for being in debt had deep roots, extending back many centuries in England and elsewhere. Nineteenth-century Americans may have perceived themselves as enlightened in penal reform, and in many ways they were. The "body execution," however—a creditor's ability to have his judgment debtor thrown in jail until he paid up—would persist in Connecticut well past the middle of the twentieth century.

12. *Report on the Penitentiaries of the United States*, William Crawford (1835), p. 69, Patterson Smith Reprint Series in Criminology, Law Enforcement and Social Problems, Montclair, N.J., 1969.

13. *Tocqueville in America*, George Wilson Pierson, Oxford University Press (1938), The Johns Hopkins University Press, 1996, p. 445.

14. The Frenchmen may have been particularly inclined to accept Welles's invitation because of their motherland's connection to this famous historic home. It was here that Washington and Rochambeau had met to plan the Yorktown campaign.

15. Pierson, *Tocqueville in America*, p. 444.

Chapter 16: Old Soldiers (pp. 137–50)

1. Report of the Directors of the Connecticut State Prison Submitted to the Legislature May Session, 1830. Printed by Order of the Legislature, p. 3.

2. Report of the Directors of the Connecticut State Prison Submitted to the Legislature May Session, 1829. Printed by Order of the Legislature, p. 10.

3. Certificate of Dr. S. B. Woodward, as reprinted in "Minutes of the Testimony Taken Before John Q. Wilson, Joseph Eaton, & Morris Woodruff, Committee from the General Assembly, To Inquire into the Conditions of Connecticut State Prison, Together With Their Report and Remarks Upon the Same," D.S. Porter's Print, Hartford, 1834, p. 14. The circumstances giving rise to this unusual document are discussed in the text.

4. These figures are reported in Martin Welles's counterreport to the committee findings, as set forth in the "Minutes of the Testimony Taken Before John Q. Wilson . . . ," p. 11.

5. "Minutes," p. 11.

6. "Minutes," testimony of John Tuller, a prison guard, p. 35.

7. "Minutes," p. 4.

8. "Minutes," p. 5.

9. "Minutes," p. 8. Here is the portion of the 1832 report to which Welles objected:

> As to the [Physician's] statement in this Report, that "Four of the prisoners have had their feet more or less frozen, one severely," it becomes our duty to remark, that until we read that statement, we were wholly ignorant that any such suffering had existed among the convicts. We have visited the Prison as often as, and indeed oftener that is required by the Statute regulating our duties as Directors; we have always inquired into the complaints of those we found in the hospital. One man in the hospital informed us, that some years ago, and before he came to the Prison, he froze his feet, and that since that time, when severe cold weather came on, his feet had troubled him; with that exception, we have never heard a complaint of frozen limbs from any of the prisoners, nor had we learnt that such was the condition of any one, either from the convicts themselves, or from the attending Physician, until we read it in his Report; nor had we reason to suspect that such might be their condition from the temperature of the atmosphere in any of the apartments occupied by the prisoners.
>
> We have enquired of the Warden, the Deputy Warden, the Chaplain, and the persons employed as overseers and watchmen in the Prison, and they all state they have never known the atmosphere, either in the work shop, or hall surrounding the cells, so cold as to render them so uncomfortable to the occupants, as that the most remote danger of injury by frost could in their estimates be apprehended.
>
> We also remark that greater efforts have been made, and greater expense incurred in endeavoring to warm the apartments of the Prison during the winter past, than in any former year; and the clothing of the prisoners has been equally warm. Under these circumstances, we learned with surprise that any of the convicts had suffered as stated by the Physician—and were no less surprised that the fact was not communicated to the Directors at an earlier day.

10. "Minutes," p. 8.

11. The *Hartford Times*, June 6, 1831, p. 3.

12. "Minutes," p. 14.

13. The vast majority of the witnesses and testimony presented to the Committee substantiated one or more of the various allegations against Pilsbury. Amos, on his

part, presented very few witnesses, and those who testified did little to advance his defense. Timothy Stillman, for instance, was called to testify on Amos's behalf, but nearly all of his direct testimony was with reference to Moses, not Amos. If Stillman's direct examination was inconsequential, his cross-examination was almost ludicrous, and certainly not supportive of Pilsbury's cause:

> *Cross Examined*—*Question:* "Do you know, whether Mr. Pilsbury was paid for his supplies, which you say, he furnished the sick so liberally? *Answer:* "I know nothing about that."
> Q. "Do you know that the sick were always supplied with food?"
> A. "I do not."
> Q. "How do you know that Mr. Pilsbury supplied the bibles and tracts which you say, you say, you saw?"
> A. "I only know he told me so."
> Q. "Did not the State pay for them; and are they not supplied by order of the Directors?"
> A. "I do not know."
> Q. "Do you know that the prisoners were supplied with the rations ordered by the Directors?"
> A. "I do not, I never saw them weighed."
> Q. "Do you know that the sick were allowed to see the Physician when they complained?"
> A. "I do not; but I have no doubt they were"
> Q. "Do you know whether the prisoners complained of bad water?"
> A. "Do not, but don't believe they did."
> Q. "You have taken an active part in the controversy, have you not?"
> A. "I have had something to do with it."
> Q. "Have you written, or carried an article for publication, to any newspaper, respecting this affair?"
> A. "I have."
> Q. "Have you ever said, that as Mr. A.P. was a member of your church, it was the duty of every member to stand by him?"
> A. "I believe, I may have said something of the kind,"
> Q. "Is not Mr. Montague, the present Warden, also a member of your church?"
> A. "He is."
> Q. "Have you thought it the duty of all the church members to stand by him also?"
> A. "I have nothing to say as to Mr. Montague."

14. "Minutes," p. 46.
15. "Minutes," p. 95.
16. "Minutes," p. 99.
17. "Minutes," p. 100.
18. "Minutes," p. 100.
19. "Minutes," p. 110.
20. Doubleday, Garden City, New York, 1957, p. 245.
21. 1922, reprinted by Patterson Smith, 1967, p. 179.
22. 1936, reprinted, Patterson Smith, 1974, p. 11.
23. See the postscript for a brief biographical sketch of Pilsbury's life after he left Wethersfield in 1845.

Chapter 17: Acidum Arseniosum *(pp. 151–53)*

1. Miller-Crane, *Encyclopedia and Dictionary of Medicine, Nursing, and Allied Health*, fifth edition, 1992.

2. The full name of the text, in keeping with the early eighteenth-century style in such matters, is *The American Dispensatory, Containing The Operations of Pharmacy; together with the Natural, Chemical, Pharmaceutical and Medical History of the different Substances employed in Medicine; illustrated and explained, according to the principles of modern chemistry: comprehending The Improvements in Dr. Duncan's Fourth Edition of the Edinburgh New Dispensatory; The Arrangement Simplified, and the Whole Adapted to the Practice of Medicine and Pharmacy in the United States.*

3. "Of arsenious acid dissolved in distilled water, in the proportion of four grains to a pint. A table spoonful of this solution, mixed with an equal quantity of milk, and a little syrup of poppies is directed to be taken every morning fasting, and the frequency of the dose gradually increased until six table spoonfuls be taken daily" (p. 239).

4. "Sixty-four grains of arsenious acid, with an equal quantity of carbonate of potass, are to be boiled together until the arsenious acid is dissolved, when as mach water is to be added as will increase the solution to one pound. Of this, from two to twelve drops may be given once, twice, or oftener, in the course of a day" (p. 239).

5. "Arsenious acid, in substance, to the extent of an eighth of a grain for a dose, combined with a little of the flowers of sulphur, has been said to be employed internally in some very obstinate cases of cutaneous diseases, and with the best effect" (p. 239).

6. Coxe, *American Dispensatory*, p. 238. An escharotic is a substance inherently corrosive in nature, capable of inflicting burns.

7. Again, the full title of Crane's work is somewhat more comprehensive: *The American Medical and Philosophical Register: Annals of Medicine, Natural History, Agriculture, and the Arts. Conducted by a Society of Gentlemen.*

8. Crane, *American Medical and Philosophical Register*, p. 452. Later treatises continued to advocate the cautious medical use of arsenic. See, e.g., Eberle, *Treatise of the Materia Medica and Therapeutics* (1822), and Wood and Bache, *The Dispensatory of the United States of America* (1833).

9. The scope of this work is made more evident through its complete title: *Modern Medicine: Being a Treatise Divested of Professional Terms on the Nature, Causes, Symptoms, and Treatment of the Diseases of Men, Women, and Children, in both Cold and Warm Climates: with Appropriate Prescriptions in English. The Whole Preceded by Practical Rules for the Preservation of Health, the Best Means for Invigorating the Human Body and Prolonging Life, and the Mode of Preventing the Extension of Infectious Disorders, as also of Annihilating Contagion.*

10. Thomas, *Modern Medicine*, p. 314.

11. Thomas, *Modern Medicine*, p. 493.

Postscript *(pp. 155–60)*

1. Prison Discipline Society, *Eighth Report*, p. 6.

2. Prison Discipline Society, *Fourth Report*, pp. 56–57.

3. Prison Discipline Society, *Eighth Report*, p. 35 et seq.

4. Prison Discipline Society, *Fourteenth Report*, p. 99.

5. During the civil war, America's prison population fell drastically, as men who otherwise might have ended up in those institutions instead made their way into the military services, primarily to collect the bounty the states paid new recruits. With the end of the war, these men returned to the general population; expectedly, the crime rate increased significantly and the prison population surged. The Auburn prisons, and to a lesser extent the Pennsylvania-plan facilities, had demonstrated that prisons could carry their own financial weight, and then some, but they had done little or nothing to rehabilitate prisoners. Dwight's vision was a financial success, but a social failure. The time had arrived for the next great leap in prison reform.

Just as Louis Dwight had led the first wave of reform, this second round would see an equally fervent leader, Enoch Wines, at the helm. Wines would introduce to prison administration such new ideas as prisoner education, indeterminate sentencing and allowing prisoners to earn small stipend for their work. Wines' most prominent disciple in implementing these changes was Zebulon Brockway, who had begun his career as a guard at Wethersfield, then moved to Albany with Amos Pilsbury. Brockway went on to become warden at the Rochester prison, and ultimately headed the prison system in Detroit.

Bibliographic Note

Since the story of Prince Mortimer has languished below the radar of historians for over a century and a half, it was not surprising that, with the solitary exception of the passage from Phelps reprinted in the foreword, I would find absolutely no secondary-source information on this poor soul's life. Even primary-source material proved to be scant: Philip Mortimer's last will and testament and the Middlesex County Superior Court information would end up as my only direct clues to Prince's eleven-decade life of captivity. Fortunately, however, information on the places and times of his subsistence was more readily available, in varying degrees.

In-depth information on life during Connecticut's and Middletown's colonial maritime grandeur came to me from several sources, mainly essays rather than books. My main sources for information on Connecticut's early political history were two articles published in the *Connecticut Bar Journal* (Volume 64, No. 5, October 1990); the first being my friend Henry Cohn's "Connecticut Constitutional History—1636–1776," and the second, Wesley Horton's "Connecticut Constitutional History—1776–1988." I also had the benefit of some excellent monographs on Middletown's early years: James L. McConaughty's "Maritime Middletown" was particularly useful, as was Albert E. Van Dusen's discussion in "Middletown and the American Revolution," both published by James D. Young Company, Middletown, 1950.

Middletown's history is inextricably tied to that of the Connecticut River, which in itself offers a story as diverse as the many communities that line its banks throughout New Hampshire, Vermont, Massachusetts, and Connecticut. Walter Hard's classic study, *The Connecticut* (Rinehart, New York, 1947, recently reprinted by the Massachusetts Audubon Society), offered me some valuable insights on Middletown's early days as a major commercial port.

Connecticut's struggle with the institution of slavery has not commanded much scholarly inquiry; initially, my primary source was Ralph Foster Weld's excellent article, "Slavery in Connecticut," written in 1933 for the Connecticut Tercentenary Commission. Fortunately, during the course of my research, an outstanding article by Joel Lang appeared in the September 29, 2002, edition of *Northeast*, the *Hartford Courant*'s Sunday magazine. In "The Plantation Next Door: How Salem Slaves, Wethersfield Onions and West Indies Sugar Made Connecticut Rich," Lang's research dispelled some long-held but mistaken notions that plantation slavery never developed in the state.

Other aspects of Prince's life also required investigation into fields I had not previously explored. For several decades, Prince toiled as a spinner in Philip Mortimer's ropewalk. In-depth information on this unique type of structure and manufacturing was not easy to come by. Ultimately, my only worthwhile source would prove to be Samuel Eliot Morison's early work, *The Ropemakers of Plymouth: A History of the Plymouth Cordage Company, 1824–1949* (Arno Press, 1976, c. 1950).

Prince's lifelong battle with yaws offered me an opportunity to delve into yet another unfamiliar area of inquiry. Even though this disease still afflicts victims in limited parts of the tropical world, in-depth medical literature on the subject is scarce. My primary source here was Cecil John Hackett's *An International Nomenclature of Yaws Lesions*, 1957, published by the World Health Organization.

Since the interrelationship between yaws and arsenic is fundamental to the mystery of Prince's alleged crime, I found it necessary to explore contemporaneous medical texts. Understandably, such material is not readily available, even in most medical libraries. Fortunately, I had the benefit of access to the resources of Cincinnati's Lloyd Library and Museum, a repository for many historical medical treatises and texts. The staff was most helpful in providing me with the several reference works cited in the notes to Chapter 17.

Even though Connecticut's Old Newgate Prison is well known, its rich history has not inspired very much by way of scholarly research or writing. The prison's place in the history of American penology is firmly established; every treatise on the subject devotes a passage to the prison, its status as America's first state prison, and its notoriety for the harsh conditions to be found in its caverns and within its walled enclosure. All of these sources, however, merely reiterate the same basic facts; none make any attempt to provide the reader with anything beyond a basic discussion of the prison. Fortunately, Richard Phelps's classic *Newgate of Connecticut: Its Origin and Early History* provides the historical depth lacking elsewhere. The value of Phelps's work is also enhanced by the fact that it was written in 1844, only seventeen years after Newgate's doors were closed.

A more recent study of Newgate, which complements Phelps's in many respects, is William G. Domonell's *Newgate from Copper Mine to State Prison* (Richard Colby, Printer, Litchfield, CT, 1998). Domonell's study, organized on a year-by-year basis, was immensely helpful in providing perspective to Phelps's tendency to disregard chronology in his discussions.

Primary source documents were critical in my effort to do justice to the story of the development of Wethersfield State Prison, but Wethersfield has also warranted the attention of several other writers on the history of prisons. First and foremost, of course, are the several annual reports of Louis Dwight's Boston Prison Discipline Society, which are replete with invaluable information on the development and administration of Wethersfield and, for that matter, all of America's early prisons.

To be sure, several important surveys of American prisons have been written at various times throughout the twentieth century, and each proved to be an invaluable resource in the course of my research, notwithstanding their uniform failure to examine more closely the events at Wethersfield State Prison. Among the more prominent: Harry Elmer Barnes, *The Story of Punishment: A Record of Man's Inhumanity to Man* (Patterson Smith 2nd ed., rev. 1972); Blake McKelvey, *American Prisons: A Study in American Social History Prior to 1915* (Patterson Smith, 1968, c. 1936); and Orlando Lewis, *The Development of American Prisons and Prison Customs, 1776–1845* (Patterson Smith, 1967, c. 1922).

Stuart Holbrook's *Dreamers of the American Dream* (Doubleday, 1957) provided me with my first exposure to the life and work of Louis Dwight. Coincidentally, Holbrook also provided me with useful information on Connecticut's colonial road system. His *The Old Post Road: The Story of the Boston Post Road* (McGraw-Hill, 1962) was an informative and enjoyable adventure into the history of a road I travel, in part, on a daily basis.

Index